In this inspired and creative book, ics ranging from character developm
literally taking the reader from Genesis to Revelation. As she
does, she teaches us history, culture, art, and science—among
other topics—beginning each lesson with a Bible verse and
ending with an innovative craft or other activity. Clearly,
Kathie Reimer has a gift for imparting deep scriptural truths
in a simple, easily understood and entertaining way.

Enthusiasm exudes from each and every lesson. This
book will be a source of deep learning as well as light-
hearted humor and general fun for all who read it. Not
only children but adults as well can learn from the lessons and activities it contains. It is an invaluable tool for
cultivating happy children and building strong families
as it teaches the relevance of the Bible to everyday life.

Beverly LaHaye, president
Concerned Women for America

Today there are a lot of pressures on our families. *1001
Ways to Help Your Child Walk with God* gives some fun and
easy ways to spend time as a family exploring God's
Word. Kathie Reimer has shown great creativity in putting this book together. I have even used some of the material as I travel as illustrations and sermon enhancers.
The material in this book can only bless you as you use it
in your family or in your church.

Jim Gerhold, children's ministries coordinator
The General Council of the Assemblies of God

A recent Gallup poll of America's teens states that over
half do not have a hero. This morning's paper says that
drug use among ten- to thirteen-year-olds is on the rise
again. Across America in public schools, fourth, fifth, and
sixth graders are learning how to use condoms (in school
colors no less). Each new Supreme Court decision puts
God farther and farther from our kids' daily lives.

1001 Ways to Help Your Child Walk with God is as creative
as a sunset over a mountain lake, as on target as a bull's-
eye in Olympic archery, as needed as a spring shower.

This book is not an entree. It is a basic-course requirement for a parent who rightfully desires a Ph.D. in raising a godly child. I urge you to read it and apply it daily. It is like having a Christian school right in your living room.

Joe White, Ed.D., president
Kanakuk-Kanakomo Kamps, Inc.

If you're struggling with how to help your children walk with God, here is an encyclopedia of ideas! For the Sunday school teacher, the homeschooler, the vacation Bible school teacher, and the parent who knows her true task each day is to teach her children to walk with God, help has arrived. Complete with a Scripture index, you'll find everything necessary to interest your children in the Bible in this helpful text.

Some kids are quiet and artistic. They learn best in focused moments. Others are boisterous and need the busyness of hands-on activities to think and process. No matter what brand of boy or girl you're raising, you'll find suggestions that work in *1001 Ways to Help Your Child Walk with God.*

Mom and Dad—this is just what you've been waiting for. Wonderful ideas to help guide your child toward God in meaningful ways. They're child-friendly, child-fun and child-participatory. And they're right here in this one volume. Sit back and relax! The homework has been done. Now your "home" work can begin.

Elisa Morgan, president
Mothers of Preschoolers International, Inc.

With so many books on the market today, it is refreshing to see one solely dedicated to producing godly principles in the lives of little children. Deuteronomy 6 tells us that we are to diligently, all day long, teach our children the principles of God, leading them to trust Jesus as their personal Savior. Kathie Reimer gives us practical ways to do this. As a mother and grandmother, and as a teacher of child psychology, I wholeheartedly recommend this book.

Beverly Lowry, professor of psychology
Liberty University

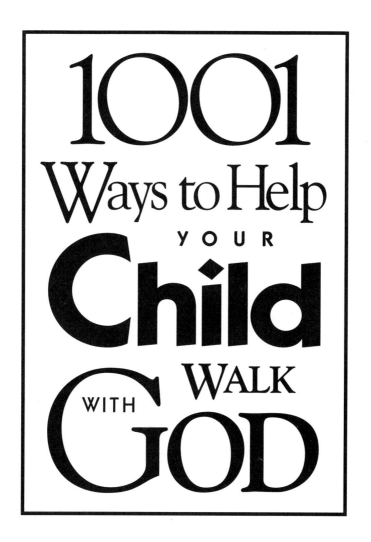

1001

Ways to Help

YOUR

Child

WITH WALK

GOD

Kathie Reimer

Tyndale House Publishers, Inc. • Wheaton, Illinois

Cover color photo copyright © 1994 by Bob Taylor
Cover black and white photos copyright © 1994 by Michael Hudson
Interior illustrations copyright © 1994 by Marty Kelley

Stories in chapter 9, "Bible Listening," are by J. Mark Reimer. Used with permission.

Unless otherwise noted, Scripture quotations are taken from the *Holy Bible,* New International Version®. Copyright © 1973, 1978, 1984 by International Bible Society. Used by permission of Zondervan Publishing House. All rights reserved. The "NIV" and "New International Version" trademarks are registered in the United States Patent and Trademark Office by International Bible Society. Use of either trademark requires the permission of International Bible Society.

Scriptures marked KJV are taken from the King James Version of the Bible.

Library of Congress Cataloging-in-Publication Data

Reimer, Kathie, date
  1001 ways to help your child walk with God / Kathie Reimer.
    p. cm.
  Includes index.
  ISBN 0-8423-4605-8
    1. Bible—Children's use. 2. Christian education of children. I. Title.
II. Title: One thousand and one ways to help your child walk with God.
III. Title: Thousand and one ways to help your child walk with God.
BS618.R45   1994
248.8′45—dc20   94-9695

Printed in the United States of America

00 99 98 97 96 95 94
 7   6   5   4   3   2   1

Contents

Dedicated to
Carol Lynne
my "daughter-in-love"
and to
Patty, my beautiful sister

A Note to Parents

The ideas and activities in this book are written in such a way that you may read them aloud to your children just as they are. Your older children may enjoy reading the book themselves or reading it to their younger brothers or sisters. Many of the activities children can do on their own; a few need adult supervision. We have endeavored to keep the ideas simple, with little or no preparation or supplies needed. (The activities in "Bible Art" and "Bible Recipes" do require a few supplies—generally things you'll have on hand.) The games, for the most part, are noncompetitive—since our goal is to help create family unity.

With very special thanks to my son Mark, who wrote the stories—and who joins with Jim, Lisa, Jenifer, and Carol as my spiritual "cheering section" and daily inspiration— as they consistently walk with God.

Introduction

Welcome, parents and kids, to the world of Bible learning through active daily devotional experiences!

We live at the greatest time in history to be alive! In your lifetime you will have the opportunity to go places, to do things, and to be the person that would not have been possible in times past. Jesus promises to give us an abundant life, and he means what he says!

But with all the excitement about what God offers kids and their parents today, there comes a warning: "Be . . . alert. Your enemy the devil prowls around like a roaring lion looking for someone to devour. Resist him, standing firm in the faith" (1 Pet. 5:8-9). One of our enemy's major evil battle plans is to take over our minds and to program into them what *he* wants us to think, to believe, and not to believe. But the Bible promises us that "the God of all grace . . . will himself . . . make you strong, firm and steadfast" to win the mind wars against Satan (1 Pet. 5:10). God even gives us his powerful weapon to hold in our hands and hide in our heart—"the sword of the Spirit, which is the Word of God," the Bible (Eph. 6:17).

Of all the books ever written—thick, skinny, simple, wordy, ancient, or hot off the press—not a single one can come close to comparing with the Bible. This book is designed to open the Bible for you, perhaps in new, fun ways you haven't thought of before.

There are lots of high-energy messages from God's Word for kids who love to go, run, and live with a supercharge of energy.

And for boys and girls who love to think, to solve mysteries, or to stir up a great dish in Mom's kitchen . . . practical kids who like to see and believe . . . budding young musicians or promising future scientists . . . there are messages in God's Word for you, too. There are activities, projects, mysteries, tough questions, answers, corny jokes, and tasty food ideas in this book to appeal to all kinds of kids, whatever your interests and abilities.

Have you ever created something? Have you ever held *nothing* in your hands, had no tools or materials to work with, and made something you could hold or enjoy looking at? Of course not! Only God can really create something from absolutely *nothing*.

But when God made you, he gave you a little bit of his "creativity," which makes it possible for you to do wonderful things like pretending, making an interesting picture on paper with pencil, crayons, or paint—or composing a great poem or melody of your very own. God is so kind to share the incredible gift of creativity with the people he loves!

One of God's most special and well-deserved names is Creator. He made the vast universe, the world, and all living things—and keeps them going in precisely the way he planned. In this chapter, many other special names for God's Son, Jesus, will be included, along with some important lessons he taught and other interesting Bible stories and truths. You will be learning a few of the wonderful, beautiful names for Jesus as you use the hands he gave you and the incredible gift of imagination to make great works of art.

See which names and truths from God's Word are your own, personal favorites—and answer the most important question: "Who is *Jesus* to you?"

Messenger Dove

When the dove returned to him in the evening, there in its beak was a freshly plucked olive leaf! (Gen. 8:11)

After the Great Flood, Noah sent out a dove to see whether the water was drying up yet. The dove came back with an olive leaf in its beak, so Noah knew there was dry land somewhere with plants growing on it.

You can make a dove from a white paper plate. Fold the plate in half and cut along the fold line. Fold one of the halves of the paper plate in half again and cut it on the fold line. Use one of those small pieces to be the wing of the dove, and glue it on the "side" of the body (which is the other half of the original paper plate). Glue the other small piece in place for the dove's tail.

Cut a circle from paper for the head of the dove and give it an eye and a beak. Color a green branch of leaves to glue in his beak, or let your dove be sitting on it.

Read Genesis 6–8 for the story of Noah and the Great Flood.

Protected by Heavenly Watch

He will not permit the destroyer to enter your houses and strike you down. (Exod. 12:23)

Have you seen the crime prevention signs that say, This Home Protected by a Neighborhood Watch? Make a similar sign for your home that says, This Home Protected by God's Mighty Angels! Then hang the sign in the house somewhere (perhaps near your room) as a reminder of God's loving protection over your family.

The homes of God's people were also watched over by a special protection in Moses' day. Read what it was in Exodus 12:22-23. See what God's people, the Israelites, did in Exodus 12:27-28.

The Path through the Sea

Then Moses stretched out his hand over the sea, and all that night the Lord drove the sea back with a strong east wind and turned it into dry land. (Exod. 14:21)

Make a construction paper diorama scene of Moses and the Red Sea. Here's how to do it:

Turn a shoe box on its side to contain the diorama scene or begin with a flat piece of cardboard for the sea bed. Cover the bottom of the box or the cardboard with brown construction paper for the dry land (or leave the cardboard brown as it is). Take two pieces of blue construction paper and cut one edge of each of them to look like a fringe, with cuts about one-half inch apart. Roll the fringed edge of the blue paper over a pencil or a stick to look like rolled back waves. Glue the blue paper onto the brown cardboard with the curled sides facing each other, leaving a path of the brown color showing between them. Trim the blue paper to fit the box or the cardboard if it is too large.

Walk some toy people or animals across the Red Sea safely, and let the bad guys, the Egyptian army, be covered by the waves. If you have no toys the right size, cut out pictures of people from magazines, catalogues, or your own drawings, and glue them in place, if you wish. Read the actual dramatic Red Sea adventure from Exodus 14:21-29.

Ten Great Rules

> Then Moses led the people out of the camp to meet with God, and they stood at the foot of the mountain. (Exod. 19:17)

Make a clay or salt dough model of the Ten Commandments on stone that God gave to Moses (and to us). If you

want to make your stone tablets look more realistic, carve letters into them with a toothpick or table knife. This is the salt-dough recipe:

- 2 cups flour
- 2 cups salt
- $1/2$ cup (or more) hot water

Mix these ingredients together, and add a teaspoon of cooking oil.

The important thing about the Ten Commandments is not how they looked, but what they said and meant. Read them together as a family from Exodus 20:3-17 and discuss their important meanings.

Oasis in the Desert

> My soul thirsts for you . . . in a dry and weary land where there is no water. (Ps. 63:1)

This interesting verse from the Bible almost makes you thirsty as you read it! What a great description of how you feel after being outside on a hot, dry, summer day!

Have you ever seen cartoons of a poor, scraggly man, dragging and clawing his way along the steaming sands of an endless desert frantically whispering, "Water! Water!"? Some of the stories picture him imagining he sees a lemonade stand or an oasis (a desert pond surrounded by shady palm trees), but when he crawls to where he thought the oasis was, it was only a mirage. It wasn't there at all!

Make a miniature oasis in a flat box by filling the box with sand or cornmeal. Make palm trees, the blue water of the oasis, cactus, desert animals, cow horns, and people out of construction paper and place them in the sand.

If you want a more realistic oasis, place a shallow lid of water in the sand and surround it with palm trees and plastic toy animals and people.

Read the very interesting true story in Exodus 15:23-27 about an oasis in the desert that was polluted until God told Moses what to do about it. When you read verse 27, think about how God's people must have felt after their long, miserable trip across the desert.

Our Fortress

Be my rock of refuge, to which I can always go; give the command to save me, for you are my rock and my fortress. (Ps. 71:3)

A refuge is a safe place to go, like a rabbit's burrow, a cave in a rock or even a hollow log, where a small animal can hide. We sometimes need a quiet, safe place where we can "escape" our problems, worries, and fears. Jesus wants to be our refuge! We can come to him with anything that is bothering us and he will protect, comfort, and help us.

Sometimes in the Bible our refuge is described as a fortress, or a "fort." In cowboy and Indian days, what advantage was there in staying in a fort? Read Psalm 18:2 and Psalm 71:3 to see that God is our fortress and refuge. Then make a "strong tower" or fort in one of these ways:

• Glue small boxes, empty toilet-paper rolls, and paper cups together.

• Cut the top edges of a medium-sized box to look like the "spires" of a castle. Then cut out doors and windows in your "fortress."

• With the help of an adult, use a large waxed paper cup to make a "candle tower." Tie a piece of string to a pencil or Popsicle stick, and balance it on the top of the cup so the string hangs down in the center of the cup. This will be the wick for your candle. Melt paraffin wax, adding pieces of old crayons to each batch to make different colors. Pour one layer at a time into the paper cup, allowing it to cool and harden before adding another layer. Use your imagination in arranging the colors and thicknesses of the layers. When the candle is the size you want it to be and the wax has thoroughly hardened, tear off the waxed paper cup from the outside. You have a candle tower! When you light it, let the light remind you that Jesus is your refuge.

Tiny Forest in a Jar

Then all the trees of the forest will sing for joy. (Ps. 96:12)

Make a miniature forest-in-a-jar paperweight or desk decoration from one half of a clear empty stocking container or a small jar (like a baby food jar). Trace around the edge of the container on a piece of cardboard and cut out a circle about a half inch wider than your line. Cover the circle with green paper.

Inside the clear container place bits of moss, bark, leaves, evergreen branches, pine needles, tiny pine-cones, acorns, or wildflowers. Glue along the edge of the container and glue the green circle to it as a base. Carefully turn the forest-in-a-jar over and allow it to dry. (When you move your paperweight, always pick it up under the base to give it support.)

Read Psalm 96:1-3, 11-13 with your family. Who is being described and what is he doing?

Sandwich in a Jar

How precious to me are your thoughts, O God! How vast is the sum of them! Were I to count them, they would out-number the grains of sand. (Ps. 139:17-18)

Make a "sandwich" in a jar like this:

• Dye sand different colors by plac-ing some in Ziploc bags, adding a drop or two of food coloring to each bag, and shaking and gently kneading each mixture. (Salt or grits may be used instead of sand.)

• Undo only the corner of one bag and pour some of the sand into a clear jar, forming the first layer of colored sand in our sandwich.

• Repeat the same action with an-other color of sand.

• Continue to build your sandwich in the same way, filling the jar to the very tip, squirting on a top layer of white glue to seal it and gluing and tightening the lid at the top.

Did you try to count the grains of sand as you mixed and poured them? Do you think you could? Why or why not? The Bible tells us something won-derful about how often God thinks about you and how very important you are to him! Read those beautiful verses in Psalm 139:17-18.

I'm a Pillar?

Our sons in their youth will be like well-nurtured plants, and our daughters will be like pillars carved to adorn a palace. (Ps. 144:12)

Make a carving of your choice from a bar of soap. Use a dull knife or the sharp end of the cap of a ballpoint pen as a carving tool.

Girls, how do you like being com-pared to a lovely carving adorning a palace? A healthy plant is a beautiful sight and so is a graceful carving! Who are these beautiful people? Read Psalm 144:15 to find out!

Closer Than a Brother

There is a friend who sticks closer than a brother. (Prov. 18:24)

Try this "stuck together" art project. With a bandanna, tie your right arm together with someone's left arm and place a pencil or crayon in each of your hands. Let the right-handed person draw a picture while the other person's left hand follows along like a shadow. Then trade sides and let the hand that didn't get to do the drawing before be the "artist" this time.

Have you ever heard of Siamese twins? What are they? That's as close as a brother or sister can "stick together"! But the Bible says that Jesus is our friend who sticks closer to us than any brother (or sister)!

It's good to see a brother or sister "stick up" for each other when one needs a friend. Families should be the most loyal friends possible on earth— but how great it is to know that we have a friend like Jesus who always sticks with us! Read what he promises in Joshua 1:5.

Our Comforter

O my Comforter in sorrow, my heart is faint within me. (Jer. 8:18)

Isn't covering up with a soft, fluffy comforter on a cold night one of the warmest, coziest feelings you can imagine? In your great-grandparent's day, people often slept on soft feather beds, warmly covered with hand-made-with-love snuggly comforters.

Make a pretty "mini-comforter" wall-hanging on heavy paper or cardboard. Glue small pieces of cloth of different patterns and colors side by side to look like a real comforter in any design you choose. When the glue has dried, make little pencil or felt-tip marker lines to look like stitches on the quilt pieces.

Jesus is our comforter. He knows that many times we need comfort: when we are sad, when disappointment or sickness comes our way, when a friend lets us down, or when we simply want to feel warmly loved.

The Holy Spirit is also sometimes called the Comforter. Read the wonderful promise Jesus gave us about the Holy Spirit in John 14:18.

Dry Bones

He asked me, "Son of man, can these bones live?" (Ezek. 37:3)

Ezekiel had a miracle dream (vision) one day that carried a special message for his people, Israel. They were discouraged and held captive by the enemy, but God promised Ezekiel that his people would be brought back to life as a great nation. Ezekiel's dream was also a picture of each person who is spiritually dead in his sins until Jesus comes along to give him life and hope.

Look at the interesting dream in Ezekiel 37:1-11 and God's promise in verse 14. Then try this lazy-bones idea:

Cut plastic drinking straws (like bones) in assorted sizes, including some with bendable joints. Collect some paper clips and bend them into S shapes to use to connect the straws together. Make a sculpture of any kind you like.

A Lion for a Pillow!

So the king gave the order, and they

brought Daniel and threw him into the lions' den. (Dan. 6:16)

Make a lion-face puppet from a paper plate or cardboard circle, gluing a Popsicle stick or tongue depressor on the back of it for a handle. Draw a lion's face on the plate and glue yellow strips of yarn or yellow paper strips all around the rim for a mane.

If you want to make a lamb's face on the other side of the puppet, glue another plate back-to-back with the first, make a lamb's face on it, and glue cotton all around the edge to look like wool. Use the lion/lamb puppet to remind you that God made fierce lions as gentle as lambs for Daniel's sake. Read or tell the familiar story from Daniel 6:8-24.

Immanuel

"And they will call him Immanuel"— which means, "God with us." (Matt. 1:23)

On a piece of glass from an old picture frame or a sheet of clear plastic, trace lightly with pencil around the edge of a small dessert plate or saucer. In black permanent marker, carefully print the word *Immanuel* in large, thick letters around the top curved line of the circle you drew. (You may want to write it lightly in pencil first and then write over the pencil marks.)

On a sheet of paper, about the same size, trace around the same plate and then color the circle to look like a globe of the world. Try to include oceans and continents, but don't worry if they don't look exactly like the "real thing"! Make black dots or draw some tiny people on the continents to represent everyone in the world.

Place the plastic sheet or the glass over your drawing of the world and glue or tape the two together. Put your "God with us" picture in a frame, if possible, and hang it in your house or your room as a reminder that Immanuel lives there with you. Read John 1:14-15 and find Jesus there—even though his name is called the Word.

Wide Road/Narrow Road

Enter through the narrow gate. For wide is the gate and broad is the road that leads to destruction, and many enter through it. But small is the gate and narrow the road that leads to life, and only a few find it. (Matt. 7:13-14)

Jesus told us about two highways we can travel in life—a wide, crowded one and a narrow one with fewer people on it. Each road goes somewhere, and just as your family chooses which roads to take when you go on vacation, all of us must choose for ourselves which highway of life we will travel.

On a piece of paper draw your own idea of what each highway is like that the Bible describes in Matthew 7:13-14. Make your road maps as simple as you wish—or add road signs, scenery along the highway, and people traveling along—but be sure you show where each road leads.

When we choose a road to follow as we travel by car, we often prefer a wide, modern superhighway; but sometimes a narrow country road is the right one to get us to the place we want to go. Jesus told us to be very careful that the road we choose to travel takes us to eternal life instead of everlasting death. The narrow road is not only the safe road—it's the happy road!

The Best Teacher

The crowds were amazed at his teaching. (Matt. 7:28)

Describe your favorite teacher to someone in your family. It can be one that you have right now or a favorite teacher from the past. Think of something valuable you learned from him or her. Be sure to thank the Lord when you pray for teachers.

Make a drawing of anything you would like. It can be simple or very complicated. Then "grade" your own paper. Think about how much time and effort you put into the drawing, not whether you are a modern-day Michelangelo (not the turtle kind)! Give yourself an *A, B* or *C* (no *F*s) on the size, the color, and the idea of your work of art. And be kind to yourself!

Jesus was the greatest teacher who ever lived! People came in huge crowds to hear him tell his fascinating stories. Can you imagine hurrying up a big mountainside to reach the top so that you could hear your teacher speak all day long and still not wanting to go home? Your teacher may be good, but certainly not that good! But read what people said about Jesus in John 7:46. When someone teaches as Jesus did—and as he does today through his Word—we want to sit up and listen!

Pearl of Great Value

The kingdom of heaven is like a merchant looking for fine pearls. When he found one of great value, he went away and sold everything he had and bought it. (Matt. 13:45)

What do you know about pearls? What do they look like? Where are they found? How are they made?

Maybe you know that a pearl is round and shiny like satin. It can be found inside the shell of a kind of oyster or a similar shellfish. Pearls are made when a tiny piece of sand or a pebble accidentally gets inside the oyster's shell and the sea animal begins to form a white layer of *calcium carbonate* around it, over and over, making it bigger and rounder until a pearl is made.

Jesus is called the "Pearl of Great Value" because he's worth more in our lives than anything else we could ever have!

Make your own string of pearls

from clay that can be baked or dried from

- 1$^{1}/_{2}$ cups flour
- $^{1}/_{2}$ cup salt
- $^{1}/_{2}$ cup (or more) warm water
- $^{1}/_{4}$ cup cooking oil

If the dough is too sticky, add more flour. Shape the dough into round "pearls" and put a toothpick in each one. Dry the pearls in a 250° oven for about 3 hours. Remove the toothpicks carefully when the dough is dry. Paint the pearls with white paint or pearly white nail polish, and "string" them on dental floss or yarn.

You can also make a "pearl-drops" picture from tiny drops of glue arranged in a design and allowed to dry.

No-Hook Fishing

"Come, follow me," Jesus said, "and I will make you fishers of men." (Mark 1:17)

Make a lightweight aquarium by turning a clear plastic bag inside out. Cut out of construction paper several small, colorful fish and decorate them with eyes, mouths, fins, stripes, or

spots if you want to. With a felt-tipped marker, write on each fish the name of someone your family wants to remember in prayer.

On one side of the bag, near the bottom, glue the cutout fish. When those fish have dried, turn the bag over and glue more fish on the other side. Add paper seaweed, coral, and shells among the fish. When all the fish are firmly stuck to the plastic bag and the glue is dry, turn the bag right-side out again and blow into it, filling it with air. Quickly trap the air in the bag by twisting the top together and wrapping a rubber band or a twist-tie tightly around it.

What kind of fish does Jesus want us to catch in Mark 1:17? Pray that God will give you the boldness and some good ideas for becoming fishers of people!

Shall We Try These Shell Ideas?

Give, and it shall [shell?] be given unto you. (Luke 6:38, KJV)

Substituting the word *shell* for *shall* may be a silly way to remember this important verse, but maybe it "shell" help! Here are two macaroni "shell" ideas to try:

- Make a macaroni shell card to give away for a special occasion, or just to share a kind thought with someone. Fold heavy paper in half to form the card, write your message inside, and decorate the front with a glued-on macaroni design. Use whatever shapes and sizes of pasta you like, and then paint the pasta designs with tempera paint or felt-tip markers when the glue is dry. Deliver your card in person. Trying to mail the card "shell" lead to smashed macaroni!

• Macaroni shells can be made into jewelry to give away, too. Glue different shapes of pasta onto plastic headbands, visors, or cardboard pieces to become pins. (A paper clip or safety pin may be taped to the cardboard to attach the pin to your clothes.) Dye the pasta with food coloring and dry it before gluing it on if you want color (or use tempera or poster paint when the pasta design is dry).

Read Luke 6:38 and talk about what it means. What would you like to have given to you? More friends? More people to like you and be kind to you? Would you like for people to say nice things about you instead of talking bad about you when you are not listening? The Bible says we should give to others what they need, and what we need will be given back to us. Try it! God's ideas always work.

Don't Worry—Be Happy!

Consider the ravens: They do not sow or reap . . . yet God feeds them. . . . Consider how the lilies grow. . . . Not even Solomon in all his splendor was dressed like one of these. (Luke 12:24, 27)

Draw an outline of several birds, or a field, or a bouquet of wild flowers. Color or paint the outlines with the prettiest colors and designs you can imagine. Your ideas do not need to look realistic, just colorful! As pretty as your picture may turn out to be, God has made real birds and flowers even prettier than your great artwork! That's because he is the Master Artist!

Do birds or flowers worry about what they are going to "put on" when they begin their day? Have you ever seen a wild flower or a bluebird frantically searching through his closet for something suitable to wear? Of course not!

Jesus tells us in Luke 12:22-30 that we do not need to worry about finding food to eat and having clothes to wear. Why not? Does God know what we need? Will he take care of us?

Only Begotten Son

For God so loved the world, that he gave his only begotten Son, that whosoever believeth in him should not perish, but have everlasting life. (John 3:16, KJV)

Make a manger scene inside an empty cereal box "stable." Lay the cereal box on its side and cut a large arched opening in it for the door of the stable. Tape together any cuts or tears in the box and close the end of it. Paint the whole box with brown tempera or poster paint, beginning with the inside of the box. If you have no paint, cover the box with a brown paper sack.

Draw and color pictures of Mary, Joseph, the manger, and baby Jesus on heavy paper and cut them out, leaving an inch-long extra piece of paper at their feet and on the legs of the manger to fold under and glue to the floor of the stable. Draw pictures of animals and shepherds, too, if you would like. (The wise men came later.)

Arrange your drawings to make a stand-up manger scene inside the cereal box, and glue or tape each one in place.

Then thank God for sending us his only begotten Son, Jesus!

I Am

"I tell you the truth," Jesus answered, "before Abraham was born, I am!" (John 8:58)

Make a banner to hang in your room to remind you who Jesus is. Here's how:

• In the middle of a piece of cloth or paper, write the words, "I am!" in bold or fancy letters. All around those words, in smaller letters, facing different directions write the words, "I was" and "I will ever be."

• Or, across a cloth or paper in huge, fat letters write the name, "I am!" Inside each letter write these phrases as many times as they will fit, "I was" and "I will ever be."

One of the most interesting and unusual names for Jesus is the two little words, *I am*. Read the fascinating story of Moses and the burning bush in Exodus 3:1-6, 12-14, and look for this name of Jesus in the verses. What do you think the name *I am* means?

Do you know what "past tense" means? Was Jesus only past tense, living a long time ago, but no longer alive and active in people's lives? Is Jesus only "present tense"? Is he the God for this day or this year only—a God only for today? Then what about tomorrow? When you have grandchildren, don't you think they should have a chance to know and love Jesus, too? Or will they be out of luck because they were born too late? The answer can be found in Hebrews 13:8. Please read it out loud and thank the great "I am," who is *always* a "present tense" God.

Jesus Is the Gate

I am the gate; whoever enters through me will be saved. (John 10:9)

Read the word picture that Jesus gave us in John 10:1-10 about the sheep and the sheepfold. A shepherd in Jesus' day took good care of his sheep during the day, and at night he led them into the sheepfold, where they were safe and content. Then, to make sure that no sheep wandered out and that nothing that was not a sheep—like a wolf or robber—got in, the shepherd would lie down and sleep across the entrance to the sheepfold, actually becoming its gate, or door.

Using white or colored paper, a pencil, crayons or markers, design several types of doors. Use your vivid imagination as you make them look modern or antique, ornate (very fancy), or plain. Add stained glass windows or peepholes to them and draw on the doors whatever type of doorknobs, handles, or locks you want them to have. One of your doors can be made to look like it belongs in a medieval castle, with a bar that slides across it to keep out enemy armies. Another door could resemble something from *Alice's Adventures in Wonderland.* Use your imagination!

God's children are his precious sheep, and John 10:3 says that he even knows us all by name. He knows all about us, and he makes it his business to take great care of us during this life, and then one day to take us safely to the "sheepfold," heaven—through the only door—the Lord Jesus Christ!

Jesus Is the Good Shepherd

I am the good shepherd; I know my sheep and my sheep know me. (John 10:14)

One of the most beautiful names for Jesus in the Bible is the Good Shepherd. It makes us think of the poor lost sheep in Luke 15:3-7 and the kind shepherd who searched for it with great concern until he found it and then gently carried it on his shoulders safely home. Read the story from the Bible.

Make a simple drawing of Jesus, the Good Shepherd, wearing a robe and carrying a shepherd's curved stick—a "staff" or "rod." Add to your picture hillsides, a stream, and a fenced "sheepfold" in the background.

Then make thumbprints all over the hillside by pressing your thumb on an ink pad or into paint. Add floppy ears, tails, legs, and curly lines around the thumbprints to make them look like sheep.

Let the thumbprint sheep remind you that all God's children are known and loved by him in a very special way because there are no two people exactly alike, just as there are no two identical thumbprints.

Jesus Is God

I and the Father are one. (John 10:30)

Have you ever tried to make a crayon-resist picture?

Make a circle (about three inches across) in the middle of a piece of white paper. Inside the circle write the word *God* in bright, bold (not black) letters. Around the outside of the circle color heavily a two-inch-wide area bright yellow—like the jagged rays of the sun—leaving no white, uncolored spots. Then, on the outside of the yellow area, color heavily a similar jagged section bright orange. Your picture should look something like a two-toned sun shining around the wonderful name *God.*

Now completely color over your beautiful picture with a black crayon, hiding it totally from sight. When all looks black, with no color showing through, use an old comb to scrape through the black crayon from side to side across your picture and watch the color begin to show through the lines!

Scrape all the black color from the center circle so that the holy name *God* can easily be seen.

Many years ago, before Jesus came to earth, people pictured God as a dreadful, unknown Power to be terribly feared—something like your picture when none of the pretty colors were showing through the dark covering on top.

But at just the right time in God's perfect planning, the Light of the World, Jesus, came to earth to shine his beautiful light on the true God—a God of beauty, grace, and love.

The Resurrection and the Life

I am the resurrection and the life. (John 11:25)

Find a short, empty brown paper tube to represent the tomb where Jesus was buried. Cut out a picture of Jesus from an old Sunday school paper or booklet—or draw and cut out a picture of him, and glue or tape it to a Popsicle stick. Slide the picture of Jesus into the tube, representing his death and burial. Push the picture up and out of the tube like Jesus arose from death and the grave.

The story of Jesus would be a tragedy if he had not come alive after he died. That would have made him just like Buddha, Muhammad, or any of the other leaders of false religions. Only Jesus Christ was resurrected from his grave, and that is very important to you. Do you know why? Read John 11:25 to find out. It's great news!

Jesus Is the Way

I am the way and the truth and the life. (John 14:6)

Here are two ways to help you remember that Jesus knows the way to God and *is* the way:

• Mark a trail through the inside of your house by making crayon rubbings of things or places along the way on a white piece of paper and numbering each one for another person to try to follow. Place a reward for him at the end of the trail.

• Use salt and flour dough (see recipe on page 3) to make a relief (stand-up) map of a make-believe place. Spread the dough over the surface of a piece of cardboard and pinch and shape it to look like mountains, valleys, lakes. Also include a road—a way to get from one side of the map to the other. Allow the dough to dry and paint your relief map to look like land, grass, and water. Paint "the way" black or brown.

What way is the Bible talking about when it describes Jesus? Where does the way lead us? Read John 14:6 to know for sure.

The Vine and the Branches

I am the vine; you are the branches . . . apart from me you can do nothing. (John 15:5)

Have you ever seen a branch trying to grow and produce fruit without being connected to a vine? Can it do that?

Jesus said that he is the Vine and we are his branches. We have a great job because we get to grow the beautiful leaves, flowers, and delicious fruit! But he has the "power and life" end of the job, since a branch can do nothing without the life that flows to it from the vine. They must be connected and work together. When we "branches" want to grow good "fruit" for Jesus, let's remember to let him be our source of power and life.

Make a picture with twigs to help you remember that Jesus is your Vine and you are his branch. Glue a thick twig or part of a branch onto a piece of cardboard or heavy paper to represent the vine. Along the vine, glue smaller twigs for branches. At the end of each branch, glue a picture of a person, cut out from magazines, or use family pictures (with permission!). On the vine, glue a picture of Jesus or the words "The Vine."

The Generous Seamstress

Dorcas . . . was always doing good and helping the poor. (Acts 9:36)

Make your own "needlework" picture card from a piece of poster board or lightweight cardboard. Draw a picture on it and punch holes about a half-inch apart along the lines you have drawn. Use a piece of yarn and a large needle for sewing, or wrap a

piece of tape around the ends of different colors of yarn to form a "needle" on each one. Then "sew up a storm"!

If you have no yarn, make a pinpunch picture on a dark piece of construction paper, using a straight pin, a hat pin, or a straightened-out paper clip. Draw a picture on the dark paper with white chalk or crayon—or staple a printed coloring book picture to the dark paper—and punch holes close together along the outlines of the picture. Hold the paper up to the light for the brightness to shine through the tiny holes.

Dorcas was a wonderful lady in the Bible whose kindness "shined" on many people. The Bible says in Acts 9:36 that she "was always doing good and helping the poor." One of the ways Dorcas often helped people was by sewing clothes for them. (People could not run down to the nearest department store for clothes in those days!) Read Acts 9:39 to see what many of Dorcas's friends did when she suddenly grew sick and died. What amazing miracle did God then do through Peter? (The answer is in Acts 9:40-42.)

The Big Fuss over Silver

*A silversmith named Demetrius . . .
made silver shrines. (Acts 19:24)*

Form a sheet of aluminum foil or shiny wrapping paper into a "silver sculpture" of some sort. Ask the other people in your family to guess what your sculpture is and give them some clues if they need help. Let someone else then make a foil sculpture for you to identify.

Can you imagine placing your foil sculpture on a table in the middle of a room and having people bow in worship and prayer to it? You would know that was wrong as well as ridiculous! How would you feel if you believed your whole life, your safety, and your future were being taken care of by a piece of metal?

In the Bible story of Paul and a silversmith named Demetrius, that was, incredibly, what was happening! Read Acts 19:24-25 to learn what Demetrius was making, what the name of his false god was, and if he was making much money from his business. Why was Demetrius angry with Paul in Acts 19:26-27?

We know that worshiping "idols" is wrong, whether they are made of gold, silver, stone, or clay. But many people do not recognize that anything in our lives that is more important to us than God is an "idol." It can be money, friends, hobbies, or other "good" things. Let's make God number one in our lives!

The True Foundation

*For no one can lay any foundation
other than the one already laid, which
is Jesus Christ. (1 Cor. 3:11)*

Make a high-rise sculpture out of paper plates and cups, blocks, paper-towel rolls, paper game cards, dominoes, or even something from your kitchen pantry, like square crackers or big marshmallows. Build your creation as high and wide as you can, but be sure that you construct it on a book, a hardwood floor, or a table. A firm and steady foundation is absolutely necessary!

That's the way it is in real life, too. A firm and steady foundation is absolutely necessary to build a life upon! Some of you are just now beginning to build your life. Others, like Mom and Dad, have done a little more building on theirs. Are you sure that your "foundation" is strong enough to construct a beautiful, solid life upon?

The Bible tells us who the foundation of our life should be. Read about him in 1 Corinthians 3:10-11. Matthew 7:24-27 tells us a familiar story about two men who built on two different foundations. Do you know what they were—and what happened to their houses? Check your answers by reading the story in the Bible.

Aren't you glad your life doesn't have to shake, rattle, and roll when it's built on the Solid Rock—Jesus!

How Rich Is God?

For you know the grace of our Lord Jesus Christ, that though he was rich, yet for your sakes he became poor. (2 Cor. 8:9)

Draw pictures of some of the riches Jesus had in the "bank" while he lived on earth. Did he have millions of dollars? How about bars of gold or silver mines? How many diamonds did he keep in his bank vault? Did he have a fancy house? (Read Matthew 8:20.)

Then how and when was he rich? Read 2 Corinthians 8:9 for a clue. Jesus is God, and how much does God own? Look in Psalm 50:10-12 for the answer. Now draw a picture of some of the riches God owns. And don't forget to draw his most valuable possession of all—you!

The Chief Cornerstone

You are . . . members of God's household . . . with Jesus Christ himself as the chief cornerstone. (Eph. 2:19-20)

What do you think a cornerstone does? Have you ever seen a city hall or old courthouse building that has one very special stone or brick in a lower corner, with engraved words and names on it? That's the cornerstone. Long ago the cornerstone actually held the walls of the building together, and without it the structure could not have remained standing.

Design and make a building from one or more of these supplies:

- A big box you can cut or paint
- A small box you can cover with frosting first and then with crackers or gingerbread
- Square candies or sugar cubes, "frosted" together to form walls and covered with a paper roof

Don't forget to make a cornerstone in your building and mark it in some special way. If it is possible to do so, write the name of Jesus on your cornerstone.

Jesus is our chief cornerstone, and we, as believers, are the bricks he uses to build his building—his church. The Bible calls us "living stones" in 1 Peter 2:5. Read Ephesians 2:21-22 to see where we fit into God's building and to see who lives in us.

Unselfish Servant

But [Jesus] made himself nothing, taking the very nature of a servant. (Phil. 2:7)

Do you know someone you think is unselfish? You know—the kind of person who would let someone else go first, let another person have his way, and share his belongings willingly?

Ask the members of your family to each draw a picture of someone they have seen being unselfish. Show your drawings to the others, and see if they can guess who the pictures are. Maybe you will see *your* face on someone's paper!

Ask each member of your family to

describe how his person was unselfish—and if your picture was not drawn, decide right now that you will act unselfishly before you play this drawing game next time.

Jesus Is Lord

. . . and every tongue confess that Jesus Christ is Lord, to the glory of God the Father. (Phil. 2:11)

Here are two special ways to write the name *Lord* or *Jesus is Lord:*

• Make the letters by squeezing and shaping pieces of aluminum foil and gluing them on a board or cardboard.

• Write the word(s) in cursive letters and outline them over and over again, placing each new line a quarter-inch away from the line beside it, and using a different color of crayon or marker each time. If someone in your family cannot yet write in cursive letters, ask another person to do the writing for him and let him do the outlining.

When we say, "Jesus is Lord," what do we mean? Years ago, in the days of the evil Roman caesars (kings), Christians were treated terribly, burned at the stake, and even fed to lions because they were brave enough to say—and mean—that "Jesus is Lord." Is he your Lord, too?

The Image of God

He is the image of the invisible God, the firstborn over all creation. (Col. 1:15)

You have probably had a good time tracing a picture sometime. Doesn't it make you feel like a great artist? All the lines and shapes are just perfect—and it is probably hard to have to admit that you traced the picture when somebody says with amazement in his face and voice, "Did you draw that?"

Find a picture that you really like and a sheet of tracing paper or waxed paper. If you are using waxed paper, trim off the rough edges first, and then staple or tape the picture and the tracing paper together to avoid a lot of "slipping and sliding" of the papers! Enjoy tracing a picture, even if you don't really need that kind of help in creating a great masterpiece!

Jesus was called the "Image of God." It is a little bit like the picture and the tracing paper. When they are together, they are one picture, but if you take out the staples, you can see two identical (just exactly alike) pictures.

God, Jesus, and the Holy Spirit are identical. They are one wonderful person. But since people on earth were all mixed up about what God was really like, God sent Jesus to show himself to us. Read Philippians 2:5-11 to see what God did in the "person" of Jesus.

The Head of the Body

He is the head of the body, the church. (Col. 1:18)

Try one or both of these art activities:

• Make the very best drawing of a person that you can. Dress him (or her) and color him however you want. He can be a famous person, someone from long ago, or a man, woman, or child who lives today. It can be a portrait of a member of your own family. There is only one requirement—don't give him a head. Leave the head off your drawing.

• Cut out paper dolls by folding a piece of drawing paper in half several times in the same direction and cutting out a half-person shape, with his back against one folded edge of the paper and his hands touching the opposite fold. Be sure that the hands and the back remain folded—do not cut them apart. Also, do not give your paper dolls a head. Open up your paper and see how your people look!

How well would anything living really do without a head? Not a pleasant thought, is it? What would tell the body how to move, to act, or even to breathe? Out of the whole body, would you say that the head is the most important part? Is the body much good without it?

When we try to operate our lives or our church without Jesus as our "head," we're trying to do the impossible! Read Colossians 1:16-18.

One Mediator

For there is one God and one mediator between God and men, the man Christ Jesus. (1 Tim. 2:5)

Jesus is like a living "bridge" between you and your heavenly Father. Make a picture to help you understand the name *mediator*. On a piece of white paper, draw a picture of a little village on top of a cliff on the left side of the paper, about three or four inches wide. On the right side of the paper, draw another cliff with a forest of trees on top of it. Pretend that the people who live in the village on the left need to get across the deep valley to the forest on the right, but there is no bridge joining the two cliffs.

Make a bridge for the poor citizens of the village in one of these ways:

• Rope bridge: Use string or yarn.
• Wooden bridge: Use Popsicle sticks, sticks, or twigs.
• Metal bridge: Roll up foil and glue it on the paper.

Jesus himself is our mediator—our "bridge" that joins us with God.

Our Savior

Our Savior, Christ Jesus . . . has destroyed death and has brought life . . . through the gospel. (2 Tim. 1:10)

What does the Bible mean when it says that Jesus is our Savior? What does he save us from? Read what the angel told Joseph in Matthew 1:21.

What did it cost Jesus to save us? Why did Jesus die to save us? Because we deserve it? Read the answer in Titus 3:4.

Make a cardboard cross to help you

think of Jesus, the Savior of the world. Cover the cardboard cross with construction paper if you wish. Write the word *Savior* clear across the side arms of the cross and also down the vertical part. (The letter *i* in *Savior* can be right in the middle of the cross where the words meet.)

To make the letters fancier, cut out small squares from tissue paper or thin colored paper, wrap one paper at a time over the eraser end of a pencil, dip it in glue, and stick it to the letters. Place the papers close together along each letter in the word *Savior.*

Now here's the big question. How does Jesus become *your* Savior? Try to answer that important question and then read what the Bible says in Acts 16:31, Romans 10:13, and Ephesians 2:8-9.

Are You an Intercessor?

> Therefore he is able to save completely those who come to God through him, because he always lives to intercede for them. (Heb. 7:25)

Have you ever been someone's intercessor? You're not sure? Let's say it another way. Did you ever "go to bat" for someone—did you ever stick up for someone? Then you have been an intercessor.

When you did that, you were doing something Jesus does for you. The dictionary says that an intercessor is someone who pleads (says, "please!") for another person or asks someone a favor for him.

Jesus sees you when you have studied hard and are taking a big test at school. "Father," he says, "please help Samantha to be able to remember the answers to the questions." Jesus notices when someone has said something that hurt you. He says to the Father, "Please soothe the hurt that Joshua is feeling and help him to be forgiving, as you are to him." Every day Jesus is your faithful intercessor.

To help you remember who Jesus is to you, trace around your hand with the fingers together. Then outline again around the thumb and fingers of your drawing (but not the back side of the hand), about a quarter-inch away from the other line. The second line will make your drawing appear to be three-dimensional, like two hands folded together in prayer.

Cut out your praying hands, punch a hole in the top, and write the word *intercessor* on them. Color the hands, if you wish, and rub a small amount of oil on the back to make a "sun catcher." Loop a ribbon or piece of yarn through the hole and hang the praying hands in a sunny window.

High Priest

> Christ came as high priest. (Heb. 9:11)

In Jesus' day, there was a special religious leader, the high priest. It was his honor to wear a special jewel-studded robe and to be in charge of the ceremonies in the temple on the Day of Atonement. His important job was to represent the people before God and to sprinkle the blood of a lamb on the mercy seat to "pay" for the sins of the people. And over and over again every year the high priest had to offer to God a sacrifice for his own sins, as well as the sins of all the people.

Make a copy of the high priest's jeweled breastplate (looking a little like a bib or a baseball catcher's chest protector), using paper and crayons, cardboard, and flat buttons painted different colors, or cardboard and a small package of assorted colored rhinestones (fake jewels) from a craft store. Make it small or large enough to wear.

Here's how the breastplate should look:

- It should be square.
- It should have rings at the four corners. You may draw and color them (gold) on your paper. If you are making a breastplate to wear, punch a hole in each corner and use shiny wrapping paper or foil to make the rings, putting them through the holes and twisting or taping them shut.
- There should be twelve jewels of several different colors glued in rows to the square breastplate.

To wear the breastplate, run a ribbon through the bottom two rings and wrap it around your waist and through the upper two rings to attach around your chest or neck.

The book of Hebrews tells us that Jesus is our High Priest. Read Hebrews 9:7, 11-12 and 10:11-12 from the Bible and see how Jesus was the only High Priest that we will ever need.

Follow His Example

Christ suffered for you, leaving you an example, that you should follow in his steps. (1 Pet. 2:21)

We often use examples in daily life: sewing patterns are kinds of examples—so are blueprints of buildings and stencils. Here's an easy way to make your own stencil:

Draw a design on poster board or lightweight cardboard. Cut it out carefully. Tape together any cuts or tears in your stencil.

You can trace around the edges of the stencil and color or paint inside the lines. Another way to use your stencil is to color heavily around the edges of it with crayon or chalk and place the colored stencil facedown on drawing paper. Rub the back of the stencil with your finger or a paper towel to leave its imprint on your paper.

Jesus was our example. What were some wonderful attitudes and actions of Jesus that you would most like to copy?

A Heart Full of Love

God is love. (1 John 4:16)

Greater love has no one than this, that he lay down his life for his friends. (John 15:13)

Draw a heart full of love on a piece of paper. Make the outline of the heart in pencil, since some of the lines may later be erased. Fill the heart with the letters *L-O-V-E*, making them fit exactly inside the whole heart.

The *L* and the *E* on the right and left sides of the inside of the heart will be smaller than the *O* and the *V* in the middle of it. When you have finished the heart-shaped word, erase any extra outside lines that are not part of the letters. Color the letters any way you like.

What has Jesus done for you to show his love? What has he done lately for your family? What can you do to "pass on" to someone else some of the love he's given to you?

King of Kings

On his robe and on his thigh he has this name written: KING OF KINGS AND LORD OF LORDS. (Rev. 19:16)

Make a crown in one or more of these ways:

- Cut a zigzag-topped strip of cardboard or poster board and cover it with foil. Form it into a circular crown by taping or gluing the ends together.
- Cut the center from a paper plate, leaving only the outside ring. Around the ring punch holes with a paper punch or a nail. Place the stems of freshly cut flowers in the holes until the whole paper ring is covered with God's beautiful flower creations. Trim the stems of the flowers and cover them with heavy tape on the underside to keep them in place.

- Collect a basketful of daisies. Make a small slit in the stem of each and thread each stem through the slit in another flower to form a daisy chain. Close the ends of the chain with a paper clip to form a crown.
- Make a paper-clip crown by joining paper clips together to form a chain—and then a circle—that will fit on your head.

It is not hard to picture Jesus as the awesome "King of kings," with flowing robes and shimmering crown! He created the incredible universe and everything in it; he's greater than anyone who has ever lived at any time. Jesus deserves to be worshiped and served as "King of all kings"! See what Psalm 72:11 and Revelation 1:5 say about Jesus.

Alpha and Omega, the First and the Last

I am the Alpha and the Omega, the First and the Last, the Beginning and the End. (Rev. 22:13)

How good are you at saying the alphabet? No problem, you say? Try repeating it backwards—from Z to A! Or try saying the Greek alphabet. That might be a problem!

Jesus was named after the alphabet of his day—the Greek alphabet, beginning with *alpha* and ending with *omega*.

Write *alpha* and *omega* or the English alphabet in fancy calligraphy (writing) that you design yourself. Start with the basic letters and add swirls, strokes, lines, and curlicues wherever you wish.

Alpha stands for the beginning. Who was alive and well at the very beginning of all beginnings? Jesus! Who will be alive and in charge of everything at the end of all ends—if there could ever be one? Jesus. Who was and is active in the affairs of life at all past and present times in between the beginning and the ending? Jesus! Are you starting to see why Jesus has that name?

When we see problems happening in our world or when we worry about our future, how is Jesus, the Alpha and the Omega, important to us? Read Revelation 22:13.

The Bright Morning Star

I am the Root and the Offspring of David, and the bright Morning Star. (Rev. 22:16)

Many times in the Bible Jesus is described as light and brightness. Isn't a bright, sunny morning a great start to the day? Don't you love to go outside on a cool, crisp night and look up at the incredible, shining stars? Even heaven is described as the place where there will be no need of light, because Jesus, the Light of the World, will be there! Read the beautiful verses about the Morning Star, Jesus, in 2 Peter 1:19.

Then enjoy this art activity as you find a hidden star. Cut an apple in half horizontally (from side to side) across the middle (not from the stem down). You will find God's little hidden star there. Remove the seeds and paint around the star with tempera or poster paint. Use the painted side of the half apple as you would a stamp on a sheet of paper, reapplying the paint to the apple as often as you need to. Make as many star stamp designs as you would like to have on the paper.

When the paint has dried, outline the stars with a fine felt-tip marker. Use the paper as a refrigerator decoration or as wrapping paper for a gift.

The Bright Morning Star is God's gift to you!

chapter

2

BIBLE

ACTING

The Bible is full of interesting and colorful people—some old, some young, some wise, some foolish, some facing big decisions, some having problems, and some just enjoying life. They sound a lot like people today, because they were!

The people we meet through the Bible worshiped the same awesome God we know and love today. He knew them, like he knows us, before they were born; he loved them with an unconditional love just as he loves us; he guided their steps as he daily wants to direct ours. We are all a part of his huge family of faith, and one day we will all live together with him.

In the pages of this chapter, you will get better acquainted with God's family of the past through acting, pretending, and discussing their lives, hopes, mistakes, and victories. So lights, camera, *acting!*

Sneak Attack

> And while they were in the field, Cain attacked his brother Abel and killed him. (Gen. 4:8)

Pretend to be a villain with a sinister plan to *tickle* someone to death. Find a feather from a pillow or a feather duster for your weapon, and hide behind a chair or the sofa to watch for your unsuspecting victim.

When someone else who wants to

be included in this dramatic situation comes merrily skipping along, jump out in front of him and begin the tickling. The victim should finally, in a great melodramatic (overacted!) flourish, fall to the floor, clutching her sides, *tickled to death!*

When was the first murder in the Bible? How and why did such an evil thing happen? Read Genesis 4:1-12 for the facts about the crime.

Noah's Newscast

Noah was a righteous man, blameless among the people of his time. (Gen. 6:9)

Pretend that you are a newscaster, reporting the news and weather of the day. Imagine that no one has ever even heard of rain before (it had never rained before the Great Flood!) and that you are trying to describe to the listening audience what is happening outside.

If you prefer, pretend to be a reporter inside the ark with a daily weather update and livestock report.

Read the reason for the big Flood in Genesis 6:5-7, the people who survived it in Genesis 6:18, what the Flood was like in Genesis 7:11-12, and what happened afterward in Genesis 9:8-11. What a happy ending to a sad story!

Water! Gasp! Water!

When the water in the skin was gone,

she put the boy under one of the bushes. (Gen. 21:15)

Pretend to be a thirsty man stranded in the desert, crawling or staggering along, clutching your dry throat and begging for water.

Choose someone to be a stranger whom the thirsty man meets in the desert. He will stand and wait as you thirstily crawl up to him and then say to you, "I'm sorry. *We* only have lemonade and soft drinks. You'll have to try three miles down the road that way." (He points.)

What a silly joke! But the story of what Hagar and Ishmael faced was no joke to them. Read what happened in Genesis 21:14-25.

Abraham's Big Test

Now I know that you fear God. (Gen. 22:12)

Act the part of Waldo the Wimpy Donkey. Waldo's problem is that he is not very strong, and his job is to carry firewood. Now that's a problem, since firewood is heavy!

Get down on all fours to be Waldo.

Ask someone in your family to stack the firewood on your back in the form of toothpicks. (Remember, you're wimpy!) Try to crawl across the room and back without spilling any firewood, and ask your master to add more wood to your back every time you pass him.

The story of Abraham and his son Isaac is not a silly story at all. In fact, their experience is one of the most touching events in the whole Bible. It pictures a father's great love for God and for his son, the son's obedience, and the rescue of the boy from death just in the nick of time!

It's also an incredible picture of the loving heavenly Father and his Son, Jesus, who carried the wooden cross on his back like Isaac carried the firewood on his.

The biggest difference in the two events is that Isaac was rescued from death because of a lamb, and Jesus is the Lamb of God who died in our place. Read the story about Isaac's rescue in Genesis 22:1-14.

The Mistreated Brother

His brothers were jealous of him. (Gen. 37:11)

How do these words and objects remind you of Joseph in the Old Testament: a colorful coat, an unusual dream, a deep well, a prison, and a palace in Egypt? If you are not sure, look in Genesis 37, 40 and 41. Tell the story in your own words. Then try telling it backwards, from Egypt back to the coat of many colors. Get your whole family to act out the story, even using costumes and props if you want to.

Baby's First Boat Ride

But when she could hide him no longer, she got a papyrus basket for him and coated it with tar and pitch. Then she placed the child in it and put it among the reeds along the bank of the Nile. (Exod. 2:3)

Pretend to be a television news reporter interviewing Miriam, Moses' sister. Imagine that the pharaoh has given his special permission for Miriam to tell her family's story on the evening news, so she is free to answer all your questions. Miriam should take all her answers from the Bible story in Exodus 2:1-10. (You may want to read the story together before you go on the air.)

Ask your own questions or use some of these:

- What were you doing today, hiding in the bulrushes near the Nile River?
- Isn't that a strange way to baby-sit?
- Why was your baby brother in a basket on the river?
- Weren't your parents afraid the basket would leak?
- Where do you think your mom got her idea of saving the baby?

- Was your family worried about the baby's safety?
- Who then came to the river to bathe?
- How did the princess discover that the baby was there?
- What did she do?
- The princess reported to our roving cameraman on the scene that you offered to go get a woman to feed and care for the baby. Is that correct?
- Who did you get?
- How are the baby and your family now?
- It has been reported that you believe that God was somehow involved in this whole experience. Would you please share your opinion on that report?

The Fireproof Bush

I will go over and see this strange sight—why the bush does not burn up. (Exod. 3:3)

Moses had an amazing adventure while he was taking care of a flock of sheep out on the desert. As he came close to Horeb, which was called the mountain of God, Moses witnessed an incredible sight! See what it was in Exodus 3:1-3.

After God had caught Moses' attention with the burning bush in the middle of the desert, what did God do? (Read verse 4.) What message and what instructions did God give Moses? Why was Moses supposed to take off his shoes? (Find the answers in Exodus 3:5-12.)

Fill a large flat pan or shallow cardboard box with cornmeal, sand, or even rice or small dried beans. Use it as the sandy desert where Moses' wilderness experiences with the children of Israel took place.

Reenact the stories of the burning bush (Exod. 3:3), crossing the Red Sea (Exod. 14:13-29), the serpent of brass (Num. 21:8-9), the fall of Jericho (Josh. 6:3-5), and other wilderness stories. Add toy animals, people, and paper cutouts to your desert scene to represent the different stories.

Adopt-a-Grandparent

Rise in the presence of the aged, show respect for the elderly. (Lev. 19:32)

Imagine that you are in charge of an Adopt-a-Grandparent program in your town because, for some mysterious reason, there are many grandparents with no grandchildren to love and appreciate them.

Pretend that you have been selected (or a team of concerned citizens has been chosen, if your whole family is involved in this activity) to advertise grandparents on television. It will be your job to promote the great qualities of grandparents, telling the viewing audience interesting and important information that children should enjoy and appreciate about older people.

Make your commercial enthusiastic and convincing, because grandparents really *are* great (as you probably already know)! If you know some older people with no grandchildren of their own in town, show special kindness to them every chance you get!

Two elderly people were so important in Jesus' life that we are still reading about them nearly two thousand years later—Anna and Simeon. Read their interesting story in Luke 2:25-34, 36-38. They had waited all their lives to see Jesus!

Stolen Treasure

It is true! I have sinned against the Lord, the God of Israel. (Josh. 7:20)

Not everyone mentioned in the Bible was a good guy! God wants us to know the truth, the whole truth, and nothing but the truth about what happens when people choose to go their own foolish ways and disregard his laws. Our loving God only wants what is best for us, and he wants us to avoid the trouble sin always brings with it. So he informs us about the good and the bad.

Read the story of Achan's sin in Joshua 7:11-12: There was sin in Israel, and God couldn't bless them because of it. God said to find out who the guilty family was (vv. 14-15). Notice how in verses 19-26 a man named Achan confessed to the sin of coveting (wanting something that wasn't his) and stealing (those two sins often go together) and was punished.

Act out the scene when Achan saw the beautiful robe, the silver, and the gold, took them, and hid them in his tent. You can turn off most of the lights since his crime probably took place at night. Make a tent by spreading a sheet between the backs of two chairs or over a table.

If you would like to, act out the rest of the story, too. And never forget its valuable lesson!

A Conversation with God

The Lord came and stood there, calling as at the other times, "Samuel! Samuel!" Then Samuel said, "Speak, for your servant is listening." (1 Sam. 3:10)

Pretend to receive a phone call from the Lord. Give only your end of the conversation, making the comments and answering the questions that you imagine the Lord would ask if he were to directly talk to you. Imagine that he is asking you to obey him and telling you about the job he has for you to do in his kingdom.

Your conversation does not have to be only serious, but it must be reverent and not silly, since listening to God in real life is the *most important* thing we will ever do!

Read the beautiful story of God's call to Samuel when he was just a young boy and see Samuel's eager willingness to listen and obey God! The story is found in 1 Samuel 3:1-10, 19.

Are you the kind of child that Samuel was? When God speaks to you through his written Word (the Bible), through your parents, or inside your own heart and mind, do you immediately say, "Speak, Lord—I am your servant, and I am listening"?

David, the Giant Slayer

So David triumphed over the Philistine with a sling and a stone. (1 Sam. 17:50)

Play this simple David and Goliath game:

Goliath must stand in the middle of the room, pretending to be a huge and powerful giant man. (He can flex his muscles and show off his might, but he is not allowed to move his feet.) The other players will represent David in the story found in 1 Samuel 17:4-11, 20-24, and 32-37.

Let Goliath remain in position while Mom or Dad reads these verses from the Bible. Then all the Davids can come close to Goliath and say to him, "The Lord will fight for us!" being careful not to let him touch them.

Everyone who gets tagged also becomes a Goliath! Continue to play until all Davids are tagged.

The true story of David and Goliath has a totally different ending, thank goodness! Read it in 1 Samuel 17:40-51.

Miracle Mountain

So Ahab sent word throughout all Israel and assembled the prophets on Mount Carmel. (1 Kings 18:20)

One of the greatest miracle stories in the Old Testament is the one found in 1 Kings 18:20-24, 26-35 and the awesome verses 1 Kings 18:38-39. Read them aloud and then act them out. Elijah showed the false prophets of Baal that he had a lot of faith, didn't he? But why shouldn't he? He knew the power of the living God!

And that same power lives in you if you are a believer in Jesus Christ. Read Colossians 1:11-12. Is there anything that God and you together can't do?

Cave Dweller

There he [Elijah] went into a cave and spent the night. (1 Kings 19:9)

Do you ever feel sorry for yourself? We all have times when we really feel deep inside that we have been unjustly treated and that we deserve better than we got or that nobody cares about us.

Elijah was a great man of God and of faith (remember the altar on Mount Carmel when God sent fire to burn up the sacrifice?), but he definitely had pity-party times. He is right in the middle of one such uncelebration in a cave, of all places, in the Bible account found in 1 Kings 19:10. Read the verse with sadness and sniffles in your voice. It wasn't like God had rejected Elijah, either. He had just done a great miracle for Elijah (in 1 Kings 18:41-46) when the land desperately needed water.

Continue Elijah's sad tale of pity in 1 Kings 19:11-13. What were the big, dramatic events that happened during Elijah's time in the cave? Was God's presence in those things? How did he speak to Elijah? Look at verse 13. Do you think Elijah felt God's presence?

Have you ever felt God's presence? Maybe it was in a church service while listening to beautiful Christian music, looking at a sunset or a snowfall, or reading a story from God's Word. If we know Jesus, or if he is calling us to come to him for salvation, he often speaks to us in a gentle, silent voice.

Wall under Construction

Let him send me to the city in Judah where my fathers are buried so that I can rebuild it [the wall]. (Neh. 2:5)

Pretend that you are in charge of a build-the-wall construction project. Give a how-to-do-it speech to your workers, including what materials you will use, how you plan to make them stay together, how tall and thick the wall will be, and so on.

Read some of these verses to your workers. Explain that Nehemiah was so upset because the people of the city had disobeyed God, and now their wall of protection was completely crumbled. There was no place of safety anymore!

- Nehemiah 2:2-3
- Nehemiah 4:6 (The wall is half done.)
- Nehemiah 4:15 (There are enemies, but the people keep working.)
- Nehemiah 6:7 (The wall is finished.)

The Girl Who Risked Her Life

I will go to the king. . . . And if I perish, I perish. (Esther 4:16)

The story of Esther would be fun to act out as a puppet show. You can make stick puppets (glue faces on sticks), sock puppets (glue or color faces on old socks and use them as hand puppets), or finger puppets (cut the fingers off an old work glove, make faces on the fingers and glue on yarn hair). You will need a lovely Queen Esther, the wicked Haman, King Xerxes, and Esther's cousin, Mordecai. When your puppets are ready, read these verses from the Bible and act them out.

- Esther 2:7, 17 (Esther becomes queen.)
- Esther 3:8, 13-14 (Evil Haman persuades the king to kill all the Jews in the kingdom.)
- Esther 4:1-5 (Mordecai is horrified about the king's command. He is a Jew, and so is Esther.)
- Esther 4:8, 11 (Mordecai asks Esther to beg the king to change his mind. For her to go to the king without his permission could cost her life!)
- Esther 5:2 and 7:3-4 (Esther begs for her people to be spared.)

- Esther 7:9-10 (Haman is hanged for his evil plan.)
- Esther 8:15-17 (The happy ending.)

Jesus, Our Redeemer

I know that my Redeemer lives. (Job 19:25)

Have you ever been a slave? Yes, you sometimes feel like one when Dad or Mom asks you to do something you'd rather not. You can pretend to be a slave with a "ball and chain" around your ankle to make sure you don't try to escape! Here's how:

Roll up a pair of socks to make a ball and tie it to a piece of ribbon or string. Attach the other end of the string to your ankle, and there you have it—instant "slavery"! Put some small, heavy unbreakable items inside the sock ball to drag around with you.

Another way to act out the idea of slavery is to make some play money from paper or buttons wrapped in aluminum foil. Place some of your stuffed animals or toys on the "auction block" (the place where slaves were sold) and let someone else in the family or neighborhood "buy" a toy to enjoy for awhile, using some of the play money.

Now, back to the question, Have you ever been a slave? The answer is *yes!* We have all been slaves to Satan and sin (Rom. 3:23), but Jesus, our Redeemer, has come to buy us ("redeem" us) and make us members of

his wonderful family! Read 1 Corinthians 6:20, 1 Corinthians 7:23, and 1 Peter 1:18-19 to see how Jesus redeemed us.

The Amazing Marvelo

He spreads out the northern skies over empty space; he suspends the earth over nothing. (Job 26:7)

Let someone in your family put on a strong-man (strong-lady) act as The Amazing Marvelo—or all join together as The Strong Family Performers. Let Marvelo prepare for his great performance in another room by putting on a long-sleeved T-shirt or sweatshirt and stuffing crumpled-up newspaper or socks inside the shoulders and upper sleeves for muscles.

Watch The Amazing Marvelo put on a fantastic display of strength, using a stick with a balloon attached to each end to look like a barbell—or other objects that can be made to appear heavy when they really are not. Applaud and cheer for his "incredible" display of strength.

Job wrote about an awesome show of God's mighty power in Job 26:7. In spite of the fact that Job lived during an ancient time of superstition and scientific misunderstanding over thirty-five hundred years ago, he was led by God to write this absolutely correct verse, describing the fact that God suspended the world in space upon nothing!

Think about it! Here we are playing, working, laughing, exercising, talking, eating, and sleeping upon a huge round ball twenty-five thousand miles around, with nothing under us to hold us up! It sounds like something unbelievable from the latest science fiction movie—but it is true!

Remember, when you hear people express incorrect ideas of how they think the world got here and stays here *without* God, that you know the true and living God, who hung the whole world upon nothing and keeps it there!

Crash, Bam, Bang! Fireworks!

The voice of the Lord is over the waters; the God of glory thunders, the Lord thunders over the mighty waters. (Ps. 29:3)

Have you ever imagined or pretended that the sound of thunder and the flash of lightning were something funny—like the giants' bowling tournament in the sky or huge barrels that keep rolling from cloud to cloud? What makes all those bright lights and commotion?

Electricity is an invisible energy that God placed in the atmosphere of his universe because he knew man would need it one day, and then he allowed man (one of them was Benjamin Franklin with his famous kite and key) to discover the invisible power and put it to use. Aren't you using electricity right now?

One time that we can see electricity is in the form of lightning. Otherwise, it's like the wind and even something like the Creator God himself: We cannot see it, but there is no doubt that it is there because of what it does!

Have you noticed that during a storm you always *see lightning* before you *hear thunder?* When the electrical energy called lightning suddenly flashes, it makes a lot of heat! The heat warms the air, which causes it to expand with a small explosion we call thunder. The lightning catches our eye first because light travels faster than sound. Read Psalm 29:3-4 with a lot of expression in your voice because these verses tell us what the thunder and lightning is saying about God. Then read Psalm 18:12-14 and enjoy God's way of picturing in words his amazing power as it is shown through thunder and lightning.

Try your talents as a sound-effects person like on radio story programs. See how nearly you can make the sounds of thunder and rain—first a trickle and then a heavy downpour. Use your mouth or something in your house to make the sound effects.

Shall I Laugh or Cry?

Put thou my tears into thy bottle: are they not in thy book? (Ps. 56:8, KJV)

Play this funny game with your family: Two players must stand facing each other and begin to sing, loudly, two *different* songs. Neither player is allowed to laugh or smile as he sings. Other people in the room should add to the confusion by describing out loud what the singers are singing and how well they are doing at maintaining a straight face. The winner of each "duet duel" (the one who keeps from smiling longer) will then be challenged to a new duet duel by someone else in the family.

Sometimes a good laugh or cry helps us feel better—but can you imagine trying to catch your tears in a bottle? That wouldn't add up to much water, would it? Even though you have probably heard the old expression "She cried buckets of tears," you know that it is not really possible to do that! If we could bottle up all the tears we shed in our whole lifetime, they would not fill a bucket—no matter how sad we have been!

A few tears, however, do not necessarily add up to a *small* amount of hurt. Our feelings can hurt terribly without a single tear being shed. But God notices our tears. That's what the writer of Psalms means in Psalm 56:8. Read this interesting verse from a King James Bible, if you have one.

God gives us tears as a blessing.

They make our eyes moist and comfortable instead of dry and scratchy. Tears help to keep our eyes clean by washing out little bits of dust or dirt that occasionally blow in. But God's great heart is saddened when he sees the tears in our eyes that mean we feel hurt, and he gives us a wonderful promise in Revelation 7:17. See what it is!

The Bible Is Trustworthy

Then I will answer the one who taunts me [Satan], for I trust in your word. (Ps. 119:42)

For this game you will need a questioner, a contestant to answer questions, and someone to taunt him. (To *taunt* in this game means to say, "I don't think you can do it!")

Pretend you are on a television game show. The contestant should stand facing his questioner (show host), with the taunter beside the contestant. As each question is read, the contestant should reply, "I will answer it." Then the one taunting him will say, "I don't think you can!" The contestant may go ahead and show him who's right by answering the question. If the contestant can't answer the question, the taunter must.

Here are the questions:

- What is the first book in the Bible?
- What color is the cover of your Bible?

- What is your favorite story in the Bible?
- Where was Daniel thrown because he prayed to God?
- What is one of the miracles Jesus performed?

Satan is our real life taunter. He whispers discouraging words silently in our hearts to keep us from believing God's Word and doing what it says. But when we know God's Word, we can answer the devil's wicked taunts.

The Incredible One-Book Library

Your word is a lamp to my feet and a light for my path. (Ps. 119:105)

Ask one person in your family to pretend to be the very *dignified* host of the distinguished and highly educational television program "Masterpiece Library," and the rest of your family to be the fascinated viewing audience. Request permission from Dad to borrow an old coat and tie (or neck scarf) for the host to wear and place your host in a chair in front of the audience, pretending to be in his own personal library as he speaks.

The television host may explain to his audience in a very dignified voice that they are about to see the world's most amazing library. He will then reach for the family Bible on a shelf or table nearby and say, "Here is a *whole* library—in just *one* incredible book!" At that amazing bit of information, the audience will gasp, look at each other, and say, "In just *one* book? Incredible!"

The host may then invite each member of the studio audience to come and be interviewed by him as he asks questions like these:

- What is your favorite book besides the Bible?
- What book have you read that has great illustrations?
- Have you ever read a book that was so interesting you could hardly put it down until it was finished?
- What is your favorite book in the incredible library, the Bible?

When your "Masterpiece Library" program is over, read Psalm 119:105 and Psalm 119:11 together and remember that you can read the Bible's exciting stories, its beautiful words of poetry, its wise advice about how to keep from having unnecessary problems and its answers to solving the ones you already have.

There has never been, and never will be, another book like the Bible!

A Fishy Story

All your words are true; all your righteous laws are eternal. (Ps. 119:160)

Take turns making up fish stories (stories that aren't really true or are very exaggerated) about a deep-sea diving trip you supposedly took, your imaginary expedition to the North Pole, or the time the president of the United

States invited you to the White House! Try to make your "fishy" stories seem as believable as possible to your listeners.

If the people listening to your stories had not been told that they were just make-believe, and you had let them believe that they were true, would that have been wrong? Is a "little white lie" so bad? What about a whopper of a lie? Which one—a white lie or a whopper—is really the truth?

Abram found out the hard way that telling a lie is a bad idea. Read Abram's lie in Genesis 12:11-13. Even though things seemed to be going all right in verses 14-16, the situation became very complicated in verses 17-20. The most important people on earth and in heaven were displeased with Abram—the king and God—and that is about as bad as a situation can get!

Actually, Abram's problem wasn't only the lie—it was also that he wasn't trusting God to take care of him and his family. His attitude was, "Oh, dear! I'd better take care of myself." He totally forgot about God's promises and power. Fortunately for Abram, God kindly delivered him from the anger of the king.

Listen to this fishy story and see if you think the truth was told:

A customer came in the door of the fish market and said to the clerk, "I want you to do me a favor."

"Certainly, sir," said the polite salesman. "What'll it be?"

"Well," said the man, "I just got back from fishing, and I didn't have any luck. To make matters worse, I promised my wife I'd bring home five big fish for dinner tonight."

"Don't worry," said the clerk, "I'll be glad to wrap you up five big fish to take home to your wife."

"Please don't do that!" said the man. "I don't want them wrapped. Just *throw* them to me!"

"I don't understand," said the clerk. "Why do you want me to do that?"

"Because I'm an honest man, and I want to be able to tell my wife that I *caught* the five fish!"

Now, how honest do you think he really was?

Fancy Restaurant!

> So the guard took away their choice food and the wine they were to drink and gave them vegetables instead. (Dan. 1:16)

Read the story of the four young men of courage and how God strengthened them and rewarded them because they refused to disobey the Lord. The story can be found in Daniel 1:8-17. Then play "fancy restaurant."

You may simply pretend to be a customer and server, or you may get really fancy, with china, silver, and long-stemmed glasses! You might even serve food!

The member of your family who is the server should show you to your

table and then try to tempt you to order things you know are wrong. In a
very distinguished, proper, manner
he should say something like, "May I
interest you in our special for today—
the rrrrichest [rolling the *R*s] of meats,
delicacies from the East, imported
aged wines, and perhaps a smoke of
homegrown marijuana to relax you after your delicious meal?"

The person who is the customer
should pretend to be a modern-day
Shadrach. Respond something like
this: "Oh, no thank you! I am a Christian from [your hometown]. I would
like to have a healthy, well-balanced
meal of fruits, vegetables, and water
to drink, please. That will be all.
Thank you very much."

The server can argue back, "Perhaps you do not understand! I have
instructions from the manager to
bring you rich food and wine. He will
be very offended, and I may lose my
job if you refuse his food!"

Reply back to the server, "Sir, I must
do what would please my God rather
than try to satisfy the management."

When the time comes in real life
when you must choose between doing
what pleases God and doing what
someone else thinks you should, be
sure to stand up strong for God's way!

Let Your Fingers Do the Writing

Suddenly the fingers of a human hand
appeared and wrote on the plaster of

the wall, near the lampstand in the
royal palace. (Dan. 5:5)

Read about the special way God used
Daniel and what Daniel's God-given
ability had to do with King Belshazzar
and the scary message on his palace
wall. It is found in Daniel 5:1-17, 22-30.
Read the story with the kind of expression that must have been in people's
voices and on their faces that night.
(Throw in a few quiet screams now
and then for effect.) Aren't you thankful that God uses you in very special
ways, too?

Here Comes the Judge!

Do not judge, or you too will be
judged. (Matt. 7:1)

Pretend you are in children's court.
Choose a family member to be the
judge and others to be the person on
trial (the defendant) and the one who
is accusing him (the plaintiff). If only
two of you are available to be in court,
one person will need to move from
one position to another, pretending to
be both the defendant and the plaintiff.

The plaintiff must make up a story
about the person he is accusing (he
stole cookies from the cookie jar; he
watched too much TV; he ate his dessert first; he left his bike in the rain; he
got his good tennis shoes muddy;
etc.). The defendant must then tell
why he did what he did, giving as
many good reasons as he can. The

judge (or judges) must then decide whether the accused person is guilty or not guilty.

Sometimes, in real life, *we* must be the judge. We must judge when we are at "school court," "neighborhood court," or even "ball team court" to make sure that who we are with and what we are doing is pleasing to God.

But we must also be careful *not* to act as the judge of whether somebody else is cool enough, smart enough, or popular enough to meet our standards. That kind of judging is unkind and unfair. We need to remember that God is pleased when we show love and kindness to others and leave that kind of judging to him. Look at 1 Samuel 16:7 to see how *God* judges people.

The Guy Nobody Liked

As Jesus went on from there, he saw a man named Matthew sitting at the tax collector's booth. "Follow me," he told him, and Matthew got up and followed him. (Matt. 9:9)

Pretend to be the guy nobody liked in the Bible—the tax collector. Act like you have come to your family's home

to collect their taxes. Find a small book to use as your "tax book" and put a small piece of paper inside it. Write on the paper the amounts of tax your family must pay as you walk from room to room.

Here are the amounts of tax they owe:

- All lamps 2¢
- All red items 5¢
- All new furniture 10¢
- All leather objects 1¢
- All cowboy hats or boots 5¢
- All thick books 10¢

Add up the total amount of tax your family owes. Tell them that if they cannot pay, you will be forced to take them to debtor's jail where they must stay until they can say, "Jack, Max, and Zack are more relaxed without tax and that's a fact!" three times very fast.

Baa! Baa! Snarl! Growl!

I am sending you out like sheep among wolves. (Matt. 10:16)

Ask one family member to read the story on this page as the others fill in the proper sound effects. Really get some dramatic action into this story—you might even get down on all fours if it will help you play the part! If the kids make the sound effects the first time the story is read, ask Mom or Dad to be the sheep and wolves the second time through.

One sunny day a flock of sheep

(say, *"Baa!"*) were munching grass on a quiet hillside. There were sheep (*"Baa!"*) of all sizes—big rams (*"Baa!"*), fluffy ewes (*"Baa!"*), and tiny baby lambs (*"Baa!"*). They ate the green grass (*"Munch, munch"*) and drank the cool water from the stream (*"Slurp, slurp"*).

But, unknown to the sheep (*"Baa!"*), a hungry wolf (*"Grrr!"*) was lurking behind the bushes, hungrily dreaming of lamb chops! Suddenly, the wolf (*"Grrr!"*) bounded out from the bushes—and found himself face-to-face with—the shepherd! Seeing the determined look on the shepherd's face, and fearing his stick, the wolf (*"Grrr!"*) retreated in a cloud of dust, leaving the sheep (*"Baa!"*) to return to their contented munching (*"Munch, munch"*) and drinking (*"Slurp, slurp"*).

When you're done, talk with your family about Jesus' words in Matthew 10:16. Who was Jesus talking to? Why did he say they were like sheep among wolves? What are some ways we might be like sheep among wolves today?

Smart Kids

I praise you, Father, Lord of heaven and earth, because you have hidden these things from the wise and learned, and revealed them to little children. (Matt. 11:25)

Have a family contest to see how many things you can think of together that children can do which adults usu-ally do not—or cannot—do. Then make up a TV commercial advertising a kid for sale. Place the kid in front of the "studio audience" and describe all the good things about him. Use all the salesmanship and enthusiasm you can express. Let's hear it for kids!

One time Jesus prayed a special prayer of thanks to God the Father for showing his truth to children. Read his prayer in Matthew 11:25. Jesus knows that many times children have more faith in God than the most edu-cated of grown-up adults. Since your faith is often strong when you are young, you can decide right now that, as you grow, you will stay the same smart person of faith that you are now.

Which Team Are You On?

He who is not with me is against me. (Matt. 12:30)

Take turns pretending to be the world's most unusual soccer player, "Two-team [your name]." Pretend that you just can't make up your mind which team to play on—so, you play on both!

Place a balloon or soft sponge ball on the floor (or a soccer ball on the grass outside) and play soccer against *yourself!* You must kick the ball in one direction and then hurry to block your own kick, aiming the ball in the oppo-site direction.

It's hard—if not impossible—to play on both teams in a ball game! Imagine trying to hit the ball in a baseball game and then trying to run and catch your own hit!

If basketball is your game, would it be possible to dribble the ball down the court and then stand in front of yourself as your own guard? Definitely not!

Jesus warned us that it is impossible for anyone to be on Jesus' team in life and on the devil's team, too. Some people try to do just that, but it is not any more possible than being on both teams or both sides in a contest. The only other position in the game of life is the referee—and that position belongs only to God!

John 3:16-18 warns us that the person who does not side up with Jesus Christ has already chosen his team in life, and Matthew 12:30 says that if we are not "for" Jesus, we are automatically against him. Read both of these important Bible passages—and be very sure that you have chosen the *right* team!

A Crowd of Kids

Jesus said, "Let the little children come to me, and do not hinder them, for the kingdom of heaven belongs to such as these." (Matt. 19:14)

Imagine that you are a radio or television announcer interviewing the children who gathered around Jesus as he preached and taught and healed throughout the land. As you ask these questions, the person being interviewed may answer them the way children in Jesus' day probably would have done.

- Why do you children always hurry to get as close as possible to Jesus?
- Does Jesus ever seem bothered because you crowd around him and want to sit on his lap?
- What do you see in his eyes and hear in his voice?
- Do you want to be a follower of Jesus all your life, too?
- Is Jesus really the Messiah, the Son of God?
- What have you seen Jesus do that helps you know he really is God's Son?

Close your radio broadcast or television program by reading Matthew 19:13-15 or telling the event as though it actually happened earlier today.

Servant Power

Whoever wants to become great among you must be your servant. (Matt. 20:26)

Pretend that you are the family's servant (you may feel a little like one at times already!) or their server in a fancy restaurant. Ask permission to use some pretty dishes or glasses, fold pieces of paper in half for menus and write on them the food that will be served for supper. Act very proper and sophisticated as you serve your family their food.

If possible, put a mint leaf, a cherry,

a lemon, or orange slice in their water or other drinks. If more than one family member wants to serve, take turns. If you do a good job, your customers might even leave a small tip!

Jesus talked about being servants, but he said nothing about expecting a monetary tip for our service. He said that our reward will be that *he will consider us great* in his sight—because we have served others and him. Read Matthew 20:28 to see who is the greatest Servant of all. Who was he?

The Huge Curtain

At that moment the curtain of the temple was torn in two from top to bottom. (Matt. 27:51)

Years ago a strong man used to do a stunt in which he would stand before a crowd, flex his massive muscles, and tear a huge big-city telephone book in half with a lot of grunting, groaning, and terribly pained looks on his face. Today, we sometimes see strong-man demonstrations where experts of all sizes show their tremendous abilities to lift weights, bend metal, and break bricks and boards. Pretty amazing stuff!

Try your own show of amazing tearing-power! First, tear a piece of paper. (Make your actions dramatic and funny.) Great! Now try something harder: a paper towel. Next, demonstrate tearing a lightweight cloth, a heavier cloth, and finally (with Mom's permission), a magazine. Point out

something in your house that you *don't* think you could tear (and please don't try!).

When Jesus died on the cross for our sins, the most amazing tearing feat of all times took place once and for all. God ripped open the huge, thick curtain that separated the very holiest place of the temple from the people. Only the high priest could go into that place to meet with God, and only once a year. When the curtain (the veil) was torn in two, God was saying that Jesus' death erased everything that separated us from God. Now we can freely come into his presence.

Jesus the Preteen

And the child grew and became strong; he was filled with wisdom, and the grace of God was upon him. (Luke 2:40)

Do you realize that in only a few years some of the members of your family who are now called children will be teenagers? In fact, some of you are already eligible to be called preteens, or "almost" teenagers.

If you have a preteen in your family, interview him for an imaginary talk show. Pretend that someone in your family is the talk-show host, asking questions of the very special preteen guest. Here are some examples of the types of questions the host may ask:

• What is it like to be a preteen?

- Are there some special benefits in being "almost" a teenager?
- What are some activities that you can do better now than when you were younger?
- What are some privileges you believe you have because you are getting older?

Then, to be fair to younger members of your family, interview someone who will not be a teenager for several more years. Let him tell the good things about being a younger child.

When Jesus was twelve years old, he had the opportunity to do something all Jewish boys eagerly looked forward to doing. He made a special trip to the magnificent temple in the city of Jerusalem. If you have ever anxiously, eagerly waited the scheduled time of a great family trip, you know a little of how Jesus must have felt about this big event! Read or tell the story in your own words from Luke 2:41-52. You will discover the upset and confusion Jesus' family felt when they discovered they needed to go back to Jerusalem and get what they had left behind.

Rich Man/Foolish Man

This is how it will be with anyone who stores up things for himself but is not rich toward God. (Luke 12:21)

Have you ever thought what it would be like to have a lot of money? Most people have. Some have even imagined or dreamed about finding money along the side of the road, winning some huge cash prize, or finding a money tree full of coins and hundred-dollar bills. Most children have pictured themselves going into a favorite store and buying anything they want for a penny—or getting it free!

Pretend that you have just been chosen to win one million dollars. Act out the scene with someone coming to your door and handing you the one-million-dollar check, and show all the surprise and excitement that you think you would express if that really happened. Make it as overly funny as possible!

What would you do with that much money? What about God's part (at least 10 percent)? How would you use the money to help other people or your church?

Most people will never be that rich. However, you (yes, you!) already *are* rich compared to millions of people in the world. Jesus told us to watch out for some dangers connected with riches. He put up big warning signs in the Bible about money. Read his Beware of Riches sign in Luke 12:15 and the story he told in Luke 12:16-21.

The Wandering Sheep

Rejoice with me; I have found my lost sheep. (Luke 15:6)

If you have smaller brothers and sisters, or if you *are* the younger sister or brother, the story in Luke 15:3-7 is a great one to act out, with one person playing the part of Jesus and the other family members or friends pretending to be his sheep. Make a real hide-and-seek game out of your acting if you would like to. You may even want to blindfold the shepherd and watch him try to find his missing sheet as they *"Baa!"* to help him—or *"Baa!"* and then run to a new hiding place to make finding the missing lambs a little more challenging.

Can you imagine anything more lovable and cute than a fluffy, frisky little lamb? Can you think, too, how much that same little lamb needs protection from enemies like wolves and other wild animals? Jesus pictures us as his much-loved sheep, and he wants to be our Good Shepherd. Look in John 14:6 to see how we become his lambs.

Son on the Run

> The younger son . . . set off for a distant country. (Luke 15:13)

Did you ever know someone who ran away? Did he pack his clothes in a suitcase and actually go somewhere overnight—or did he just walk down the street and sit on the curb? Running away always creates new problems and usually worse ones than the person had before.

That's exactly what happened to the "son on the run" that Jesus told about. He thought he had problems before—but they got much worse!

Read his story out loud from Luke 15:11-24. Does it have a happy ending?

Here are three ideas to help you remember this important story from the Bible:

- Act the story out as a family and put a lot of energy and emotion into it. (Maybe you'll win an Academy Award!)
- Draw and color a picture of the part of the story you think is most important, or make a comic-strip version of the whole story.
- Celebrate with your family by getting an ice cream cone or frozen yogurt together.

Hey! Watch Me Pray!

> Two men went up to the temple to pray, one a Pharisee and the other a tax collector. (Luke 18:10)

News release! News release! Two men went to the temple to pray! Pretend that you are a television announcer, informing the viewing audience about what has happened that day in your town.

In your own words, describe how different the two men were in their ways of praying. Speculate about (guess) what will happen to their prayers. Will they be heard? Will they be answered by God? Announce that you will return after a commercial announcement. Give an advertisement for good things a customer can expect to receive from praying. Try to really sell your product—prayer.

When you return to your nightly news program, read Luke 18:9-14 as you spread the news about the man who pleased God by the way that he prayed.

Lamb of God

> Look, the Lamb of God, who takes away the sin of the world! (John 1:29)

Make a lamb puppet from a white or brown paper sack. On the folded bottom of the sack, glue construction paper eyes, nose, and ears. Make an oval-shaped white tail on the back of the puppet and cover the entire sack with cotton or cotton balls. Make up a puppet monologue (the puppet doing all the talking) about the day the lamb met the Good Shepherd.

Lazarus, Come Forth!

> I am the resurrection and the life. He who believes in me will live, even though he dies. (John 11:25)

Read the story of Lazarus's death in John 11:1, 11-14, 38-44. Act out the resurrection of Lazarus by wrapping a member of your family in an old sheet or blanket. (Or if Mom doesn't mind, wrap him around and around in a roll of toilet paper to look something like people did when they were buried in Bible days.) Put "Lazarus" under the kitchen table and instruct him to stay there until someone shouts as Jesus did, "Lazarus, come forth!"

At the signal, Lazarus must see how quickly he can get out and stand up. Then let another Lazarus in the family try it.

What three simple words brought Lazarus back to life? Do you know anyone who is very much alive right now in heaven?

The Happiest Day of All

> This same Jesus, who has been taken from you into heaven, will come back in the same way you have seen him go into heaven. (Acts 1:11)

Play "my happiest day" in much the same way as you would play charades. Take turns acting out the happiest day you can ever remember, without saying a word, and see if the other family members can guess what it was.

If everyone in your family had the same kind of happiest day (like the day when Jesus became your Savior and Lord), act out the *second* happiest day in your lives.

The mother of a famous minister told about the happiest day of her life. She said that her daddy had been drafted to go fight in the Civil War when she was just a little girl, and she felt so sad and so worried! She was afraid he would be hurt or killed and she would never see him again. Her mother and all the other children in her family cried and prayed for their daddy every night.

Then one day a telegram arrived at the door that gave the awful news that her father had been killed in battle! The little girl couldn't believe that it was really true! Her mother cried until the girl thought she would never stop.

But then one day the mother and the little girl were sitting on the porch swing shelling peas when they saw a man approaching from far away. They watched as he came closer, and the mother said, "Honey, that man sorta walks like your daddy used to walk."

The mother and her little girl sat quietly for a while longer, still watching the man coming closer. Suddenly, the mother stood up and peas rolled all over the porch. "Honey, that man *is* your daddy!" she cried as the two ran and hugged the man they loved so much. They realized that he had not really died after all—and the battle scars he wore on his face and hands only made them love him all the more! That was the happiest day of her life.

As believers in Jesus Christ, *we* will have the happiest day of our lives when Jesus comes back to earth. Jesus promised to come back—and he will! If you have never given your life to him and received his gift of forgiveness and eternal life, would you like to do it now? Here is how you can:

- *Admit* that you have sinned. (Rom. 3:23)
- *Believe* that Jesus died to forgive you and give you eternal life. (Acts 16:31; John 3:16)
- *Call* upon Jesus in prayer, ask him to forgive your sins and become your Lord. (Rom. 10:13)

Purple Power

One of those listening was a woman named Lydia, a dealer in purple cloth. . . . (Acts 16:14)

Lots of kids like the color—and even the flavor—of purple. Do you? How could you make the color purple if you had only the colors red, yellow, blue, black, and white? If you had a bucket full of beautiful purple paint, what would you paint with it? Do you prefer light or very dark purple? What things in God's world of nature are purple?

Give yourself twenty seconds to think about the color purple and then give a short, convincing speech advertising the color as you would on television. Tell why it is pretty, what objects you have seen that are the color purple, and even how it sometimes tastes. Did you sell the color to your audience?

Tentmakers

Paul went to see them, and because he was a tentmaker as they were, he stayed and worked with them. (Acts 18:3)

Do you enjoy spending the night in the home of special friends? If your family could spend the night tonight with someone else, where would it be?

Paul often stayed in the home of two friendly Christian people, Aquila and Priscilla. Which name, do you think, was the man and which was his wife? Paul even worked at the same kind of job they did when he was not busy preaching. Make a tent from a big sheet draped over the furniture, leaving space underneath for the *whole* family (yes, Dad and Mom too!) to get in and sit down.

Read Acts 18:1-4 from the Bible as you sit in the tent—to see what Aquila and Priscilla did for a living. Use a flashlight to help you see the Bible if your tent is dark.

Discuss how the home of Aquila and Priscilla must have been different from yours, what kind of furniture they may have had, how many rooms there were, and where they probably kept their tentmaking supplies. Thank the Lord for your house and for the kinds of work the members of your family are able to do.

Weak Is Strong!

For when I am weak, then I am strong. (2 Cor. 12:10)

Make a set of barbells (weights) from a stick with a pair of rolled-up socks

attached to each end. Pretend to be having a strong-man (or strong-lady) competition, trying to put on a convincing job of lifting the heavy weights. Try to make your audience believe that the barbell weighs hundreds of pounds and that even though it is almost impossible to lift, you can do it!

Next, pretend that a small pillow is an enormously heavy rock. Think of all the different ways you can carry the heavy rock across the room (on your head, your shoulder, under your arm, on your foot, between your knees), and try them all, much to the absolute amazement of your audience! (It would be great if they would clap and cheer you on.)

Talk about the ways that people in Bible days—and today in many other countries—carry loads such as water pots or baskets. Look in 2 Corinthians 12:9-10 to see when we—as Christians—are most strong. How can weak be strong? Who has the power to turn our weaknesses into strengths?

Doctor Luke

Our dear friend Luke, the doctor, and Demas send greetings. (Col. 4:14)

Pretend that your family is a medical team in Paul's day, taking care of a patient or performing surgery upon him on the kitchen table. Use a big pillow or a stuffed animal dressed in a robe or pajamas for the patient.

As you treat the sick patient, pretend that a time machine brings you a newspaper reporter from modern times. As the reporter asks you these questions to try to get the latest medical news for his paper, answer him the way you imagine a doctor or nurse would have answered in Paul's day.

Luke was a good friend of Paul's who often went places with him. Discover Luke's occupation from Colossians 4:14 and tell why you think Paul may have sometimes needed him along as the two men traveled from country to country, sharing the wonderful news of Jesus Christ with the people. Here are the kinds of questions the newspaper reporter may ask:

- What kinds of sicknesses and injuries do you often treat?
- What kind of medicine and instruments do you use?
- Do you have hospitals or ambulances?
- Do you think people live as long or stay as well in Paul's day as they do in my time?
- Does God help people get well in the first century just as he does in the twentieth century?

Be sure to thank the Lord for your own doctor and for all the medicine we have today to help us get well fast. Also, remember that whether God makes a person well in an extraordinary fast manner of healing or uses the skills of doctors to help us, it's only God who can make a person well. He's the greatest doctor of all!

Did you know that the Bible has a lot to say about food? Every book in the Bible tells stories, miracles, and events that have food or eating situations in them. Here are a few Bible verses that make us think of food:

Taste and see that the Lord is good. (Ps. 34:8)

How sweet are your words to my taste, sweeter than honey to my mouth! (Ps. 119:103)

Like newborn babies, crave pure spiritual milk, so that by it you may grow up in your salvation, now that you have tasted that the Lord is good. (1 Pet. 2:2-3)

The whole idea of appetite and food comes from God—and so it seems very proper that we can enjoy the experience of cooking, eating, and kitchen "experiments" as we learn his truth and principles. So get out those bowls and spoons, rattle those pots and pans, and see what God has to say to you through cooking and fun in the kitchen!

From One to Ten

And God spoke all these words: "I am the Lord your God. . . ." (Exod. 20:1-2)

Bake these ten-layer cookies to remind you of the very important Ten Commandments that God gave in Exodus 20:3-17. Read these special rules from God in your Bible and pray for his help to always obey them. Talk with your family about what each commandment means.

Ten-Layer Cookies

Melt one stick of butter in an eight-by-eight or nine-by-nine-inch baking pan in the microwave oven (if it is a glass pan) or a 350° oven. Take the pan from the oven and sprinkle in these ingredients in the order given, making ten layers (including the butter).

- 1 cup of graham cracker or cookie crumbs
- 1 6-ounce pkg. of chocolate chips
- 1 6-ounce pkg. butterscotch chips
- 1 can sweetened condensed milk
- 1 cup chopped nuts
- 1 cup miniature marshmallows
- 1 more cup cookie crumbs
- $\frac{1}{2}$ cup more chocolate or butterscotch chips or nuts
- shredded coconut

Bake at 350° until golden brown. When cool cut into squares and serve.

Surprise Inside!

Man looks at the outward appearance, but the Lord looks at the heart. (1 Sam. 16:7)

What do a kiwi fruit, an avocado, a pomegranate, and a peanut have in common?

Think for a minute about how each one looks on the outside. If you are not sure how they look, find them the next time you go to the grocery store and see for yourself. The outside of each of these kinds of food is not really beautiful. Some are bumpy, lumpy, or scratchy; others have a weird shape; and none of them is a very pretty color. But what about the inside of them?

Have you ever seen what happens to a fruit salad when kiwi is added? If you are a person who likes avocado, you thoroughly enjoy the taste under the dark, bumpy skin. When you crack open a pomegranate for the first time, you are amazed at the beautiful little jewels of flavor compactly arranged inside! And who doesn't love the taste of a yummy peanut?

If we only looked at the outside of these foods, we would probably never even try them, and look what we would miss! The Bible says to watch out because we often spend way too much time considering the outside of things—and especially of people—and miss the real beauty and value they have.

The shell, the skin, the crust, the "package" is not the important part of the product. It's what is inside that counts! Let's remember that Bible truth the next time we catch ourselves judging another person by his looks, his size, or the clothes he wears. It's the person inside that counts!

Here's a recipe to try with a great "surprise" inside:

Mint Surprise Cookies

Cream together 1 cup butter, 1 cup

sugar, and $^1\!/_2$ cup brown sugar, firmly packed. Add 2 eggs, 1 tablespoon water, and 1 teaspoon vanilla. Blend in the following dry ingredients:

- 3 cups sifted flour
- 1 teaspoon baking soda
- $^1\!/_2$ teaspoon salt

Mix together, cover, and chill in the refrigerator for at least 2 hours. Shape tablespoonfuls of the dough into balls, "hiding" a small chocolate mint in the center of each. Place the cookies on an ungreased cookie sheet, top with a pecan or walnut if you wish, and bake at 375° for 10 to 12 minutes.

The recipe makes about $4^1\!/_2$ dozen cookies.

Brr! Snow!

He says to the snow, "Fall on the earth." (Job 37:6)

Here's an idea for wintertime fun—if you live somewhere that it snows! Collect a glassful of clean snow and make a snow slush by pouring slightly diluted fruit juice concentrate or soda over it.

Enjoy these Bible verses that tell us about snow:

- Job 38:22
- Psalm 147:16
- Proverbs 25:13

Whiter than Snow

Wash me, and I will be whiter than snow. (Ps. 51:7)

Try one of these "snowy" projects as a reminder of the wonderful fact that when we ask Jesus to forgive our sins and become our very own Savior and Lord, he makes our hearts as clean and white as snow!

Snowball Cookies

- 4 cups powdered sugar
- 2-3 cups finely grated coconut
- 1 small pkg. cream cheese
- 1 teaspoon almond flavoring

Beat the cream cheese by hand and add the sugar, almond flavoring, and coconut. Shape the dough into little balls and roll them through powdered sugar "snow." Place the snowballs on waxed paper to cool in the refrigerator. Eat and enjoy!

"Mountain of Snow" Game

Fill a pie pan or plastic bowl with flour, cover it with a larger plate or pan, and slowly turn the pan of flour upside down. Carefully remove the pie pan or bowl, leaving a "mountain of snow" on the plate. Place a chocolate chip, candy, or raisin in the center of the mountaintop.

Take turns removing "slices" of flour away from the mountain with a table knife without letting the chocolate chip fall off. The player who finally causes its fall must put his hands behind his back and pick up the chocolate chip with his *teeth!*

No Busy Signal Here!

He will call upon me, and I will answer him. (Ps. 91:15)

From pancake mix or using the recipe on this page, make telephone-shaped pancakes. If the telephones you are used to do not have a very interesting shape, try pouring the batter into the form of older-style phones, with the receiver shaped more like a curved "barbell" that fits over a nearly triangular-shaped base, with a round dial on the front. Add a "curly" cord by drizzling batter if you can. Mom and

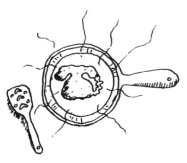

Dad will probably remember that type of phone from their childhood, or perhaps you have seen them at telephone stores or in magazines. Here's the pancake recipe:

Mix these ingredients together until smooth:

- 1 cup flour
- $^{1}/_{4}$ teaspoon salt
- 1 teaspoon baking soda
- 1 teaspoon baking powder

- $^{1}/_{4}$ cup sugar
- 1 egg, beaten
- $^{3}/_{4}$ cup milk
- 1 teaspoon vanilla

What is the point of making and eating telephone-shaped pancakes? To remind you that when you call upon God in prayer, he will hear you and give you his answer at the right time!

East/West Snacks

As far as the east is from the west, so far has he removed our transgressions from us. (Ps. 103:12)

Go outside or look out a big window in your house. Can you tell which way is east? If you are not sure and there is no one else at home who knows, take a guess and call that direction east. How far does east go and where does it end? Talk with someone about what lies east of your house if you were to keep going and going. Use your imagination and a globe if you have one. Now locate west. It will be the opposite direction from east. If you were going to take a truckload of trash as far east or as far west as you could possibly go, would you ever come to the end of east or west?

Jesus gave us a wonderful promise in Psalm 103:11-12. He said that he would take away our trash—our sins—as far away as the east is from the west, so far it cannot even be measured!

Do you think Jesus leaves our sins

there far away, or does he keep hauling them back to show us and scold us?

Those sins are gone for good, and we *don't* want to ever have them, or any other trash like them, back in our lives. But when we do sin again at times and we ask his kind forgiveness, he goes on trash removal service again!

Oriental countries such as China and Japan are often considered the "East." The words "out West" sometimes bring cowboys and their desert travels to mind. Here are an "East" and a "West" recipe to try just for fun:

Far East Fortune Cookies

- $^3/_4$ cup soft butter or margarine
- 2 cups sugar
- 1 teaspoon vanilla
- 3 eggs
- 1 cup sifted flour

Cream butter and sugar until fluffy and blend in vanilla. Add one egg at a time, beating well after each one is added. Mix in flour thoroughly. Grease and flour cookie sheets and drop 6 rounded teaspoons of dough on each set, about 2 inches apart. Bake in preheated 375° oven for 15 to 20 minutes, until edges are well browned. Remove from oven and gently loosen the fortune cookies with a wide spatula. Keep the pan warm as you gently fold each cookie in half, placing a Bible verse inside, and then pinching the two points together.

Wild West Cactus Candy

- 4 cups powdered sugar
- 3 cups coconut
- 1 small pkg. cream cheese
- $^1/_2$ teaspoon vanilla flavoring
- 2 drops green food coloring

Beat the cream cheese until soft and add sugar, vanilla flavoring, 2 cups of coconut, and the green food coloring. Blend the ingredients well, shape the dough into cactus shapes, and sprinkle or roll in the remaining coconut. Chill and eat.

O Happy Day!

This is the day the Lord has made; let us rejoice and be glad in it. (Ps. 118:24)

Make one of these "happy day" recipes, depending upon what time of God's day it is.

Top o' the Morning Pizza

This breakfast pizza is made from an English muffin topped with butter, scrambled eggs, grated cheese, and bacon strips or crumbled bacon.

Minipizza

A later-in-the-day minipizza can be made with spaghetti sauce, pepperoni, hamburger or mushroom, and grated cheese toppings.

Leading the Blind

Trust in the Lord with all your heart and

lean not on your own understanding. (Prov. 3:5)

This verse from Proverbs 3 will probably become one of the most valuable and best-loved verses for your whole life, because you can use it as your "guide." Here's a way to help you remember it:

Find a recipe to try and a partner who will help you prepare it. You will need to operate on the buddy system, because one of you will be blindfolded. The cook who cannot see will be the one doing the mixing and stirring, but his partner will read the recipe, help him measure, and place the food in the oven to bake. The blindfolded person will have to trust his partner to tell him what to do and how to do it.

That's the way it is when we "trust in the Lord with all our heart." We depend upon him to show us the right things to do and to direct the way we go in life, and he will!

Soft and Gentle

A gentle [soft] answer turns away wrath, but a harsh word stirs up anger. (Prov. 15:1)

Try this recipe for soft-as-a-cloud "fluffernutters." They are great for breakfast, snacks, or anytime!

Toast half an English muffin, and while it is still warm, spread it with creamy or crunchy peanut butter. Top the peanut butter with a soft, fluffy layer of marshmallow creme. Yum!

Once there was a boy with a very bad temper. Anytime someone spoke harshly to him, he answered back with mean, angry words, always turning the small problem into a big, terrible fight!

One day the boy became a believer in Jesus Christ, and the Lord kindly washed away all his past, angry sins. The boy was so happy and grateful, but he was also very troubled about all the mean words he had said to so many people. *How can I take them back?* he wondered. His pastor made this suggestion:

"Make a list of all the people you can remember saying mean, angry words to. Ride your bike past their houses, and place a feather from an old pillow on their front porches. Go home and pray for every person, and then go back the next day and collect the feathers you left." Do you think the boy was able to do as the pastor suggested? Why, or why not?

When the boy returned to the pastor's office, he was brokenhearted. "All the feathers were gone. I couldn't take them back," he said sadly.

The boy understood the pastor's message about what happens to the words we say, but the kind pastor encouraged the boy to "start right now and ask God to help you do what he tells us to do in Proverbs 15:1—answer mean talk with kind words. It is hard—but nothing's too hard for the God who lives in you!"

Being a Friend

A friend loves at all times. (Prov. 17:17)

Put up a lemonade or "slush" stand (or hot chocolate, if it is winter) outside your house or in your garage. Make a sign that people can easily read, and make your lemonade stand a "giveaway stand." Do not charge for the drinks. Use this opportunity to give away some kindness, a lot of smiles and friendly conversation, and even some little tracts (booklets) about Jesus if you can. You can get the tracts at a Christian bookstore. Here's the Giveaway Slushes recipe:

Pour lemonade or fruit juice into a blender and gradually blend with crushed ice until the mixture reaches "slush" consistency. Or pour the juice into a nonmetal bowl and freeze it until it becomes slushy.

Being a friend always means having friends. A friendly, kind person who really cares about others is almost irresistible.

Have you ever heard of a barnyard "pecking order?" That funny expression means that the chickens in the barnyard have an order of "importance." None of the chickens bother the most "important" chicken, some of the chickens pester the "next important" chickens, and all the chickens pick on the poor chicken on the bottom of the pecking order. It's just not fair for the one pitiful little chick to get all featherless and hurt!

Is there a "pecking order" at school or in your neighborhood? Child number one is the "cool" boy (or the popular girl), even if he is a bully and picks on other kids (or if she makes unkind remarks about other girls' clothes or hair or size).

Then there are the "number two" kids in the neighborhood pecking order. They almost all say unkind, hurtful things about each other some of the time, but they also know how to be nice when they want to.

The last kids in this unfortunate arrangement are treated nice by no one and are picked on by all the others for no good reason. Is that fair? Does it have to be that way?

Jesus would never treat anyone like that. He loves all people just exactly the same. Decide right now that you are going to stick up for the people at the bottom of your school's pecking order and not be a part of unkind talk and actions toward anyone else, either.

Give Me a Hand

Whatever your hand finds to do, do it with all your might. (Eccles. 9:10)

Make Strong-Hand Cookies to help you remember this verse by rolling out sugar-cookie dough and tracing around your hand several times with a toothpick or a knife. Bake the handprints in different poses—some flat, some making the OK sign with the thumb and forefinger pressed together, some rolled into a fist, and some pointing with three fingers folded over and pressed down. Decorate with frosting or candy to look like rings or fingernails.

Big Crop, Few Workers

The harvest is plentiful but the workers are few. (Matt. 9:37)

Find a comfortable spot in your house, lie down on your back or relax in a chair, and close your eyes. Imagine that you see a big field of cotton, white and fluffy and ready to be picked. Now picture a child about your age entering the field with a big sack over his shoulder. He begins to pick the cotton because it is his job to pick all the cotton in the field by himself. He works as hard as he can in the hot summer sun, since he wants to do his job well. Can he finish the work?

Next, imagine a huge field of golden wheat, rippling in waves in the gentle breeze. The grain is ready to harvest and must be picked before it is too late. Picture the workers entering the wheat field, two little girls with sand buckets. How can they possibly pick all that wheat?

Finally, think of a field of huge, golden sunflowers, stretching as far as you can see, and simply bursting with tasty seeds. They must be picked, packaged, and sold in the stores right away. The problem is that the only sunflower picker who is trying to pick the sunflowers is a little gray-headed, stooped-over grandmother, placing as many sunflowers and seeds as she possibly can in the pockets of her apron! Will she be able to get the whole job done by nightfall?

The field Jesus described is full of the most important crop in the world—people! These people do not yet know Jesus Christ as their Lord and Savior, but they are ready for someone to come and tell them about him. In every neighborhood, town, and school there are people ready to be harvested for Jesus. None of us can do the whole job alone, but many of us working for Jesus where we live and play can make a big difference. Will you be one of the workers who will serve Jesus and do your part to bring other people to him?

Think about this important question as you make an "edible picture" of a ripe and ready-to-harvest plant.

Use a whole rectangular graham or saltine cracker for the background on which to make your picture. Decide whether to make a picture of a ripe cotton plant—or of a sunflower full of seeds. (Your choice may depend upon what you have available in the pantry.)

First spread margarine, cream cheese, peanut butter, honey, or something similar on your cracker to stick the parts of your picture to. Begin by shaking a small layer of "dirt" (instant cocoa mix or cookie or cereal crumbs) over the spread of your choice at the bottom edge of the cracker. Add a pretzel stick or a thin strip of celery for the stem of your plant and a piece of lettuce or half a round cracker or potato chip for a leaf on the stem.

Finish your harvest picture by adding marshmallows or a spoonful of marshmallow fluff at the top of the stem to make a cotton plant or a cluster of shelled sunflower seeds for a sunflower plant. Enjoy eating the tasty "harvest!" And don't forget the important lesson Jesus taught!

Dress the Teddy

I needed clothes and you clothed me. . . . Whatever you did for one of the least of these brothers of mine, you did for me. (Matt. 25:36, 40)

Use frosting to "dress up" teddy-bear-shaped graham crackers or animal cookies. Add tiny clothes, hats, hair, fur, shoes, or whatever your imagination tells you. Use a cake decorator bag and attachments if you have them, or put the frosting "clothes" on with a toothpick, Popsicle stick, or table knife. The important thing is to get those poor, cold teddy bears covered!

An important message about clothing from the Lord Jesus Christ himself comes from Matthew 25:35-40. Read what Jesus asks his followers to do for other people that really, truly is being done for him as we help those in need.

Love Them for Jesus

Whatever you did for one of the least of these brothers of mine, you did for me. (Matt. 25:40)

Who are the least? They are people whom Jesus loves so much that he wants us to treat *them* just like we would treat *him*. The least may be someone who is not famous or rich, maybe not as beautiful or handsome as a movie star, or as intelligent as Albert Einstein. It is probably someone who is not very important or popular by the world's standards. It might be somebody just like us! The very least important person in the world is of great value to Jesus.

Plan and prepare a meal for someone who needs it because he is poor, sad, sick, very busy, or just because you want to show him kindness and friendship. If you prefer, have the person in your home for a meal or take the food to him in the form of groceries. (If you take groceries, try to include some snack items that you like, just for fun.)

Remember that you are doing your kind deed for Jesus!

Gone Fishing

Follow me . . . and I will make you fishers of men. (Mark 1:17)

Have you ever eaten "fish cracker" casserole? Here's how to make it:

In a glass bowl, place a layer of fish crackers. Top it with layers of salted nuts, pretzels, small crackers, popcorn, and finally, fish crackers again. (You may substitute dry cereal, miniature marshmallows, or whatever you have in your kitchen cupboard instead.)

Each layer in this snack mixture represents a generation of people who have chosen to follow Jesus. A "generation" means all the people born in the same period of time. Your parents and their friends belong to one generation, your grandparents and their friends belong to another, and you and your friends belong to the "right-now" generation.

Mix all the snack layers together to form a larger, tastier combination of flavors! That's the way we will one day be in heaven—all the followers of Jesus from all generations will live together as a wonderful happy family.

Better than Gatorade!

Anyone who gives you a cup of water in my name because you belong to Christ will certainly not lose his reward. (Mark 9:41)

Have you ever been so thirsty after playing hard on a hot, summer day that you could hardly even think about anything except a drink of cold water? If so, Jesus has a Bible verse just for you. Read it in Mark 9:41.

Just imagine! The one who created the whole incredible universe, who keeps the gigantic planets circling in perfect orbits, who controls the seasons and even the ocean tides, is concerned that his little ones get a drink of cold water when they need it. Wow! What a great God we serve!

Remember, too, that when we give a drink to the hot and thirsty mailman or to Dad mowing the lawn, or when we help smaller children at church get a drink from the drinking fountain, God sees us and will bless us, too. So let's join the cool-drink-giver gang!

Enjoy one of these refreshing drinks, beginning each with a glass of cold water and then following these directions:

• Purple Cow: Pour the water into a blender or a larger glass or bowl and add $2/3$ cup of grape juice concentrate and a large scoop of vanilla ice cream or whipped topping or 1 cup of dry milk. Stir or blend thoroughly.

• Lemonade Delight: Add to the cold water $1/2$ cup frozen lemonade concentrate or the juice from several lemons (and sugar or sweetener till it tastes right), a slice of orange, a maraschino cherry, and crushed ice. If you have any sherbet in the freezer, add a scoop of that, too, and blend all the ingredients together. (The orange slice and cherry are there to add color and flavor.)

It's My Favorite

Do to others as you would have them do to you. (Luke 6:31)

Think of the meal (or dessert) your

family makes at home that is your very favorite. Work together with your family to prepare it to give to someone else, or double the recipe so you can share it with another family, either at your house or theirs. If the cost of the extra food is a problem, save up for this special occasion or offer to give some of your own savings to help pay for it.

By doing what you would want someone else to do for you, you will be obeying the Bible verses in Luke 6:27-31, and you will be sure to receive back a wonderful, good feeling yourself!

If you have trouble deciding what to fix for your dinner or dessert, try this recipe:

Chocolate Cheese Cupcakes

- $1\frac{1}{2}$ cup flour
- 1 cup sugar
- $\frac{1}{4}$ cup cocoa
- 1 teaspoon soda
- $\frac{1}{4}$ teaspoon salt
- 1 cup water
- 5 tablespoons vegetable oil

- 1 tablespoon vinegar
- 1 teaspoon vanilla

Chocolate chip filling:
- 8-ounce pkg. cream cheese
- $\frac{1}{3}$ cup sugar
- 1 egg
- 6-ounce pkg. chocolate chips

In a large bowl, stir together flour, salt, sugar, cocoa, and soda. In a second bowl, beat together the water, oil, vinegar, and vanilla. Gradually add this to dry ingredients, beating until smooth. To make filling, beat cream cheese, sugar, and egg together and stir in chocolate chips. Fill paper-lined cupcake tins about half full of batter. Top each with 1 tablespoon filling. Sprinkle tops with finely chopped nuts. Bake at 350° for 25 minutes.

Measure for Measure

For with the measure you use, it will be measured to you. (Luke 6:38)

Try this experiment in measuring, using only flour or sugar, with clean hands and measuring cups and spoons. Place a clean paper towel or waxed paper on the counter to catch spills so the flour or sugar can be poured back into their canisters (containers) when you are finished. Remember, this is only a measuring exercise.

Measure these amounts of flour or sugar:

- 1 cup
- $\frac{1}{3}$ cup

- $^1/_2$ cup
- 2 tablespoons (one rounded and one level)
- $^1/_4$ cup
- 1 teaspoon (one rounded and one level)

An old Jewish folktale goes something like this:

Once there were two brothers who lived side by side on a big farm they shared. One brother lived alone since he was not married. The other brother was married and had seven children.

Both brothers worked hard, and the farm produced good crops every year. At harvesttime, the brothers would divide the wheat they had grown evenly—half of the grain in each brother's barn.

But one night the unmarried brother tossed and turned on his bed and could not go to sleep. "It just isn't right!" he said to himself. "My brother and I receive the same amount of grain, but I have one mouth to feed, and he has nine!" So the unmarried brother began to secretly carry some of his grain into his brother's barn each night.

At the same time, the married brother couldn't sleep either! He was worried about his brother, who was all alone, with no children to take care of him when he would one day be too old to work. "He needs more grain to sell for money he can save for later," he told himself. So every night the married brother secretly put some of his grain into his brother's barn.

Every morning both brothers noticed that their barns were just as full as the night before, even though they had both given grain away. They wondered how that could be possible!

They learned the secret one dark night as they met each other halfway between the barns. When they realized what had been happening, each brother cried tears of happiness for the kindness of his brother.

The Bible promises that we will receive back what we give to others. If we give kindness away, people will give us kindness back. When we smile at other people, we will be amazed at how many friendly people there are! If we greet someone with friendly, happy words, he is almost sure to answer us back in the same way—and even if that person doesn't, someone else soon will.

What a great way to live!

The Best Christmas Gift

For God so loved the world that he gave his one and only Son, that whoever believes in him shall not perish but have eternal life. (John 3:16)

You do not have to wait until the holidays to enjoy "Every Day Is Christmas" Pretzels. Here's how they are made:

With the help of an adult, melt 6 ounces of vanilla-flavored candy, white chocolate, or almond bark candy with 2 tablespoons margarine in a medium saucepan over low heat or in a microwave oven.

When the candy is thoroughly melted, add a few pretzels at a time to the mixture, stirring them and turning them over to coat thoroughly. Immediately roll the pretzels in red, green, or multicolored candy sprinkles—or place the candy-coated pretzels in a plastic bag containing sprinkles and shake them up. Enjoy the "taste" of Christmas whatever time of year it is right now!

Read the beautiful story of God's gift of himself that he gave to us from Luke 2:1-7 or Philippians 2:6-11.

Along the Way

Jesus answered, "I am the way and the truth and the life." (John 14:6)

Here's a recipe for trail mix to pack and take along "the way."

- dried fruit or raisins
- nuts of your choice
- chocolate or carob chips
- granola

What way, you say? How about taking a hike along a nearby nature trail, a walk through your neighborhood with a friend, or a "walk and talk" with one of your great parents? Give your friend or parent a bag of "along-the-way" trail mix to enjoy with you.

Jesus not only promised that he watches over our way (Ps. 1:6) and

that he will go with us on the way (Matt. 28:20), but he also assured us that he *is* the Way (John 14:6)!

How can we ever go wrong if we stay close to him?

Around the World

You will be my witnesses in Jerusalem, and in all Judea and Samaria, and to the ends of the earth. (Acts 1:8)

Make Round-the-World Soup from a mixture of whatever vegetables you have in your refrigerator. Begin with water and beef or chicken bouillon cubes, and then cut up and add carrots, potatoes, celery, tomatoes or tomato sauce, meat, rice, or whatever else your family would enjoy. Add salt and seasonings that you like.

The soup represents a mixture of a lot of different ingredients and flavors, all blended together to make something good—like God's great big family made up of all kinds of people from around the world. The very sad truth is, however, that not everyone in the world has heard the wonderful news about God and his Son, Jesus Christ.

Some of the people who have not yet "met" Jesus for themselves are in your school, neighborhood, and town like "Jerusalem" in Acts 1:8.

Other people who do not know Jesus Christ live in your state or country—your "Judea or Samaria." Many more people live in our big, wide world who still have not gotten to hear the Good News that we know about every day!

Here is a game to play as a reminder to be ready to "pass on" God's Good News every day:

"Soup roll" is played by taking turns rolling an unopened can of soup across the room to a finish line on the other side. Each player will get three turns and five points for every time his can touches or crosses the finish line. When the game is over, you may add the contents of the soup can to your Round-the-World Soup if you wish.

Buzzy Bees

Believe on the Lord Jesus Christ, and thou shalt be saved! (Acts 16:31, KJV)

Make Buzzy Bee Cookies to help you remember that the way to *be* saved and forgiven is to *believe* on the wonderful Lord Jesus Christ with all your heart and for all your life! Here's how to make the "bees."

Mix well together in a bowl:

- $3/4$ cup graham cracker crumbs
- $1/2$ cup dried fruit bits
- $1/2$ cup peanut butter
- 1 tablespoon honey

Shape the mixture into oval-shaped balls and roll them in 2 tablespoons of graham cracker crumbs. Place the balls on a plate and decorate them to look like bees. Chocolate frosting could be used to make stripes, the wings could be almond slices (or round little crackers or cereal flakes), and a chocolate chip or half a raisin would make a good eye. For the stinger, use an almond sliver or a pretzel stick. Enjoy your Buzzy Bee Cookies, but much more important than that, remember to *believe* on Jesus!

Grab-Bag Giveaway

. . . remembering the words the Lord Jesus himself said, "It is more blessed to give than to receive." (Acts 20:35)

Make "grab-bag giveaways" to hand out to your friends. Mix some of the following snack items together in a bowl. Then divide the mixture into smaller amounts, putting some in several small plastic bags. Tie or twist the tops of the bags shut and put them in a bigger paper "grab bag." Take the treats to school, church, or your neighborhood and let people reach into the grab bag for a "giveaway" treat.

Here are some ideas of what you could mix:

- dry cereal
- popcorn
- mixed nuts or dry roasted peanuts
- pretzel sticks
- shredded coconut
- miniature marshmallows
- raisins
- M&M's
- dried fruit
- chocolate or butterscotch chips
- chow mein noodles
- tiny crackers

As you willingly give to others, remember the words that Jesus Christ himself said—that the blessing and the good feeling you will have when you give is much greater than the fun you have when you get!

All Blended Together

And we know that all things work together for good to them that love God, to them who are the called according to his purpose. (Rom. 8:28, KJV)

Add all the ingredients in this recipe together, one at a time, tasting each one (except the egg) before you add it. You do not have to take a big bite! Just dip your (clean) finger in each ingredient and see how it tastes by itself. Then cook the pancakes and taste the finished product. Here's the recipe:

Chocolate Pancakes

- 1 cup pancake mix
- $1/4$ cup unsweetened cocoa
- $2/3$ cup milk
- 2 tablespoons oil
- 1 egg (don't taste raw eggs—they can carry bacteria)

First, blend the pancake mix and the cocoa together well. Then add the milk, oil, and egg; stir only until you can see no more dry mix. Pour about $1/4$ cup batter for each pancake onto a hot skillet. Cook 1 to $1^1/2$ minutes until little bubbles form and begin to break; then turn the pancakes over for one more minute. Serve them with syrup, strawberries, chocolate sauce, or whipped cream.

How did each ingredient taste by itself? Was the cake better tasting when the ingredients were all blended together and cooked? Did you like the taste of some things you added better than others?

Your cooking and tasting experience was a lot like real life. As we live each day as people who love God, some great things happen to us—like the good-tasting ingredients. But now and then, some not-so-good events interrupt our happy days, and we plainly don't like the "taste" of them!

God promises that, even though not everything that happens to us as Christians seems good at the time, he will blend the bad and good together and make the finished product always turn out for our good. Read Romans 8:28 in your Bible—and remember God's great promise to you.

Swimming Upstream

Do not conform any longer to the pattern of this world, but be transformed by the renewing of your mind. (Rom. 12:2)

Have you ever seen an old black-and-white Superman show? It always starts by describing Clark Kent, a "mild-mannered reporter for a great metropolitan newspaper" who is able to suddenly change into the amazing someone who can "leap tall buildings in a single bound," with X-ray vision and super strength. Pretty amazing stuff! And even though almost everyone watching realizes it is all fake, they still watch eagerly to see what the "amazing Superman" will accomplish in this week's episode.

Just think—the huge transformation of quiet, shy Clark Kent to daring, powerful Superman took place in a matter of minutes in a phone booth!

Did you know that God wants a transformation to take place in us? Look at 1 Peter 2:9. God wants us to be transformed (changed) from the kingdom of darkness (the devil's rule in you) to his wonderful kingdom of light (God's control in your life). When we give our heart and life to Jesus, that happens. Presto!

But he also wants our minds to be transformed to think his good, pure, honest thoughts—not to do the kind of thinking that people do who don't know him. Jesus wants us to go the opposite direction from the way the world without him is going and to fill our minds with his Word, his attitudes, and everything that will please him.

Try this fun snack idea to help you remember to be *transformed* and not to *conform:*

Arrange fish-shaped crackers on a plate like they are swimming in a "school" of fish, all headed in the same direction. Mark one fish to look different from the rest by spreading it with butter, cream cheese, or frosting. Turn that fish (representing a Christian in his world) in the opposite direction of all the rest. A Christian should not conform to anything that doesn't please God, no matter how many other "fish" are going that way!

Getting Even

Do not repay anyone evil for evil. . . . Do not take revenge . . . for it is written, "It is mine to avenge; I will repay," says the Lord. (Rom. 12:17, 19)

Make these Revenge Cookies, following the directions exactly, and making sure you measure every ingredient *evenly.* To make sure that you are making your measurements *even,* fill the right size measuring cup full each time you add an ingredient, and scrape and smooth across the top of it with the edge of a table knife. Now, that's *even!*

Mix together:

- $^3/_4$ cup margarine, softened
- $1^1/_2$ cups sugar
- 1 egg
- $^1/_4$ cup water
- 1 teaspoon vanilla

Stir in:

- $1^1/_2$ cups flour
- 1 teaspoon salt
- $^1/_2$ teaspoon baking soda
- 4 cups toasted oat cereal
- 1 cup oats

Mix the dough well and drop it by spoonfuls about 2 inches apart onto a greased cookie sheet. Bake until the cookies are light brown—10 to 12 minutes. (If you would like, you may add one or more of these to the cookie dough: raisins, coconut, chocolate chips, nuts, or $\frac{1}{2}$ cup peanut butter.) Now let's see why they are called "Revenge Cookies"!

Do you ever feel like getting even? Remember as you made the cookies it was important that all the ingredients be *evenly* measured? Sometimes we think and act like that. When someone treats us unkindly or unfairly, embarrasses us, or gets us in trouble, we often want them to get back exactly what they gave us. In the Old Testament that attitude was called "an eye for an eye and a tooth for a tooth." It's like saying, "If you gave me a 'cupful' of trouble, you deserve a 'cupful' of the same trouble back!"

But is that what Jesus tells us to do when someone wrongs us? Read Romans 12:17 and 19 to see what we should not do in those unfortunate situations. Then read Ephesians 4:32 to see what we should do instead.

When we do what Jesus told us to, sometimes we still have a little feeling of "what if they do it again and again—will they just keep getting away with it?" Then we need to remember the last part of Romans 12:19—that only God can decide if anything needs to be done and what it should be. So let's leave matters in his hands! And how about giving some Revenge Cookies with love and for-giveness to someone who has been unkind to you?

The Christian Sandwich

Do you not know that your body is a temple of the Holy Spirit, who is in you . . . ? You are not your own; you were bought at a price. Therefore honor God with your body. (1 Cor. 6:19-20)

Did you ever think of yourself as a "pocket sandwich"? Here's how to make a tasty sandwich from pocket (pita) bread:

• Cut the round, flat pocket bread in half. Save one half in a plastic bag or share it with a friend or relative.

• Carefully open the "pocket" in the bread and spread the inside of it with mayonnaise, mustard, butter, catsup, or the dressing of your choice.

• Fill the empty pocket with anything that sounds yummy to you (lettuce, tomato, olives, alfalfa sprouts, cheese, ham, avocado, turkey, tuna, or whatever your taste buds desire).

• Enjoy with a prayer of thanks for the good food God gives you every day!

Think about how you are like the

pocket sandwich: As a believer with Jesus Christ living in you there is the outside you—your body, your face, and even your hair, hands, and feet. But inside you lives Jesus your Savior. He fills you up with his goodness and presence, and now you are not just an empty "pocket." Your life is full and complete and satisfying.

Spread the Fragrance

Thanks be to God, who . . . through us spreads everywhere the fragrance of the knowledge of him. (2 Cor. 2:14)

Try these good-smelling experiments:

• Put a small amount of three or four different spices or seasonings in separate plastic bags. Close the top of each bag. Make another identical bag for each spice you used, and place all the bags together on a table.

Ask a member of your family to close his eyes and use only his nose to find the matching bags of spices.

• Soak some whole cloves and allspice in water for a few days or until they are soft. Thread a needle with dental floss or heavy thread and run it through the spices in whatever interesting arrangement you choose to make a fragrant necklace.

Whenever you use spices or enjoy the pleasant smell of potpourri, remember that Jesus wants us to spread his lovely "fragrance" with us everywhere we go. He did! Read Ephesians 5:1-2.

Which Is Your Favorite?

There is neither Jew nor Greek, slave nor free, male nor female, for you are all one in Christ Jesus. (Gal. 3:28)

Prepare a fruit basket to put in the bedroom of a special guest who comes to your house or make it for your own family to enjoy.

As you add each piece of fruit to the basket, ask yourself or someone else in the family, "Is this your favorite kind of fruit?" Ask the same question as you add oranges, apples, bananas, pears, or whatever fruit you have. Do you have one fruit that you like better than all the rest?

Sometimes we really believe that God thinks about people like we did about the different kinds of fruit. We imagine down deep in our hearts and minds that he really does have special "favorites" when it comes to types of people—their color, their nationality, maybe even their sex or age! But Galatians 3:28 makes it very clear that God does not have "favorite" people or kinds of people. He loves all his precious children just the same (and we should, too). Read Acts 10:34-35 from your Bible, and thank God today for someone who is different from you.

Fruit Treats

The fruit of the Spirit is love, joy, peace, patience, kindness, goodness, faithfulness, gentleness and self-control. (Gal. 5:22-23)

Here are some fun ideas with fruit to help you remember the "fruit" of the Spirit:

• Make "fruity faces" by dipping apples in melted caramel and giving them faces made from candy pieces, chocolate chips, raisins, or nuts. Top the faces with coconut "hair"!

• Make fruity animal faces from canned pears, apricots, peaches, or pineapple. Pineapple rings make a good lion's mane; a mouse or monkey can be made from an upside-down pear or peach half with apricot ears; peach slices make good ears for a rabbit. Use raisins or nuts for eyes and noses—and pieces of apple peel for mouths.

Watch What You Plant

A man reaps what he sows. (Gal. 6:7)

Make Pillow Cookie Surprise. Here's how:

Blend 8 ounces of cream cheese with 1 cup of butter or margarine. Stir in 2 cups of flour and chill the dough for 2 to 3 hours. Combine 1 cup of your favorite jam or jelly with 2 teaspoons sugar (and some chopped nuts, if you wish).

Divide the cookie dough into 4 parts, working with 1 part at a time while the others stay chilled. Roll the dough very thin on a lightly-floured surface and cut it into two-inch squares. Place half the squares on an ungreased cookie sheet, spread them with a small amount of the jelly mix-

ture, and cover them with another square, pressing the edges together with a fork. Bake at 350° for 12 to 15 minutes. Dust with powdered sugar.

It may be a surprise to the lucky people who get to eat your cookies to find the hidden treat inside, but it was no surprise to you, was it? You knew what to expect because you put the surprise there before you baked the cookies!

God wants to make absolutely sure that we do not have to face any surprises when it comes to our actions and attitudes and their consequences. Over and over in the Bible, he warns us to be careful and on our guard, because doing wrong will bring to us bad results, and he wants only good for his children. Read Job 4:8 and 2 Corinthians 9:6.

If a farmer sows (plants) green bean seeds, he will soon grow green bean plants. When he puts corn into the ground, he will later have a field of corn stalks producing golden ears of corn. That's no big surprise!

When we plant God's good "seed" in our garden of life, we will see beautiful, healthy plants growing later on, and the Bible says we will bring forth much fruit.

Turn Down That Anger!

In your anger do not sin. (Eph. 4:26)

Anger is here to stay! We *all* experience anger when it sneaks up on us and, *suddenly,* we're mad. Or anger gradually grows and grows inside us like a smoldering hot coal in a barbecue grill. Even Jesus, the only perfect person, experienced *anger* because anger has a good face and a bad face.

Most of the time our anger is the bad kind, the *sinful* kind—like when we don't get our way, when we feel jealous of someone else, or when we have to obey a rule we don't like.

You can demonstrate *that* kind of anger with a Pyrex pan (with the help of an adult). Fill the pan half full of water and place it on the stove at the highest temperature.

As the water begins to grow hotter, notice the tiny bubbles forming, growing bigger and more active, and finally, erupting into a full, steamy boil. If that kind of anger "spills over," someone will get *hurt!* Jesus said to *avoid* that kind of selfish anger, and he will help us do that if we ask him to.

There is a good purpose for anger, however. Jesus showed us that *good* kind of anger when he forced the evil money changers out of the temple of God because they were dishonoring his holy name and cheating innocent people. Read what happened in Mark 11:15-17. It is right to be angry about sin, because *God* is. That kind of anger makes us want to stay away from anything that doesn't please God.

Put the boiling water to good use by adding to it (carefully!) an egg or some kind of pasta. Pray that God will help you aim your *anger* in the right direction, too—against sin and evil.

Check Your Programming

Whatever is true, whatever is noble, whatever is right, whatever is pure, whatever is lovely, whatever is admirable . . . [let us] think about such things. (Phil. 4:8)

Have you ever heard of "lettuce" (let us) Christians or computer salad?

Make a "computer salad" from lettuce, tomatoes, cucumbers, carrots, or whatever your family prefers in an ordinary salad. Computer salad, however, is no run-of-the-mill, everyday salad, but it should be served often as a reminder to us of an important computer fact: that we must *program in* thoughts that are true, noble, right, pure, lovely, and admirable if we want good things to come up on the screen of our lives!

Here are some other lettuce ("let us") Scriptures to look up, read, and program into the database of our lives:

- Hebrews 4:16
- Hebrews 12:1-2
- James 1:5-6
- 1 John 2:18
- 1 John 4:7

Kneading Needed

My God will meet all your needs according to his glorious riches in Christ Jesus. (Phil. 4:19)

Have you ever heard of a recipe that needs "kneading"? What does that mean? The dictionary says that *knead-*

ing means "pressing and squeezing dough with the hands." Here's a recipe to let you try out your kneading skills. (Note: this recipe calls for quite a bit of flour and several hours of time!)

Light-as-Air-Buns

Mix together and let stand for 10 minutes:

- $1/2$ cup lukewarm water
- 1 envelope yeast
- 1 teaspoon sugar

Mix in a large bowl:

- $1/2$ cup sugar
- $1/2$ cup shortening or margarine
- 1 teaspoon salt
- 2 tablespoons vinegar
- $3^1/2$ cups warm water

Blend together the yeast mixture, the dry ingredients, and 8 to 10 cups of flour (add more flour if the dough is too sticky to handle). Grease the sides of the bowl and the dough with a small amount of cooking oil or margarine. Let the dough rise in a warm place for 2 hours. Knead the dough several times and let it rise again for 1 more hour. Knead the dough once more and shape it into small balls. Set them several inches apart on greased cookie sheets or muffin pans. Cover with a cloth and let the rolls rise 3 more hours.

Set the oven at 400° and bake the rolls until they are golden brown.

In order to turn out well, the rolls needed to be kneaded, didn't they?

And all people have things they need, too. What does God promise us in Philippians 4:19?

Cooking to God's Glory

Whatever you do, whether in word or deed, do it all in the name of the Lord Jesus, giving thanks to God the Father through him. (Col. 3:17)

How can you bake something to the glory of God? We know we can sing a beautiful song of praise to him or read his Word and bring him glory, but to honor him through our *cooking?*

Read what kinds of things we can do to bring glory to God in Matthew 5:16 and Colossians 3:17. What do these verses tell us? Do you think if you thanked God for your hands, for a kitchen in which to bake, and for the ingredients you use, and if you then were to share the finished product with one of God's special servants at your church—a Sunday school teacher, a minister, a secretary, or a custodian—that you would be glorifying and honoring God? Then here's a recipe to use!

Impossible Pie

- 4 eggs
- $1/2$ cup margarine
- $1/2$ cup flour
- 2 cups milk
- 1 cup sugar
- 1 cup coconut
- 2 teaspoons vanilla

Mix all the ingredients in a blender for a few seconds until they are well blended. Pour the mixture into a greased ten-inch pie pan. Bake at 350° for approximately 1 hour, until the center is firm.

Special Tools

Make it your ambition to lead a quiet life, to mind your own business and to work with your hands . . . so that your daily life may win the respect of outsiders. (1 Thess. 4:11-12)

Here are some cookies that need measuring, mixing, rolling, and molding—in other words, you will have to "work with your hands" to make them. Besides all the fun, you and your family will get to have the "eating pleasure," too. This is the recipe:

Cream 1 cup shortening and 2 cups sugar together. Add 4 eggs, one at a time, beating well after each addition. Blend in 2 tablespoons milk or cream. Sift 4 cups flour with 4 teaspoons baking powder and $\frac{1}{8}$ teaspoon salt; add to creamed mixture. Mix well; add 1 teaspoon vanilla extract. Chill for 20 minutes in the refrigerator.

Now you have tasty cookie dough to roll out about $\frac{1}{4}$ inch thick on a floured surface and then to cut or mold into your favorite alphabet letters, animal shapes, flowers, hearts, or whatever your imagination instructs your hands to do!

God did us an incredible favor when he made us with hands! Our hands can be two of his most useful "tools" to help other people for him, to give a pat or a hug when someone needs it, to extend a friendly wave, to fold in prayer, or to lift in praise to the wonderful God who gave us our hands.

"Thanks" Gloves

Give thanks in all circumstances, for this is God's will for you in Christ Jesus. (1 Thess. 5:18)

There was once a little girl who had a great deal of difficulty hiding her feelings when she was sad or mad, and she often was one or the other. The little girl rarely found much to be happy about—or thankful for—at least until one Christmas when she was in the fourth grade.

The exciting day had arrived for the Christmas party and gift exchange, and for a change, the little girl was *happy* and very eager to see what her gift would be! But her eagerness soon turned to anger and sadness, because she opened her present to find an old pair of mittens, torn and worn, and given by someone who obviously had no money to buy her a new gift.

In anger, and without even taking the mittens from the box, she marched over to the trash can and threw them in. Then she sat down to pout and sulk and missed the fun of the rest of the party.

Later, as the other happy children worked to help their teacher clean up the room after the party, one child suddenly cried out, "Look! There's something *inside* the fingers of these mittens!" Sure enough, each finger contained a tasty piece of wrapped candy or a shiny penny.

That day the angry little girl learned a valuable lesson: a person is very fortunate who learns to be thankful!

The Bible tells us that in 1 Thessalonians 5:16-17. Read it aloud to your family and decide right now to live your life with a happy "attitude of gratitude."

Make a "thanks" glove by placing wrapped candies in the fingers of a clean, inexpensive pair of gardening gloves or mittens. Tie a ribbon or piece of string licorice around the wrist opening of each glove and then tie them together. Give the "thanks" gloves to someone whom you want to *thank* for their kindness to you.

Money to Love

The love of money is a root of all kinds of evil. (1 Tim. 6:10)

Make "coin" cookies from frozen cookie dough, or make your own dough from a favorite recipe. Roll the dough into balls and flatten them. Carve a funny face on your coin cookies with a toothpick, or try to copy part of the designs from a real coin. You could even carve a coin design deeply on a Styrofoam meat wrapper and press the design onto the cookies with it. Make little lines around the edges of your cookies like some real coins have. Bake them, cool them, and eat them!

Play this guessing game with pennies, giving yourself one coin for each right answer you give to these money questions from the Bible. You may look up the answers if you need to.

- How many pieces of silver did Jesus' enemies give Judas to betray him? (Matt. 26:15) (thirty)
- What did Solomon want God to give him more than riches? (1 Kings 3:9-12) (wisdom)
- Did Jesus call his disciples to take along a lot of money when they went out to preach? (Luke 9:3) (no)
- What did God say people often steal from him—objects from the church or the money (tithes) they should give his church? (Mal. 3:8) (tithes)
- How much was the tithe that the Bible said people should give back to God? 10 percent or

75 percent? (Lev. 27:32) (10 percent)

After you finish the game, add more pennies to your "earnings" and give them in the church offering next Sunday. Every penny we give helps God's work and pleases him.

Forever the Same

Jesus Christ is the same yesterday and today and forever. (Heb. 13:8)

Do this experiment in your kitchen to see if you can "bend" water!

Rub a plastic comb against your clothes or on the carpet to "charge" it with static electricity. Hold the charged-up comb near (but not touching) a thin stream of water coming from the kitchen faucet. Watch what happens to the water. (It "bends" toward the comb as the static electricity attracts it.)

Now, wait fifteen minutes and do the same experiment again exactly as you did before, without looking at the instructions. Were you able to do the experiment exactly as you did before? Were you the same person you were fifteen minutes ago? Do you look and act the same as you did fifteen minutes earlier? Of course!

But do you think you could do the same experiment in thirty years and then again in seventy-five years without looking? Will *you* look and act *exactly* as you do today in seventy-five more years?

People change a bit—or quite a lot—over time. The changes in what we are like and how we act can be good or bad, depending much upon the good or bad choices we make in our lives. But Jesus Christ never changes (Heb. 13:8). He can always be depended upon to be the same loving, powerful, saving, awesome God he has *always* been!

Perfect Presents

Every good and perfect gift is from above, coming down from the Father of the heavenly lights, who does not change like shifting shadows. (James 1:17)

Make "present cookies" from a packaged cookie mix, softened frozen cookie dough, or from the recipe that follows:

Lemon Squares
Combine $1/4$ cup powdered sugar, $1/8$ teaspoon salt, and 1 cup flour; mix well. Work in $1/2$ cup butter. Press mixture into eight-inch square pan. Bake in preheated 350° oven for 15 minutes. Remove from oven. Combine 1 cup sugar, $1/2$ teaspoon baking powder, and $1/8$ teaspoon salt. Blend in 2 eggs and 2 tablespoons lemon juice. Spread over baked mixture. Return to oven. Bake for 20 minutes longer. Remove from oven; cool completely. Cut into squares to serve.

Decorate the cooled cookies to make them look like little "presents," with frosting, string licorice ties, or whatever you have handy. Share your "gifts" with a friend or your family.

And the next time you go to the store for food, a new jacket, or the cool tennis shoes you have wanted for so long—or anytime you get a present from somebody who likes you—remember that "every good and perfect gift is from above, coming down from the Father!" (And thank him!)

Fancy Doors

Here I am! I stand at the door and knock. If anyone hears my voice and opens the door, I will come in and eat with him, and he with me. (Rev. 3:20)

Make a big batch of gingerbread cookies! Here's the recipe:

- 1 pkg. butterscotch pudding and pie filling (4-serving size)
- $^1/_2$ cup butter or margarine
- $^1/_2$ cup firmly packed brown sugar
- 1 egg
- $1^1/_2$ cup flour
- $^1/_2$ teaspoon baking soda
- 1 teaspoon (or less) ginger

- 1 teaspoon cinnamon

Cream the pudding mix with the butter and sugar. Add the egg and blend well. Mix the flour with the baking soda, ginger, and cinnamon. Blend it thoroughly with the pudding mixture. Chill the dough until firm.

Spread the dough about one-fourth-inch thick on a cookie sheet or large, flat pan. Bake it at 350° for 10 to 15 minutes.

Before cooling the gingerbread, cut it into "door" shapes: rectangles with straight or arched tops. Carve "details" on the doors with a toothpick—doorknobs, small windows, locks, and fancy carvings—while the gingerbread is still warm and pliable.

If you would rather frost the gingerbread doors and use raisins, peanuts, or chocolate chips for the details, let the cookies cool before decorating them.

Eat the cookie doors as a reminder of the Bible verse, Revelation 3:20, or give them away with a copy of that important verse to someone who might not know Jesus.

O ur God is an awesome God! Listen to what the Bible says about him and his creative handiwork:

The heavens declare the glory of God; the skies proclaim the work of his hands. (Ps. 19:1)

Before the mountains were born or you brought forth the earth and the world, from everlasting to everlasting you are God. (Ps. 90:2)

You are worthy, our Lord and God, to receive glory and honor and power, for you created all things, and by your will they were created and have their being. (Rev. 4:11)

Why did God create the awesome universe, the incredible earth, and everything else with them? The Bible says that God created all things for his glory and to show himself clearly to man. "For since the creation of the world God's invisible qualities—his eternal power and divine nature—have been clearly seen, being understood from what has been made" (Rom. 1:20). Hebrews 3:4 says this: "For every house is built by someone, but God is the builder of everything."

Does it make sense to say that your house *just happened* to crash together with the order, arrangement, and beauty that it has when some boards, nails, bricks, carpet, tile, and plaster came rolling in from different directions? Of course not! And it makes much less sense to claim that the whole incredible universe "just happened" to come into being by a lucky chance event!

Day after day, in every part of the world, God shows himself to us through his marvelous creation. The experiments in this chapter of Bible science are intended to point to his power, his majesty, and his love. Isn't our God great to work that hard to let us know him?

The Big, Wide Sky

God called the expanse "sky." (Gen. 1:8)

One of God's most important creations was the sky with its space and its air. Try these experiments with air:

- Hold a sheet of thin paper in front of your face, just below your lips, and blow steadily over the top of the paper. What happens?
- Lift a pile of books using only your breath. Pile the books on a

large plastic bag and blow into it. Take your time and watch the books rise off the table.

What else did God create by using air? Read Genesis 2:7 to find out.

Water, Water Everywhere!

God called the dry ground "land," and the gathered waters he called "seas." (Gen. 1:10)

Genesis 1:6-10 says God created two kinds of water: water above the earth and water upon the earth. What did he mean? Is there water in the sky? Talk with your family about the water vapor in the earth's atmosphere.

We are very familiar with the water on our earth. We drink it, we bathe in it, we use it to water our plants, and we love to have fun in it during the hot summers. Thanks, Lord, for the gift of water!

When God told the water what to do, it obeyed his words! Water began to fill up gigantic empty ocean beds; it quickly ran down the mountainsides in rushing rivers and sparkling streams. It filled up lakes where boats would one day navigate and ponds where animals would drink. God knew exactly where his water would need to be placed. Our God is an awesome planner and Creator.

Try this water-go-where-I-want-you-to experiment. Tie one end of a string to the handle of a pitcher. Fill the pitcher with water. Pull the string tightly over the pouring spout of the pitcher and hold the end of it over a glass. Tell the water to flow down the string and begin to pour it slowly from the pitcher. It will obey!

Too Much Water!

The floodgates of the heavens were opened. And rain fell on the earth forty days and forty nights. (Gen. 7:11-12)

Sometimes no rainfall can cause a big problem called a drought. When rain is scarce, there is not enough water to meet all the needs of the plants, animals, and people, and there begins to be a shortage. If the water shortage occurs in a populated place (one that has many people living there), people have to be much more careful how much water they use. They can't water their lawns as often or have water at restaurants without specially ordering it.

The opposite problem occurs when there is too much water, like in Noah's day. Read in Genesis 7:11-12 about the major water problem that God saved Noah and his family from. See what happened next in Genesis 8:1-5. Good news for Noah and his gang!

When it was God's time for the rain and flood to stop, it did. Try this easy experiment with a piece of cardboard, a drinking glass, and water, and watch a flood of water stop.

Place the cardboard over a glass that is filled to the brim with water. Make sure that the cardboard is pressed tightly against the glass so that no air bubbles can get in. Then turn the glass upside down over the sink and take away your hand that is holding the cardboard. Amazing! No flood!

What did God promise about a worldwide flood ever happening again? (See Genesis 8:21 for the answer.)

Incredible Rainbows

Whenever the rainbow appears in the clouds, I will see it and remember the everlasting covenant between God and all living creatures. (Gen. 9:16)

God knew something incredible even before he made color—that light can be split up into different colors. Sunlight or the light from an electric light bulb appears to have no color at all, doesn't it? Wrong! It is really made up of a mixture of other colors that can be seen when the light shines through something transparent, like water or glass. When light shines through water or glass, its colors separate. Perhaps you have seen a tiny row of rainbow colors appear on your wall or ceiling when the sun shines through a chandelier or a decorative windowpane.

Try this experiment to copy God's rainbow of colors inside your house:

On a sunny day, fill a dish with water and lean a flat mirror against the inside. Place the dish where the sunlight falls on the mirror. Hold a white piece of paper in front of the mirror and move the paper and the mirror around until a rainbow of colors appears on the paper. Can you name the seven colors of God's incredible rainbow? (Red, orange, yellow, green, blue, indigo, and violet.) Read Genesis 9:13 to see why God gave the rainbow to Noah and to us and to learn the comforting promise God made to Noah and everyone else who lives on the earth.

Samson the Strong/Weak

The woman gave birth to a boy and named him Samson. He grew and the Lord blessed him. (Judg. 13:24)

Samson was a young man who began his life and ministry strong for the Lord, got weak because of sin, and ended up strong again because of God's grace. But he had terrible scars from his time of sin and disobedience to God. (His eyes were blinded.) Read Judges 13:5 to see the special rule (vow) that God meant for Samson to keep as a sign that he would be Israel's special leader.

How strong is strong? Is a piece of paper strong? Find out with this experiment:

Find four pieces of notebook or typing paper. Fold them into four different shapes. Fold one paper in half, standing it on its edges like a tent. Fold another paper in thirds and tape the edges together to form a triangular 3-D shape. Fold one paper like an accordion and lay it flat on the table. Roll the last piece of paper into a cylinder and tape it together.

Place a small paperback book on top of each paper and see which shapes are strong enough to hold it. Add more books and decide which of the four shapes will support the most weight.

See Samson at his strongest (Judg. 14:5-6; 15:4-5, 14-15), at his weakest (Judg. 16:15-21), and at the end of his life (Judg. 16:23-30). The most important lesson Samson would teach you is to stay true and strong for God every single day of your life so that you will never have to bear any scars from sin.

Everlasting Oil

For the jar of flour was not used up and the jug of oil did not run dry, in keeping with the word of the Lord spoken by Elijah. (1 Kings 17:16)

Read the story of Elijah and the generous lady and her jug of oil, found in 1 Kings 17:7-16.

Then make an oil and honey "sandwich" (no, thank you, I'm not hungry!). Into a narrow jar, pour two tablespoons of oil, two tablespoons of water, and two tablespoons of honey, molasses, or syrup. Cover the jar. What happens? (The honey or syrup sinks because it is heavier and more dense than the water. The oil floats because it is lighter and less dense than the water.) Now, did you really think we were going to use bread?

(After making your sandwich, read 1 Kings 17:17-24 to see what happened later.)

Naaman's Big Problem

Now Naaman was commander of the army of the king of Aram. He was a great man in the sight of his master and highly regarded . . . but he had leprosy. (2 Kings 5:1)

Try this spot-removing trick, with your parents' permission, on a piece of scrap cloth. Make a spot with ink, spray it with hair spray, and see what happens!

Naaman would have given anything if a spray of hair spray would have removed his problem. What was it? Read 2 Kings 5:1 to find out. Then continue the story by reading verses 2-15. Who led Naaman to know the true and living God? Did Naaman become a believer? (See 2 Kings 5:15, 17.)

The Floating Axhead

When he showed him the place, Elisha cut a stick and threw it there, and made the iron float. (2 Kings 6:6)

Which of these things do you think would float in water and which would sink?

- a dried bean
- a piece of dry cereal
- a scrap of paper
- a sponge
- a pencil
- a nail
- a nickel
- a rubber band

Try floating some or all of these items and see if you were right. Do you think something heavy like brick or iron would float? Read the miracle of the floating iron found in 2 Kings 6:1-7 and thank God that making iron float when it needs to is a simple thing for him!

Chariots of Fire

He looked and saw the hills full of horses and chariots of fire all around Elisha. (2 Kings 6:17)

There was a huge, angry enemy army of King Aram surrounding the little house where Elisha and his servant had spent the night in Dothan. When the servant got up in the morning and went outside to stretch, he almost dropped his teeth! The city was completely surrounded by the enemy army with horses and chariots.

The servant rushed back in with knocking knees and chattering teeth to report the bad news to Elisha. The prophet of God showed his servant that a much more mighty army of God's angels was surrounding their enemy! What does that say to you? Read the beautiful story of Elisha and his worried servant in 2 Kings 6:13-18.

Try this protective shield experiment with an empty glass and a sink or tub of water. Push the empty glass (upside down) into the water, keeping it in a vertical position. Does water enter the glass? Why not? Now tip the glass slightly and see what happens. Why can the water get in now?

To learn more about the protective shield of angels guarding God's children, read Psalm 91:11 and Matthew 18:10.

Ask the Animals

But ask the animals, and they will teach you. (Job 12:7)

Take a piece of clay or modeling dough and make an animal. Now make it come alive. Can you? Blow on it—does that help? Did you create your clay animal from nothing? What did you begin with?

If you could make your animal come alive (create it) how could you keep it alive and well (sustain it)? Those are two of the many things only God can do.

Sometimes we think we keep ourselves alive and well. We keep clean to kill germs, we eat good food, drink water, try to get enough sleep. But who really makes our breathing and our beating heart possible? Our Creator and Sustainer, God.

Would we have life without him? Isn't it right that we should give our whole life back to him for his use? The book of Job says that there are four things from nature that could teach us important lessons about God. See what they are in Job 12:7-10.

God's Frozen Wonders

The breath of God produces ice, and the broad waters become frozen. (Job 37:10)

God's frozen wonders are some of the most fascinating of his creations. If you live where you experience some below-freezing days in the winter, pay special attention to these amazing frozen spectacles:

- Icicles: They form anywhere that water drips when the air is very cold.
- Snowflakes: They form when water vapor freezes in the cold sky.
- Ice: Ice crystals make beautiful, complicated patterns on cold windows when water vapor freezes slowly.
- Blankets of ice: These cover the surfaces of puddles, ponds, and lakes. They are tempting to step on or skate out on, but they often are not thick enough to be safe.

For winter fun, place a small piece of black poster board or cloth in the freezer to chill it. Then catch snowflakes on the black surface and study them with a magnifying glass. Each one is different, but all snowflakes have six sides because they are designed by the Master Creator, who is a God of amazing order. If snowflakes just happened by chance, they would simply be clumps of snow with no lovely design or arrangement. What an amazing God we have!

A Kind God Sends Rain

He brings the clouds to . . . water his
earth and show his love. (Job 37:13)

Have you ever had "rain, rain, go away!" days when you were hoping for bright sunshine, and a downpour spoiled your plans? Next time you wish the rain would "go away, come again some other day" (or not at all!) try making a rain gauge.

Find a clear plastic bottle, a pencil, and a ruler. Cut the top off the bottle and fit the top part upside down into the bottom half to form a funnel. Use the ruler to make inch marks on the side of the bottle.

Set your rain gauge in an open place, firmly in the ground where it will not get blown over by the wind.

Check the amount of water that has accumulated after the next rain.

Even though rainy weather can spoil our plans sometimes, we know that we really do need the rainy days. We need to remember that God's massive universe does not revolve around only our plans, and there is a great need for rain in every part of our world. Our world would be an impossible place to call home if it were not for God's gift of rain.

Counting Clouds

Who has the wisdom to count the clouds? Who can tip over the water jars of the heavens when the dust be-

comes hard and the clods of earth stick together? (Job 38:37-38)

Here's how to make a miniature cloud in your kitchen, with the help of an adult. Heat water to boiling in a tea-kettle (be careful—steam and hot water can burn!) and watch the steam clouds form as water vapor escapes from it and meets the colder kitchen air. If you want to see the cloud of steam rain like a cloud in the sky, put on a hot pad oven mitt to protect your hand, and hold a cool spoon in front of the teakettle spout. The water vapor will turn back into water and drip off!

Have you ever looked up at a cloudy sky and studied the cloud shapes? Have you ever tried to *count* the clouds? Probably not! Read Job 38:34-38 aloud to hear a beautiful description of the great God who planned the clouds and rain as his gift to a thirsty earth.

Mysterious Drops of Water

You care for the land and water it; you enrich it abundantly. The streams of God are filled with water. (Ps. 65:9-10)

Did you ever go across the lawn bare-foot on a bright, sunny morning, only to find your feet wet for no apparent reason? Have you sometimes wondered how water drops collect on leaves when there has been no rain for days? Look at Hosea 14:5 in the Old Testament for a clue.

Be a dew catcher for several days by breaking off a dew-spotted leaf each day and bringing it into the house for observation. Look at the little diamondlike dewdrops through a magnifying glass. You can see the same type of formation of water drops on a cold can of pop that sits on the kitchen table in the warm air for a few minutes. How does that happen?

When a cold surface meets warm air, some of the invisible moisture in the air condenses or turns into little drops of water. We call those water drops *dew.* The collecting of dew on grass and plants is part of God's amazing plan to keep his creations alive and well even though every day is not a rainy day!

Read the interesting questions that Job asks about dew in Job 38:28 and then answer Job's questions for him.

Dance for Joy

This is the day the Lord has made; let us rejoice and be glad in it. (Ps. 118:24)

Try this "dancing for joy" popcorn experiment. Pour one heaping tablespoon of baking soda into a tall glass. Add one tablespoon of vinegar to a smaller glass filled with water. Holding the glasses over the sink to catch drips, pour the vinegar and water mixture into the tall glass with the baking soda in it and watch it bubble. When the bubbling subsides, drop a few unpopped kernels of popcorn into the water, one at a time. They will "dance" for joy!

Read Psalm 118:24 from your Bible and try to make this special verse a part of every day. Each new day is a gift from God!

I'm a Plant?

Our sons in their youth will be like well-nurtured plants. (Ps. 144:12)

Enjoy some of these planting activities:

• Cut one section from an egg carton and place an eggshell half in it. Fill the eggshell with dirt and plant a few flower seeds in it. Water it gently.

• Cut a grapefruit in half, scoop out the inside, and eat it. Poke two or three small holes in the bottom of the grapefruit half and fill it with dirt. Place the grapefruit in a plastic container that is a little larger than the grapefruit. Plant seeds in the dirt and water them every few days.

• Cut the top off a carrot, radish, turnip, or beet. Place it in a shallow bowl lined with small pebbles. Add water only to cover the edge of the vegetable and replace the water as it is needed. Watch your garden grow!

What is a well-nurtured plant like? *Nurtured* usually means "fed." What and how do plants eat to be strong and well nourished? Read about plant life in an encyclopedia or science book. Who provides the nutrients in the dirt for the plants' food?

What kind of spiritual diet should a boy or girl have to grow strong and healthy as a Christian? Has God provided food for Christians to grow on?

A Breathtaking God

Let everything that has breath praise the Lord. (Ps. 150:6)

Try this experiment, using your breath, an apple cut in half, and a lighted birthday candle. The object is to blow out the candle with the apple in the way. Think you can? Try it!

Stand the candle on end on the kitchen counter by sticking it into a piece of clay or a slice of bread, and light it (with the help of an adult). Set the half apple between you and the candle with the flat side toward you. Blow! Does the flame go out?

Next, turn the rounded side of the apple toward you and blow. What happened this time? Why do you think there is a difference? (The rounded side presents less wind resistance.)

Industrious Ants

Go to the ant, you sluggard [lazy person]; consider its ways and be wise! (Prov. 6:6)

What are some lessons that you think we can learn from this tiny member of God's created kingdom? Share your ideas with your family and then read God's ant lesson from Proverbs 6:6-11.

Did you ever watch ants? They are fascinating, aren't they? They scurry around, picking up grains of sand or crumbs that are two or three times their size, weaving and tottering under the weight of their loads but abso-lutely determined to transport their cargo to its destination! Haven't you almost wanted to shrink down to ant-size and take a tour of their intricate underground tunnel system? (That is, if you wouldn't be considered and treated as an enemy!)

Make an ant farm in a jar like this:

Fill a clear glass jar about half full of dirt. Find a busy anthill and dig it up with a small shovel or scoop, in-

cluding some surrounding dirt and debris (bits of sticks, bark, and leaves), and put it all into the jar. Cover the jar with a screen or a lid with a few air holes, and wrap black paper around it to encourage the ants to go underground. Give them a water supply by putting a piece of wet cotton on the dirt and moisten-ing it occasionally. Feed them crumbs of bread, crackers, or cookies every few days. For a treat, add a spoonful of honey to the jar occa-sionally. Before long, you will be able to watch the ants work in their tun-nel by unwrapping the black paper. (Do not keep the ants for over a month since a jar is not their natural habitat.)

Here are some ant facts:

- Ants live together and work together in an ant community (like a city).
- Some ants have the keeping-the-place-clean jobs, others take care of ant eggs or tiny new ants, and others handle the food storage.
- Ants talk to each other by sending out a puff of a chemical smell that sends a message to another ant's antennae. It's a silent language!

Like Oil and Water

If your enemy is hungry, give him food to eat; if he is thirsty, give him water to drink . . . and the Lord will reward you. (Prov. 25:21-22)

Have you ever heard the strange expression "They're like oil and water—they just can't mix"? That usually describes two people who have trouble getting along—who always have problems and arguments when they are together.

Try this kitchen experiment to see if oil and water really do not mix:

Put a tablespoon or two of oil and an equal amount of colored water into a soda bottle. Cover the end of the bottle and shake it well. Although the two liquids seem to mix together when you shake the bottle, they separate again when you put the bottle down. Which liquid stays on top?

What kinds of things do enemies often do to each other? Who ends up

the winner in a battle between enemies—whether they fight with looks, with words, or with fists? How does Jesus tell us to handle an "enemy situation?" Did Jesus ever have to face an enemy himself? Look in Luke 23:34 to see what he did.

Rose of Sharon

I am a rose of Sharon, a lily of the valleys. (Song of Songs 2:1)

Aren't flowers beautiful? There are thousands of kinds, colors, and sizes of flowers in the world—all made by the Master Artist's creative hand.

Since no one name can really describe how magnificent Jesus is, the Bible pictures him in many ways, and two of those names are beautiful flowers—the Rose and the Lily.

Try this art "experiment" with a piece of paper, a pencil, scissors, and a bowl of water. Draw a flower shape with four or five petals and cut it out. Color the flower, if you like. Fold the petals up toward each other like a closed flower.

Place the closed flower to float in the bowl of water. Watch the petals begin to open up, just like a real flower.

Grass Guys

The grass withers and the flowers fall, but the word of our God stands forever. (Isa. 40:8)

Make a funny-looking guy from a Styrofoam cup or half of an eggshell or half of an empty egg-shaped container for stockings. Glue the half-shell to a cardboard base so it will not tip over. Decorate the cup or eggshell (carefully!) with a felt-tip marker to look like a face, and fill it with dirt. Sprinkle grass seed or bird seed on the dirt and keep it moist. After a few days, the guy's hair should begin to come in, thick and green. When you think he needs a haircut, scissors should do the job!

Do you know why grass seed sprouts so quickly? It doesn't need much root. The same is true of many kinds of flowers. And because they don't have much root, they wither and die very easily. But the Bible tells us about something that doesn't wither and dry up ever! What is it? Read Isaiah 40:8 to see.

Feeling Really Down!

They lowered Jeremiah by ropes into the cistern; it had no water in it, only mud, and Jeremiah sank down into the mud. (Jer. 38:6)

Have you ever had a really down day? Jeremiah sure did! Read about Jeremiah's terribly, awfully, disgustingly bad day in Jeremiah 38:4-13. Jeremiah definitely needed a shower after *his* bad day, didn't he?

Do this ice-rescue experiment to remind you of Jeremiah's experience. Float an ice cube in a glass of water. Rescue the ice cube, using only a string and some salt! Hang one end of the string over the edge of the glass and place the other end on the ice cube. Sprinkle a little salt on the ice, wait ten minutes, and rescue the ice by pulling up on the string.

Did Jeremiah have such a bad experience because he was doing evil? No! He was boldly speaking God's words, and some people didn't like that. It is much more important to do God's will and speak up for him than to do what the crowd says and thinks.

White as Snow

His clothing was as white as snow; the hair of his head was white like wool. (Dan. 7:9)

Daniel saw a vision of God (the "Ancient of Days") on his throne. One thing Daniel remembered afterward was the dazzling white color of God's clothing and hair.

White is a very important color, isn't it? We often think of it as no real color at all—just something to mix with other colors in order to lighten them. But white is really a package of seven rainbow colors mixed into one. We can show that by this simple science experiment:

Cut a circle out of heavy paper or poster board. Divide it into seven equal sections, as nearly as you can. (If a teen or adult in your family has a protractor, ask him or her to help you measure the seven sections of your circle. Each section would measure about 51° wide.) Color each circle section one of the rainbow colors: red, orange, yellow, green, blue, indigo (dark, purplish blue), and violet. Push a sharp pencil into the middle of the colored circle and spin the end of the pencil as you would a toy top. What happens to the colors when the circle is spinning fast?

Wouldn't you think that the spinning mixture of all the colors would be a muddy sort of brown? What color do they make? When the circle spins quickly, your eyes cannot see each color that exists inside white separately, but they are still there, aren't they?

Other people in the Bible saw similar visions of Jesus. Read about them in Mark 9:2-4 and Revelation 1:12-14.

Hey, Salty!

You are the salt of the earth. (Matt. 5:13)

Put an egg in a glass half full of water. What happens? Add several spoonfuls of salt, stir gently, and see what happens to the egg. (If it is not floating on top of the water, add more salt.)

What made the difference in whether the egg sank or floated? It was that salt! Salt can actually lift things.

What are some other uses for salt? If you are not sure, look up the word *salt* in an encyclopedia or dictionary.

Jesus wants us to be his "salt" on the earth. Like the salt that could lift the egg, he wants us to lift other people to a better, happier life on earth and to eternal life forevermore. How can you be his salt at school, on your ball team, or in the neighborhood? Think of three "salty" things, and start to do them.

A Toothpick or a Telephone Pole?

First take the plank out of your own eye, and then you will see clearly to remove the speck from your brother's eye. (Matt. 7:5)

People in Jesus' day must have been a lot like they are today, because he talked about real-life situations we face almost every day. He knew that we often are much harder on other people than we are on ourselves—and that, if we are not careful, we can get really busy examining their faults with a big magnifying glass while we pay no attention to our own!

A simple experiment with a drop of water will help us to see what we sometimes do to other people.

Straighten out a paper clip or a short piece of wire and make a small loop at one end of it. Rub a little butter, margarine, or cooking oil on the loop, and dip it into a glass of water. When you lift the loop out of the water, you'll have a lens, like a tiny magnifying glass. Use the lens to read some words from the newspaper, a telephone book, or your Bible.

Jesus told a funny word picture about someone trying to get a tiny speck of dust out of someone else's eye when he had a big log in his own!

Instead of magnifying other people's faults, Jesus wants us to work on our own—and then to be kind and helpful to other people.

Solid Rocks or Sinking Sand

Everyone who hears these words of mine and puts them into practice is like a wise man who built his house on the rock. (Matt. 7:24)

On a kitchen saucer, place a pile of sand (or a sand substitute such as sugar, salt, or Jell-O powder). On another saucer place a flat rock. Add drops of water, one at a time, to both the sand and the rock. What happens when the water hits the sand? the rocks? On which one do the water drops sink? Can you think of anything that would sink into a rock? Could a bead or a pebble sink into the sand? Is sand steady and strong? Is a rock?

Why is Jesus often called our Rock in the Bible? Read Deuteronomy 32:4 and Psalm 18:2. If you were actually building a house, would you want its foundation to be on rock or sand? Several years ago, during a strong San Francisco earthquake, the houses that suffered the most damage were those that were built on sandy soil.

When you grow up and are ready to build your home—your marriage and your family—do you want to build it upon the solid Rock, Jesus Christ, or upon some other shifting, sinking sand foundation? How about the life you are building right now? (Read Matthew 7:24-27.)

The Sower

The one who sowed the good seed is the Son of Man. (Matt. 13:37)

Plant a seed in a bag so that you can watch it sprout. Dampen a paper towel, fold it, and place it in a clear plastic sandwich bag with several bean seeds (or grass seed, or even birdseed!). Close the top of the bag and check every day to see what's happening. When a root or sprout has grown, you may plant it carefully in a cup of dirt or outside in the ground.

Jesus is pictured in the Bible as one who plants (or *sows*) seeds—a *sower*. Read with your family Jesus' story found in Matthew 13:3-8, 18-23, and talk together about the meaning of this parable. See what kind of seed you are—or want to be!

Awesome Angel Armies

Do you think I cannot call on my Father, and he will at once put at my disposal more than twelve legions of angels? (Matt. 26:53)

God's Word tells us that he sends his angels to be our shield of protection against danger and our enemy, the devil. Try this experiment to see how an amazing invisible shield of air can keep newspaper dry. Crumple a sheet of paper and stuff it into the bottom of an empty glass. Be sure to pack it in tightly enough so that it won't fall out when you turn the glass upside down. Push the upside-down glass deep into a pan or sink full of water and hold it in place while you count to twenty-five. Pull the glass straight out of the water and remove the paper. It will still be dry! Why? Because water cannot get into the glass since it is already filled with air. The air protects the newspaper.

There was one time when God's mighty angels did not protect Jesus, even though he could have called for thousands of them to rush to save him. That time was when Jesus was about to die on the cross. He could have saved himself by calling that awesome angel army; but who, then, would have died to pay for our sins? Thank Jesus for his love for you.

The Lady Who Impressed Jesus

They all gave out of their wealth; but she, out of her poverty, put in every-thing—all she had to live on. (Mark 12:44)

Try this "coin brightening" trick with several dull, tarnished pennies. Put at least enough lemon juice or vinegar in a small glass or paper cup to cover one penny at a time. Leave each coin in the juice for five minutes and then remove a shiny coin!

If you are wondering how lemon juice or vinegar can shine a coin and soap and water cannot, here's why: the acid in the lemon juice acts chemi-cally to remove the "oxide," which is the name for the dull coating on the surface of the copper coin.

A poor widow lady once impressed Jesus with her two very small copper coins. In the touching story, found in Mark 12:41-44, the main characters are Jesus, the lady, some very rich people, and the people in the temple who heard his words. Find out what hap-pened as you read the Bible story to-gether.

Remember, too, that even when you give a small offering to Jesus from a heart of love and thanksgiving, he notices your gift.

Living Water

If you knew . . . who it is that asks you for a drink, you would have asked him and he would have given you living wa-ter. (John 4:10)

"Whoever believes in me . . . streams of living water will flow from within him. (John 7:38)

Only God can provide living water for you, but you can make a glass of water "come alive" and blow up a balloon before your very eyes! You will need an empty soda bottle, vinegar or lemon juice, water, and baking soda.

Stretch the balloon to make it easier to inflate and keep it near you on the kitchen counter. Dissolve a teaspoon of baking soda in a small glass con-taining about one ounce of water. Pour the mixture into the clean soda bottle and add the juice from one lemon or two ounces of vinegar. Quickly attach the balloon to the top of the bottle, and watch the water come "alive," blowing air into the balloon!

Who offers to give us living water, or the water of Life? Look at John 4:13-14 to find the answer, and then read Revelation 21:6. With all the kinds of drinks in cans and bottles that can be bought at the grocery store, cool water is still the best thirst quencher there is. And the best Thirst Quencher for our souls is Jesus!

Water Going Up?

"Sir," the woman said, "you have nothing to draw with and the well is deep." (John 4:11)

We usually think of water running *down* rather than moving *up*, because we see that happening as rivers run downhill, as water pours down from the faucet, and rain falls down from the sky.

Try this experiment to see if you can lift water up. Put some water in the kitchen sink or in a bowl. Dip a glass into it so that it fills with water. Then turn the glass upside down in the water. Slowly lift the glass until the rim of it comes close to the surface of the water, but not above it. Are you able to actually *lift* the water inside the glass? What happens if you lift the glass clear out of the water? What do you think holds the water in the glass? (Air)

There was also a time in the Bible when water traveled up. Read about the woman whom Jesus asked to lift water in John 4:4-10, 39.

Water of Life

Whoever drinks the water I give him will never thirst. (John 4:14)

Make a water sculpture. Here's how:

Use a nail (with the help of an adult) to make five holes in a row, side by side, near the bottom of a plastic container. Space them about a quarter-inch apart.

Hold the container under the kitchen faucet and watch the five streams of water coming out. Pinch the five streams together between your fingers—and you'll see that you have molded them like a sculptor does clay!

When you want to reshape your water sculpture into the five streams of water, brush your hand across the water, and they should separate as before.

When Jesus said, "Whoever drinks

the water I give him will never thirst," he was not talking about "wet" water—he was talking about the "thirsting" to know God that is in every person's soul. Millions of satisfied customers all over the world, over centuries of time, have met Jesus, the Water of Life, and are not thirsty anymore.

Jesus Draws Us

When I am lifted up from the earth [on the cross], [I] will draw all men to myself. (John 12:32)

Design a kitchen magnet sculpture from a strong refrigerator magnet and some small metal paper clips. Make each paper clip magnetic by rubbing it on the magnet in one direction. Once the paper clips are magnetic, the magnet will "draw" them to it, and they can then be made to stand up end to end in an original sculpture "creation."

Now take two plain magnets and place them together in such a way that they push against each other instead of "drawing" together. That pushing away is called resisting or repelling. (It's the same thing kids have been known to do when they didn't want someone to give them a big kiss or hug!)

The Bible says, "Choose for yourselves this day whom you will serve" (Josh. 24:15). It is your choice to come to Jesus when he draws you, or to "resist" his loving invitation. No one else can choose for you!

Jesus the Life

I am the way and the truth and the life. (John 14:6)

Make a terrarium (a small "garden" of plants) in a large jar, turned on its side. Place a thin layer of pebbles or gravel in it, then a thicker layer of rich dirt, and then small plants, rocks, shells, or tiny ceramic or plastic toys. Water the plants thoroughly, close the wide lid, and place them near a bright window. You now have a lovely indoor garden, filled with plant life!

Jesus says that he is "the Life." Have a round-table discussion (around the table or sitting together on the floor) with your family to decide why Jesus is called the Life. Try to name things from the living world he created that start with the letters *L-I-F-E*, and don't forget to thank him for the great gift of *everlasting* life!

The Holy Spirit

But when he, the Spirit of truth, comes, he will guide you into all truth. (John 16:13)

Do one or both of these wind experiments as a reminder of the coming of the Holy Spirit:

• Blow the Paper Away: Place two thick books about four inches apart on a table. Lay a piece of paper over the books. Blow underneath the paper to try to lift it and make it float away. Does it work? Why or why not?

• Jumping Circle: Wind can lift things off the ground! We've seen it happen as leaves and papers are carried along by the wind in our neighborhoods. Try to lift a round piece of cardboard or a plastic game token into a nearby saucer just by blowing on it. Place both the cardboard circle and the saucer on a table or shelf in front of you and practice blowing hard until you can lift the circle into the saucer.

The Incredible Death-to-Life Miracle

But Christ has indeed been raised from the dead. (1 Cor. 15:20)

Have you ever thought of what Jesus' death on the cross would have meant if he had not been raised from the dead? Give each member of your family, starting with the youngest to the oldest, a chance to tell what he thinks would have happened if Jesus had died and then stayed buried in the tomb. Then try to name some other religious leaders who died and whose graves can be visited today. If you could go to their graves, would their bodies still be there? (Dad and Mom, be ready to help with the answers.)

Try one or more of these "rising" tricks as a reminder of what Jesus did and who he is. Remember, too, that Jesus' incredible resurrection was no trick—it was God's mighty miracle!

• Fill a small-mouthed jar or bottle to the top with water. Take the cap from a ball-point pen and wrap a small piece of modeling clay or dough around the bottom edge and the pointed end of the pen's top. Place the top upright in the water so that it is barely floating. If the pen does not float well, you may have to add or subtract small amounts of clay until it does. Cover the jar's mouth with a thin sheet of rubber and secure it in place with a rubber band. (A piece of balloon would be a good thing to use.) Press down gently on the stretched balloon, and the pen top should sink. When you remove your hand, the pen should rise again.

• Tie a string around the neck of a small glass bottle. Fill it with hot water. Add two or three drops of food coloring to the water. Then carefully lower the small bottle into a large bottle or glass bowl containing water. The colored water will rise upward.

If you have a large family Bible, see if it contains a photograph of the empty tomb of Jesus. No other person who claimed to be God ever has or ever will rise from the grave as Jesus did. That's because Jesus is the only one who really is God! Read 1 Corinthians 15:20-23.

Are You Full?

Be filled with the Spirit. (Eph. 5:18)

Pour yourself a cool drink of water, but don't drink it quite yet! See how full you can get the glass without spilling it. Pour the water slowly into the glass, and you will notice that the liquid forms a little dome (a rounded top) that is slightly higher than the top edge of the glass. Now *that's full!* But how can that be?

The top surface of the water is held in place by a pressure called "surface tension," which acts almost like a thin "skin" spread over it.

The Bible tells us to be "filled with the Spirit" of God. Let's compare that experience to the glass of water. What is the "job" of the glass? Is its purpose to "contain" something? If it is empty, a glass may look good and sit nicely on the cupboard shelf, but it is not useful.

We are like that glass. God made us to "contain" Jesus Christ in our hearts and lives. But sometimes our lives are so full of other things that there is no room for Jesus to live in us and to fill us with his Spirit. A glass that is full of dirt, rocks, or cobwebs has no room to be useful or filled with anything else.

The same is true of us if we have not asked Jesus to come into our lives, to wash out the "dirt, rocks, and cobwebs" of sin that are there and to pour himself into us clear up to the little "dome" at the top of our hearts. He will do it if we just ask. Read Galatians 2:20 to see where Jesus wants to live.

God the Three

For there is one God and one mediator between God and men, the man Christ Jesus. (1 Tim. 2:5)

God is one God, right? But he is three persons, too. How can that be?

That hard-to-understand truth is called *the Trinity.* The Trinity means God the Father, Jesus Christ the Son, and the Holy Spirit. (Read 1 Timothy 2:5-6.) Although our minds are not great enough to completely understand all that God is like, we can understand as much as we need to know to love him and serve him. The following illustration from God's world may also help.

Water is water, isn't it? Water is one substance that exists in three different forms. You have all three in your own home every day. Turn on the faucet. What kind of water is that? (Liquid.) Look in the freezer. Is water there? In what form is that water? (Solid or ice.) Heat some water on the stove to boiling (under a parent's watchful eye!). What form does the water turn into? (Vapor or steam.) Is steam water? Is ice water? Is water water?

God shows himself to us, too, in three persons, each one of which has a special job to do. All of them together are called the Godhead, or the Trinity, and each job that God performs through his three persons is very important to us. You can see all three members of the Trinity at once at Jesus' baptism in Matthew 3:16-17.

Be an Example

Don't let anyone look down on you because you are young, but set an example for the believers in speech, in life, in love, in faith and in purity. (1 Tim. 4:12)

The Bible makes it very clear that even children have influence upon other people. That means that what you do affects other people either for good and for God, or for evil and the devil. We all make a difference in somebody else's life.

Try these "influence experiments" in your kitchen:

• Sprinkle talcum powder into a bowl of water. Add a drop or two of dishwashing liquid and see what happens. The dishwashing liquid pushes the powder away as it spreads out its "influence" over the surface of the water. How is that like the good influence of a Christian?

• Arrange six toothpicks or matches like the spokes of a wheel in a bowl of water. Place a sugar cube in the center of the circle of toothpicks. What happens?

Now remove the sugar cube and place a piece of soap in the center of the toothpicks instead. Does something different happen to the toothpicks?

As children of God, we either act as his "sugar," drawing people to him— or as the soap, causing people to go away from his goodness because of the "bad taste" they get from our actions, words, and attitudes.

Let's be God's sugar and set an example for others to follow!

Jesus' View of the World

In the past God spoke to our forefathers through the prophets . . . , but in these last days he has spoken to us by his Son, whom he appointed heir of all things, and through whom he made the universe. (Heb. 1:1-2)

Jesus told us why he came to earth. Find his words in Luke 19:10 and John 3:17.

Try this experiment to help you see the world like Jesus did. Draw a two-inch-high cross shape on a card using a pencil and a ruler. Cut out the cross to leave a cross-shaped hole in the card. Hold the card upright at a right angle beside a picture or photograph of the world or of a city. Stare down at the picture through the cross for several seconds, until the picture begins to look somewhat three-dimensional.

Remember that when Jesus sees us or the world, he sees us through the Cross. He came to seek and to save us!

Watch Him Flee!

Submit yourselves, then, to God. Resist the devil, and he will flee from you. (James 4:7)

Try this kitchen experiment with a glass of water, some liquid detergent, and some pepper. Let the pepper represent the devil, who wants to "cover" you with his evil plans and make you be and do what *he* wants. The detergent will represent the protection from the devil that God gives us, and the water will be our everyday life. Watch what happens!

Sprinkle some pepper into the glass of water. Dip your finger into the liquid detergent and then into the middle of the glass of water. Amazing! What happens to the pepper?

The Bible promises us that when we submit (give ourselves completely) to God and refuse to obey the devil (get tough!), he will leave us alone. Great! And when he comes back with his crafty, wicked schemes, let him know that you are God's child and you will not obey him! (But remember: God is your power source!)

Salvation, the Stain Remover

If we confess our sins, he is faithful and just and will forgive us our sins and purify us from all unrighteousness. (1 John 1:9)

Though your sins are like scarlet, they shall be as white as snow; though they are red as crimson, they shall be like wool. (Isa. 1:18)

Have you ever gotten a big stain on a favorite shirt or jeans? Isn't that upsetting?

Here's an experiment to do in your kitchen to demonstrate the power of stain. You will need an old white handkerchief or a piece of white cloth and a small amount of brightly colored grape juice, cranberry juice, or the juice from blackberries or raspberries. Dip your finger or a cotton swab into the juice or press a berry against the cloth to make a pattern. Leave it on the shelf to dry overnight. The next morning, wash the handkerchief under the kitchen sink. Use soap if you wish. How does the cloth look?

Scarlet and crimson are the deepest of all possible reds. How can our sins go from darkest red to whitest white with no trace of a stain? You must:

• Admit that there is a stain in you—the stain of sin.

Have you ever done even one wrong thing? A bad thought, an unkind look or word, a selfish act, an angry attitude, a careless habit—those are all stains in our hearts. And we all have them! (Read Romans 3:23.)

• Believe that Jesus died on the cross to take your stain away. John 1:29 says, "Look, the Lamb of God [Jesus], who takes away the sin of the world!" You can't wash it away by yourself. (Read Ephesians 2:8-9.)

• Confess to Jesus that you need the stain of sin removed and ask him to forgive you and make you clean. First John 1:9 says, "If we confess our sins, he is faithful and just and will forgive us our sins and purify us from all unrighteousness."

Do you know that you have the stain of sin in you? Do you believe that only Jesus can wash it away? If you haven't already asked him to make you clean, why not do it now?

Wash Up

Unto him that loved us, and washed us from our sins in his own blood . . . to him be glory and dominion for ever and ever. (Rev. 1:5-6, KJV)

Can you make a miniature washing machine? You say you are not that mechanically minded? Sure, you are! Here's how to do it:

Find a plastic container with a lid that fits tightly. Place in it a block or a small waterproof toy, a pair of your socks to wash, and a little bit of laundry or dishwashing detergent, and then fill it three-fourths of the way to the top with water.

Tighten the lid and shake the container for about one minute. There you have it—a tiny washing machine! And you supply the power! The block or toy acts like the "agitator" in the center of your family's real washing machine. (It helps to separate the clothes and break up the dirt.)

The Bible says that Jesus washed us from our sins. He supplied the power! How did he do it? Read Revelation 1:5-6 to check your answer. What did he use to clean us?

Is everybody automatically washed by Jesus, just like your mom would dump a big pile of clothes in the washing machine? That would mean that everyone who ever lived—the evil King Herod, Judas, wicked murderers today—would all be in heaven one day, and there would be no hell. But is that what the Bible teaches? Do we have a choice about being washed—or not? Find out in Acts 10:43 and 1 Corinthians 6:9-11.

BIBLE
MUSIC

Music is an important part of the Bible from Genesis to Revelation. Very early in our existence on earth, music was already important. Genesis 4:21 introduces to us a man named Jubal, the first musician, the inventor of the harp and flute. God placed in his greatest creations the ability to sing, to enjoy the beauty of sound, melody, harmony, and rhythm—and the know-how to make musical instruments. Why?

Because God did everything possible to make our life beautiful and satisfying. He made people able to enjoy the flavor of food, the colors and textures in his wonderful world, the fragrance of flowers, and the lovely sounds of the trilling birds, the babbling brooks, and *music!*

The most important reason God made music—and only God could!—was so that we would have a way to praise him. Since we were made to give honor and glory to God (Isa. 43:7), we needed a way to express our praise—naturally, spontaneously, with beauty and order. Nothing allows us to express the praise and worship inside our hearts like music! We can *please* God through the use of our senses, our intelligence, and our work, but we can *praise* him through music. Through music we come into the very presence of God.

The Bible shows us that we can worship and praise God through musical instruments of all kinds, through clapping, marching, and dancing, through shouting, and, of course, through using our voices as our own happy "instrument."

In this chapter we will enjoy and praise the Lord our God in all these ways. So . . . let the music begin!

The Very First "Strings"

His brother's name was Jubal; he was the father of all who play the harp and the flute. (Gen. 4:21)

The harp is the very first musical instrument mentioned in the Bible. Another Bible name for the harp is *lyre*. It was small enough to be carried in someone's hands, and David the shepherd boy probably took his harp with him to the hillsides to play while he watched his father's sheep. Read what 1 Samuel 16:18 says about David's musical ability. Read verses 21-23 to see how God used David's talent (and it must have required a lot of practice in order to play the harp for a king!) to help King Saul.

Did you know that you can use your musical talent to bless other people and to honor your King?

Here is a way to make a simple harp: Place rows of rubber bands around two different sizes of cake pans. Strum the rubber bands, watch them vibrate, and compare their sounds. Thick rubber bands will make lower sounds than thin ones, because they vibrate more slowly.

A Clanging Cymbal

The Miriam the prophetess, the sister of Aaron, took a tambourine and led the women in dances. (Exod. 15:20)

There were two kinds of cymbals in Bible times. One kind looked like two flat metal plates held in each hand and struck together.

The other kind of cymbals were more like cups in their shape. One was held still, while the other one was brought down sharply upon it.

The Bible also mentions the timbrel and tabret. Those funny-sounding twins were kinds of tambourines. They were always associated with joy, gladness, and feasting. God's people have always had much to celebrate!

Read Exodus 15:20 to see when a tambourine was used in praise to the Lord. What was the happy occasion all about? (See verses 19 and 21.)

Make a row of hanging, clanging cymbals by tying metal cups, silverware, and lids from pots and pans to strings that are attached along the length of a ribbon or belt and suspended between two chair backs. Bang your cymbals with a long-handled spoon and enjoy knowing the Lord.

The Bible also says that not every sound of a cymbal is good. When is our life compared to a noisy, unpleasant-sounding instrument? What do we need for our lives to make "beautiful music"? Read the answer in 1 Corinthians 13:1.

Hard Water

> Strike the rock, and water will come out of it for the people to drink.
> (Exod. 17:6)

Line these items up in front of you on a table: a glass containing water, an empty glass, a small empty box, a hardback book, a cereal box, and a set of keys. Describe how you think each item will sound when you tap it with a stick or an unsharpened pencil. Which will sound the most like music? Tap each item and see if you are right.

Moses had an interesting tapping experience with a stick, a big rock, and a crowd of thirsty, griping people. Read the story in Exodus 17:3-7. Then go get a drink from your kitchen with a grateful heart.

Animal Instruments

> Have seven priests carry trumpets of rams' horns in front of the ark.
> (Josh. 6:4)

Have you heard of a trumpet, a cornet, or a horn? Of course you have! Those wind instruments had the same names in Bible days as they have now, although their appearance has probably changed over the years.

Some early horns really were *horns*— animal horns. Then, in time, their design was copied and molded from metal. Look in Joshua 6:4-5 to see God's people blowing animal horns. What kind were they?

One kind of horn used in Bible days to call people to come to special occasions (remember, loud speakers and telephones weren't around yet!) was the *sopar*—a long wind instrument with a turned-up end. It was the official, national instrument of the Israelites and looked very impressive. It is still used today in some Jewish synagogues.

In Numbers 10:1-10 Moses is instructing God's people about how and when to use the trumpet. Read the verses, and after each use of the word *trumpet*, hold your hands to look like a trumpet and make the sound effect.

Marching Around

> Advance! March around the city.
> (Josh. 6:7)

Play a friendly game of musical chairs in one of these ways:

• Mark one chair with a taped X. Circle around the chairs to a familiar Christian music tape (a lively one would be fun). Whoever sits on the marked chair when the music stops must sing or hum the next line of the song on the tape. Don't remove any chairs from the circle.

• Play "musical hats" or "musical rings." Place the same number of hats or rings as there are players in the center of the floor. Circle around them until the music stops. Then quickly grab one hat or ring and put it on, and sing together the next words of the song—or make something up if you are not sure what the words are!

Jericho March

On the seventh day, they got up at daybreak and marched around the city seven times. (Josh. 6:15)

Instruments played an important part in the story of Joshua and the walled city of Jericho. Read about it in Joshua 6:2-5, 20 and answer these questions:

- Who told Joshua what to do? (v. 2)
- Did God promise the people that they would defeat Jericho? (v. 2)
- For how many days were God's people to march around Jericho? (v. 3)
- What kinds of instruments were they to blow? (vv. 4-5)
- What would happen to the wall? (v. 5)
- Did God keep his promise? (v. 20)

Now play "Jericho march" with all the members of your family or a group of your friends. Here's how to play:

Form a circle and march around the room to a music tape or record (or sing a song that you all know well as your march). One player will be designated

as the leader, and he will need to know the number of players in the game.

As the leader marches around with the other players, he will call out a number that is smaller than the number of people playing the game. The "marchers" must immediately form new circles containing that number of people.

For example, if the leader calls out, "Two!" the players must immediately form small circles containing *two marchers* each and continue to march around Jericho. If the leader calls, "Three!" circles of *three* will form. If there isn't the right number of players for everyone to be in the right-sized group, extra marchers will continue their walk around the room without being in a circle. The object of the game is to make the changes into different sizes of groups as quickly and smoothly as possible, while the music continues.

Blow That Flute

And all the people went up after him, playing flutes and rejoicing greatly. (1 Kings 1:40)

The Bible also tells us about wind instruments like we have in modern-day orchestras. Which kind of musical instrument would you prefer to play—a stringed or a wind instrument?

A man named Jubal, way back in Genesis 4:21, had the great idea of cutting a piece of a hollow reed (like bamboo, perhaps), punching holes in the top of it, and blowing. Who would have imagined all the kinds of wind instruments there are today, and all the incredibly beautiful sounds they make! Wouldn't Jubal be surprised?

Read Isaiah 30:29 to learn one type of occasion where a wind instrument was used in Bible days. What was it? Read also 1 Kings 1:40 and Matthew 9:23 to see other times a pipe or flute was used. Wind instruments can be used in joyful as well as sad times, but most of all, they can be used to bring honor and praise to the great Creator of music.

Make your own simple flute from a straw. Pinch the end of a drinking straw flat at one end and cut off the corners of it to form "reeds." Poke three small holes along the top of the straw, about an inch apart. Put the straw far enough into your mouth so that your lips don't touch the corners of the reed and blow. Cover one or more of the holes each time you blow on your straw instrument.

All Kinds of Praise

So all Israel brought up the ark of the covenant of the Lord with shouts, with the sounding of rams' horns and trumpets, and of cymbals . . . and of lyres and harps. (1 Chron. 15:28)

Try these unusual, found-at-home instrument ideas to give praise to the Lord as you sing or listen to Christian music:

• Make a "pin piano" on a piece of wood. Draw a line down the wood with a ruler and nail straight pins along it, each one nailed into the wood a little farther than the one before it. Play it by tapping or strumming the row of pins with another straight pin that has been stuck into the eraser end of a pencil.

• Place a cookie tin in a plastic grocery bag and tie the corners of the bag with a string to hang around your neck. If you tap the cookie tin with a wooden spoon, you have a drum!

Orchestra of Praise

. . . the sounding of the trumpets and cymbals and for the playing of the other instruments for sacred song. (1 Chron. 16:42)

Enjoy being a family "orchestra" with one or all of these types of instruments:

• Soda bottle flutes. Give everyone an empty plastic soda bottle and a place in the orchestra lineup. For a different effect, add a little water to one or more of the bottles. Blow in unison.

• Empty oatmeal-box drums.

• Crystal chimes. Fill glasses with different levels of water to provide different sound pitches. Line up the glasses, wet your fingers and rub them around and around the edges of the glasses.

Draw the Music

The trumpeters and singers joined in unison, as with one voice, to give praise and thanks to the Lord. (2 Chron. 5:13)

Play an instrumental Christian tape that alternates between loud and soft volume and fast and slow rhythms. Give each person a sheet of paper and two or three crayons.

When the music begins, each player may choose the color of crayon that seems to best describe the "color" of the music and make the crayon do what the music indicates—hopping or skipping across the paper, swirling around and around, zigzagging, or coloring softly or very brightly on the paper.

Read about some Old Testament musicians in 2 Chronicles 5:12-14 and decide if you think God was pleased with their praise. Is the Lord God pleased when his children worship him today?

Joyful Hearts and Feet

For the joy of the Lord is your strength. (Neh. 8:10)

Line up enough chairs side by side for each person in your family. Ask everyone to sit down and pretend to be a wooden puppet, remaining perfectly still until the invisible "puppeteer" pulls your strings.

Request that one family member turn on a lively Christian tape. Then move only your feet and legs (while seated) to the first verse of the music. When the chorus or next verse begins, move only your hands and arms to the music, keeping the rest of your body as still as possible. Finally, move only your head and change facial expressions as you enjoy the joy of the Lord through music.

Read Nehemiah 8:10 and do what the first part of the verse says: "Go and enjoy choice food and sweet drinks" (or "Go have a good snack or refreshing drink" together). Remember, too, that the "joy of the Lord is your strength"!

Nature Praise

. . . while the morning stars sang together and all the angels shouted for joy. (Job 38:7)

Did you know that scientists have discovered the planets actually give off "sounds" as they circle in their orbits? How did Job know that thousands of years ago? How does all nature point to the one who made everything in perfect order and balance?

Ask your family members to take turns demonstrating how they *think* the planets may sound as they "sing" (or make humming sounds) in their orbits in space (yes, this demonstration could get a little silly).

Then read the interesting word pictures about nature's praise in Psalm 96:11-13, Psalm 148:7-10, and Isaiah 55:12.

Whose praise and worship does God want and deserve most? Find that important answer in Psalm 148:11-13.

Carry On, Singer!

I will praise you among the nations,
O Lord; I will sing praises to your name.
(Ps. 18:49)

Have you ever seen a *relay* race? Talk about what happens in a relay race, or actually run one around the outside of your house with the members of your family. If you choose to run the relay race, ask one member of your family to be the starting runner at the front of your house. He will carry the "baton" (a rolled-up section of newspaper with a rubber band around it) in his hand, begin to run, and then pass it to the next runner, who will be waiting at the side or the back of the house. Position other family members around the house, with the last person carrying the baton back to the starting place.

Time yourselves to see how long the relay takes you and then try it again, attempting to beat your own time. Watch out, though, for obstacles in the yard you might trip over—like shrubs, toys, rocks, or pets!

When you come back inside the house, play this *singing* relay (after you catch your breath). One player will sing the first line of a familiar Christian song. He will then point to someone else, who must sing the second line and point in turn to another singer, and so on. When the song is finished, the next person in order may begin another song.

The Bible compares the Christian life to a race much like a relay race. Read what Hebrews 12:1-2 says about running the race for Jesus. The "baton" we carry is the gospel of Jesus Christ. Look back in Hebrews 11 to see who some of the other runners were who carried the baton before you. Remember to thank God for their faith.

Shake It Up!

Rejoice in the Lord and be glad. (Ps. 32:11)

Make a "shake-a-ma-jig" like this: find a sturdy stick, a piece of dowel rod or broom handle, a twirling baton with rubber ends, an old baseball bat, or even a bathroom plunger! Transform this ordinary "stick-a-ma-jig" into an authentic (and one-of-a-kind) "shake-a-ma-jig" by taping things on it that will rattle when it is shaken. Use a ring of keys, old jewelry, bells, beads, spools, baby rattles, a bandanna or plastic bag containing some coins or buttons, or whatever your great imagination suggests.

Play a lively Christian tune on the tape player or radio and keep the rhythm going as you tap your "shake-a-ma-jig" on the floor.

Then read Psalm 32:11 and Psalm 33:4 in rhythm as you keep time with your new instrument. Remember that the *psalms* were once *songs* that God's people sang to praise him.

A Brand-New Song

He put a new song in my mouth, a hymn of praise to our God. (Ps. 40:3)

Did you ever feel like singing after having a drink of water? Would you want to sing after narrowly escaping death? What if you had just gotten married? Would you sing?

The people of Israel sang after a refreshing drink cooled their dry, parched lips. Read about their song in Numbers 21:17-18.

David sang after he escaped a close brush with death at the hand of his enemy, King Saul. Read about David's song in 2 Samuel 22:1-4.

The whole Song of Solomon is written about a newly married couple. The Bible is full of occasions to sing.

There are songs in the New Testament, too. Mary sang a "solo" at a very special time of celebration in her life. Look in Luke 1:43-45 to find the special occasion. Then Zechariah, the priest and the husband of Mary's cousin, Elisabeth, sang his own praise song because of the birth of his son. Who was his son? What had Zecha-

riah just been through that made him really feel like singing? He probably sang at the top of his grateful lungs! Read Luke 1:20, 62-64.

Anytime is a great time to sing, especially when you are together as a family. Sing around the piano, the guitar, or the kazoo. Sing along with a tape as you ride in the car or harmonize together as you wash the dishes!

The next time you are taking a bath or shower, use the opportunity to sing in the tub! You will be able to find plenty of things to sing about as you think about the goodness of the Lord.

Clap Your Hands

Clap your hands, all you nations; shout to God with cries of joy. (Ps. 47:1)

Clap your hands with enthusiasm to a happy Christian tape or a song on the Christian radio station. After you have tired of clapping in the ordinary way, try this:

Sit with your family in a circle on the floor. Start the music! First, clap your knees with your arms crossed; next, clap on your shoulders; then clap behind your back and in front of you, being careful not to miss a single beat. Repeat the same pattern of clapping until the song is over.

The Bible says we should clap our hands for joy because God is good to us. Play the rhythm game as you sit in your circle: Slap your knees, then your hands in front of you, snap your fingers, slap your knees again, and so on, maintaining a rhythm. Each time you snap your fingers, let a person in the circle in turn name something he is thankful for or happy about.

Sing a Scripture

My heart is steadfast, O God . . . I will sing and make music. (Ps. 57:7)

You probably have noticed that many praise choruses get their words directly from verses in the Bible. Give each member of your family a Bible verse to "sing." If you prefer to sing "duets" instead, pair up the people in your family. Send each person or pair into a separate room to make up their own tune and to practice it. Here are some verses you may want to use:

- Psalm 59:16 or 17
- Psalm 66:1-2
- Psalm 66:5
- Psalm 67:1
- Psalm 121:7-8

You may use the whole Bible verse or just take a part of one and repeat it several times in your song. Come back together to share your songs and then try to join in singing the Bible verses your other family members have composed.

The important thing is that we use our voices to praise our God!

South of the Border Praise

From the ends of the earth I call to you. (Ps. 61:2)

People all over the world express their praise to the same wonderful God you love and serve. In some places they beat their drums, strike their tambourines, or shake their Mexican maracas.

Some churches around the world enjoy the music of instruments or small orchestras, and others simply use their voices alone to praise our great God.

Make a simple rhythm instrument that sounds like a Mexican maraca from an empty plastic container with a tightly fitting lid or from a small paper sack. Decorate your instrument with paints, permanent markers, or bright-colored crayons.

Put dried peas, beans, or unpopped popcorn inside the plastic container and close the lid tightly, sealing it with glue or tape. If you are making your maraca from a paper sack, put the beans inside, blow air into the sack, and close the opening tightly with a rubber band or string.

Shake your praise to the Lord as you sing a favorite song or play a Christian tape that you like. Read Psalm 19:1-4 from your Bible and talk about the ways you think people in other parts of the world may worship God.

Presto Chango, Musico!

Shout with joy to God, all the earth! Sing the glory of his name; make his praise glorious! Say to God, "How awesome are your deeds!" (Ps. 66:1-3)

Sit in a circle on the floor with your family. Instruct each person to decide what instrument he will *pretend* to play in this activity. You will also need a conductor to get the "orchestra" started, but he may then play his own make-believe instrument. Here are some suggestions to choose from, or think of your own:

- a harmonica
- a flute
- an accordion
- handbells
- a xylophone
- a trombone
- a bass violin
- a tuba
- snare drums

When the conductor counts to three, all musicians must raise their instruments and pretend to play without making any sound at all. The rule is, however, that two people cannot play the *same* instrument at once. If a player notices someone with the same instrument as his, one or both people must quickly change to another instrument and continue pretending to play.

Several times during this activity, the conductor must shout, "Presto chango, musico!" and all players must change imaginary instruments until everyone is pretending to play something different.

After changing instruments several times, the conductor must say, "All play [the name of a tune everyone knows]." At that signal, all the musicians will begin to play that tune out

loud on their imaginary instruments. (It may take several seconds of playing before everyone gets on the same notes and rhythm, but let the music play!)

Ask one family member to read Psalm 66:1-5 and another to lead in a prayer of thanks to God for his goodness.

Comb Chorus

It is good to praise the Lord and make music to your name, O Most High. (Ps. 92:1)

Organize a "comb chorus" from the members of your family. Give everyone a comb and a small square of waxed paper or tissue paper to fold over it. Place the paper against your lips and practice humming into it, making a funny vibrating sound.

Decide what Christian tune you all know and hum it together into your comb "instruments." Harmonize with each other if you can, or you may all hum the melody. Ask someone in the family to read Psalm 92:1-5 to the others.

Musical Instructions

Let us come before him with thanksgiving and extol him with music and song. (Ps. 95:2)

Write these musical instructions on strips of paper and place them in a basket or paper sack. Give each family member a turn to pick a piece of paper and follow its instruction.

- Hum a verse of a Christian song you know well. Your family must guess the name of your song and join in humming with you.
- Imitate the rhythm of a Christian song that your family knows well by tapping two pencils together or by tapping a pen against a table or wooden chair. See who can name the song correctly.
- Try to whistle a Christian song that you like. Then, ask your family to join in whistling with you.
- Begin to sing a familiar praise song, but stop singing after the first line. Point to someone in the family to continue the song. After he sings the next line, he must stop and point to another person to continue or to finish the song.
- Be a music conductor, with your family acting like a choir or chorus. Stand them side by side according to size, from the shortest to the tallest, and direct them in a verse of a Christian song of your choice.

When you have completed these musical activities, take turns reading Psalm 95:1-7 and pray together as a family.

A Joyful Noise

Make a joyful noise unto the Lord, all ye lands. (Ps. 100:1, KJV)

Play a funny sound-effects game as a reminder that the Bible tells us to "make a joyful noise unto the Lord."

Assign each person one of these sounds to make, using only his voice, hands, or feet (clapping, stamping feet, clicking tongue, etc.):

- a drum
- cymbals
- a trombone
- a tuba
- a horse galloping
- a clock ticking and chiming
- a train passing by

Then ask one member of the family to sing his favorite Christian song as the others "accompany" the singer with their assigned sound effects.

Read Psalm 100 together and talk about other ways of making a "joyful noise" to the Lord. Ask everyone to tell something about God or Jesus that makes him want to celebrate!

Hum-a-thon

I will sing of your love and justice; to you, O Lord, I will sing praise. I will be careful to lead a blameless life. (Ps. 101:1-2)

There are a number of ways to enjoy music and to give our praise to the Lord. One way is by humming. Humming a familiar praise chorus or a hymn we love can be a very worshipful experience as we produce a lovely, quiet musical sound.

Share a "hum-a-thon" with your family as you sit together in a circle on the floor or as you ride in the car. First, read Psalm 101:1-2 from the Bible (or quote a familiar Bible verse from memory, if you are in the car), and then let each member of your family take a turn beginning to hum his favorite Christian tune. As he hums, join in with him, humming in harmony, if you can.

Try to be ready to immediately begin a new tune when one finishes, to make a continuing "marathon" of humming. When you get tired of humming, break into song with words. Talk about what Psalm 101:2 means to you, and think of ways to lead a "blameless life." Then, with God's great help, do them!

Rattle, Bang, Crash!

Praise him with the tambourine and dancing, . . . praise him with the clash of cymbals. (Ps. 150:4-5)

Aren't you glad for noise! Not that you would want it all the time or too much of it at one time, but what if there were always only silence? Some noise is clatter and clamor and chaos, but some noise can give enthusiastic praise to God. Read 2 Samuel 6:5 to see one of those happy, noisy, worshipful occasions.

Try singing to the Lord or listening to Christian music and keep time to the music with a percussion "orchestra" of spoons, rapping on a table.

Percussion instruments can be used in praise to the Lord, as strings and wind instruments can. In fact, the combination of all three kinds of music makes some of the most wonderful sounding music of all. Have you ever been to hear a great orchestra? Does your church have an orchestra or use different kinds of instruments in your worship services?

Exodus 39:25-26 tells about a percussion musical instrument being worn! What was it? Exodus 39:1 tells us who wore it.

Symphonic Strings

Praise him with the strings and flute. (Ps. 150:4)

Transform two family members into a human musical instrument by standing them face to face with their hands held up at shoulder level, palms pointed outward and fingers apart. Attach large rubber bands, elastic, fishing string, or twine back and forth between their hands, forming a "human guitar." If there are four people in your family, make a three-person *triangular* guitar and ask the fourth person to strum the strings. If you feel silly enough, connect the strings between your toes instead of your fingers!

Read Psalm 150 and sing a Christian song together as you strum your guitar.

Breathe a Song of Praise

Let everything that hath breath praise the Lord. (Ps. 150:6)

What are you doing right now? Sit very still, don't make a sound—don't move a muscle. There! Good! Wait—not so good—you're doing something! Your eyes are blinking. Why is your chest moving up and down like that? What are you doing? Breathing? Why do you do that? Name as many reasons as you can for breathing.

Did you list praising God? Can you praise the Lord through even your breath? Read Psalm 150 to see a whole list of ways to praise the Lord.

Then make three breath instruments. Here's how:

• Fill a soda bottle three-quarters-full with water. Put a straw down into the bottle as you blow across the top of it. Lower the straw in the water to get a lower pitch. You've made a straw trombone!

• Use the paper tube from a roll of paper towels or aluminum foil to make a simple kazoo. Put a piece of waxed paper or tissue paper over one end and hold it in place with a rubber band. Punch a hole in the side of the tube with a pencil, and hum or sing into the open end of the tube.

• Place a piece of waxed paper or tissue paper over a comb and hum or sing. You have a comb kazoo!

Rhythm Verses

The mountains and hills will burst into song before you, and all the trees of the field will clap their hands. (Isa. 55:12)

Try repeating (or memorizing) some of these familiar Bible verses as you play the game rhythm:

• Genesis 1:1
• John 3:16
• Acts 16:31
• Ephesians 4:32
• Revelation 3:20

Here's how to play:

Sit cross-legged in a circle on the floor. Slap your knees and then snap your fingers. Repeat these actions over and over, saying a word of the Bible verse each time you snap or slap. (The verses may be spoken by your whole family at the same time, or each member may take a turn saying a verse.)

If you want to make the activity a little more challenging, try three actions rather than two: *slap, snap, clap; slap, snap, clap!* Or, if you wish, you may begin the verses slowly and pick up speed as you say them.

Answer Me, Please

Call to me and I will answer you. (Jer. 33:3)

Read the wonderful promise God gives us in Jeremiah 33:2-3. Who does God say he is? How is God able to tell us things we do not know? How much does God know?

Play this "answer me" game as a reminder that God *will* answer our prayers and is always ready to teach us wonderful new things about himself, his world, and his Word. Here's how to play:

Give each player two pencils, pens, sticks, spoons, or table knives. One player must begin the game by tapping a rhythm with his sticks and then pointing to someone else to answer him with the very same rhythm. The second player may then tap a new rhythm and point to someone else to copy it.

Continue the tapping and answering as long as you like, making the rhythms progressively harder (but not *impossible*) to answer.

Musical Trouble

As soon as you hear the sound of the horn, flute, zither, lyre, harp, pipes and all kinds of music, you must fall down and worship the image of gold. (Dan. 3:5)

Some funny names for other Bible instruments are the psaltery, the lute, the dulcimer, and the sackbut. Do you have any of those tucked away in a closet somewhere? Does your school orchestra have a sackbut section?

Read the names of the instruments in Daniel 3:5. Then read Daniel 3:5-12 to see how these instruments were being used. Can musical instruments be used to either honor or dishonor God? If you play an instrument, how do you use yours?

Make a silly musical instrument by stringing fishing wire, dental floss, or big rubber bands (perhaps looped together to form rubber-band "chains") between the backs or legs of two kitchen chairs. Think of different ways to play your instrument (with your feet, while lying on your back on the floor? with your elbow?). Make up a funny name for it!

Musical Humility

There are some Jews . . . Shadrach, Meshach and Abednego—who pay no attention to you, O king. (Dan. 3:12)

When the three courageous young men, Shadrach, Meshach, and Abednego, were told to bow down to an enormous golden idol when the music began to play, they refused. Take turns telling the incredible events in order, like a "chain" story.

Then play "musical humility" as a reminder that believers in Jesus Christ bow down their hearts and bend their knees in worship only to the living God!

Play the game somewhat as you would musical chairs, but when the music stops, kneel on the floor and stay there until the music begins, and then begin to march around the room again. To make the game more challenging, have all players place a small Bible or New Testament on their head and keep it balanced there as they march and kneel. If it falls off, they must sit on the floor where they are and let the others march around them until all the players are out of the action. (It shouldn't take long.) Then begin the game again.

Palm Branch Praise

Many people spread their cloaks on the road, while others spread branches they had cut in the fields. (Mark 11:8)

Sit in a circle on the floor as a family. Pass a small branch with leaves or a palm branch cut from green construction paper around the circle as you sing together a praise song of your choice. Each time the music stops, the one holding the branch must start a new song or the next verse of the same song.

After a few moments of singing together, read the story of Jesus' triumphal entry into Jerusalem from Mark 11:7-10.

March the Right Way

Jesus answered, "I am the way and the truth and the life." (John 14:6)

Even though we want to follow Jesus all our lives, sometimes we aren't sure which way he is leading us. Satan tries to trick us into taking the wrong road every chance he has, so we must always be on our guard! God's Word will be our road map and guidebook to keep us from wondering which direction to go in life. Play this musical game as a family to help you remember which road is right:

Write each of these sentences on a piece of paper and give one to each member of your family. Ask each person to hold onto his sentence until it is his turn to read it out loud.

- You have been invited to take small gifts to children in the hospital with your Sunday school class.
- A popular boy (or girl) at school wants you to sneak out and go somewhere with him without your parents' permission.
- A group of kids at school are going to paint the name of your school on the walls of several buildings in town and want you to come along for the "fun."
- It's Sunday morning and time to get ready for church.
- A neighbor boy or girl doesn't seem to know much about God, and you feel like you should tell him.
- You have broken a family rule and feel badly about it, even though no one else knows. You are very tempted to keep it quiet or to lie about it if anyone finds out.
- Some bigger kids want you to try drugs or alcohol.

- Your mom and dad need your help around the house, but you don't really want to work.
- You really believe that Jesus wants you to give him your heart and life.

Begin to march in a circle in the direction you decide to call "the right way." As you march in the "right" direction, sing the following song together to the tune of "Are You Sleeping, Brother John?"

Follow Jesus,
Follow Jesus.
He's the way.
He's the way.
We will follow Jesus.
We will follow Jesus.
He's the way.
He's the way.

Then ask one family member to read his statement. If it is the right way to go, continue marching and singing as you are. But if the statement would not be God's way to go, turn and march around the circle in the opposite direction and sing these words instead:

That's the wrong way.
That's the wrong way.
Please don't go!
Please don't go!
We will follow Jesus.
We will follow Jesus.
He's the way.
He's the way.

Jump for Joy

He jumped to his feet and began to walk. Then he went with them into the temple courts, walking and jumping, and praising God. (Acts 3:8)

Can you imagine how you would feel if you had never, ever known how it was to walk, and then Jesus' power made you well? What do you think you would do? That very thing happened to a man in the days of Peter and John. Read the exciting story in Acts 3:1-9.

Did you know that a number of God's creations jump and dance from place to place? Even some seashells, much like snails in the garden, have a "foot" on which they can slide and hop.

These sea animals have something to "jump for joy" about! They have a Creator who gives them a wonderful place to live and provides food, good care, and *everything* they could possibly need. Doesn't that give us a reason to do a little "dance for joy"—since God does much more for us?

Put on some Christian music and give the members of your family a chance to demonstrate their own creative "jumps for joy" because of what God has done for them.

"My Name Is . . . "

The disciples were called Christians first at Antioch. (Acts 11:26)

Did you ever think about how good it

is to have a *name?* Having a first and last name (and maybe a middle name, too) is a way of saying that you are special and important. Besides that, a name identifies you with other people. It tells that you are a part of a *family.*

Play this musical name game. Take turns chanting your name in a natural speaking rhythm, such as "My name is Stacy Brown," or "My name is Christopher Bolin." When all family members have chanted their names in rhythm, say all together, "*Our* name is [your last name(s)]." To end the chant, all the family may say, "Our name is *Christian!*"

The Bible is very clear about the value of a *good* name. Read Proverbs 22:1 to see how much our good name is really worth.

If we had valuable jewels or riches, how would we protect them? How can we protect our good name? Why is it important to act and live in such a way that we will not harm the valuable name that our parents and family have given us?

What extra-special name do we wear if we are believers in Jesus Christ? Find out by reading Acts 11:26.

Jailhouse Duet

About midnight Paul and Silas were praying and singing hymns to God. (Acts 16:25)

Pretend to be Paul and Silas in the jail in Philippi. Read Acts 16:25-34 to see

- why they were there;
- what condition they were in;
- what they did in their darkest hour.

Play "jailhouse duet" as you would musical chairs, but use pillows or couch cushions (one less than the

number of "teams") laid on the floor in a circle in place of chairs. You will need at least four players, and preferably more. Players need to pair off, and each team of two must link elbows and walk around the circle together. When the music stops, they must plop down on the pillows together. The pair(s) of players that had no place to plop may continue to play and try to do better the next time the music stops.

Upside Down Praise

These that have turned the world upside down are come hither also. (Acts 17:6, KJV)

Two players may perform this stunt for the rest of the family, but the others should not know what will happen ahead of time. They will be the audience.

Stretch a sheet across a doorway or between two chair backs, about four or five feet above the floor. The two "Upside-Down Praise Singers" will squat down or kneel behind the sheet and put their shoes on their hands. Announce that the famous Upside-Down Praise Singers will be performing!

As the Upside-Down Praise Singers sing a song or chorus they both know, they will hold their hands up in the air inside the shoes, allowing the toes of the shoes to show over the edge of the sheet. They will look like they really are upside-down.

The New Testament Christians were so busy serving the Lord and telling people about his great love and salvation that people said they had turned their whole world upside down! If today's Christian boys and girls, dads and moms will do the same, we can turn our neighborhoods, towns, and even our country "upside down" for Jesus, which is really "right-side up."

Invisible Band

Do not offer the parts of your body to sin, as instruments of wickedness, but rather offer yourselves to God . . . as instruments of righteousness. (Rom. 6:13)

Organize a musical band, with everyone playing an invisible instruments. Let each musician decide what instrument he will play (no cost or lessons involved), polish up his instrument, and practice tuning up and making its sound. Assign someone to be your conductor, to either lead the band or start you off by saying, "One, two, ready, begin!" Choose your song, tell everyone what instrument you are playing, select your pitch, and one, two, ready, begin!

At the conclusion of your concert take a well-deserved bow. Then read together Romans 6:13, talk about what it means, and pray together that your lives really will be God's instruments.

Human Chimes

If I speak in the tongues of men and of angels, but have not love, I am only a resounding gong or a clanging cymbal. (1 Cor. 13:1)

Line up the members of your family like a set of human church chimes, side by side. One person may volunteer to be the chime director, who will *gently* tap the "chimes" on their heads with a yardstick one at a time to make a musical note (*any* old note will do).

After practicing your note-making skills a little, try to "chime" an actual melody that you all know well, making the sound of the next note in the song when the director taps your head.

Read 1 Corinthians 13:1 and see what Paul says is better than the ability to make beautiful music. Read on in verses 2-3 to find out some other things that people could do that would still not compare with the very best thing of all. What is the best?

Conduct Your Life

> Whatever happens, conduct yourselves in a manner worthy of the gospel of Christ. (Phil. 1:27)

Pretend to be a famous conductor, leading a member (or a whole chorus!) of your family in a verse of the famous "opera" melody "Row, Row, Row Your Boat." Since you are the conductor, the singer(s) must follow your leading exactly as you direct them to sing loudly, softly, very fast, slowly, suddenly loud or suddenly soft! Use your hands and your gestures to let them know what you want. Be sure to take the bows you deserve—even if you have no audience!

Why is a conductor important in producing beautiful music from a choir or orchestra? A conductor helps to bring order and control to what could otherwise be a bunch of noisy instruments!

The Bible says that we have a life to "conduct." Philippians 1:27 encourages us to lead our own lives in such a way that we will make beautiful music for Jesus Christ.

United Music

> Sing psalms, hymns and spiritual songs with gratitude in your hearts to God. (Col. 3:16)

Sit with your family in a circle on the floor with backs facing each other and elbows linked together. Choose a Christian song that everyone in the family knows and begin to sing it together. As you do, try to stand up together without unlinking arms, move around in a complete circle to where you began, and sit back down before the last note of the song is sung.

Then read what Colossians 3:15-17 tells us to do together.

BIBLE AGENTS

Nearly everyone sometimes enjoys a good detective adventure—a story or activity that requires you to look for clues, find something that is missing, or solve a puzzling situation.

The whole Bible is full of secret agent material. Sometimes the "detective work" involves actual spying, like Joshua and Caleb did in the Old Testament, but in other cases where no actual sneaking around is involved, there are still plenty of questions to answer, complicated situations to figure out, identities of fascinating people to guess, and crimes to solve.

This chapter is all about an important Bible secret agent—you! You will be guessing, figuring, answering, analyzing, and just doing some ordinary thinking as you and your family enjoy learning more about the very real people who lived in the days of the Bible. So let the clues begin!

The Mystery of the Disappearing Water

> He draws up the drops of water, which distill as rain to the streams. (Job 36:27)

You have probably investigated the mysterious *appearance* of dewdrops early in the morning, but what about *disappearing* water? Try this experiment the next time it rains and a puddle collects on your driveway or sidewalk. Draw a chalk circle around the puddle as soon as the rain stops. Wait a little while and see if the puddle is any smaller. If it is, draw around the smaller puddle, too. Continue to draw around the edge of the shrinking puddle until it is completely gone.

God's words about nature are always up-to-date. Job 36:26-27 tells us exactly what happens when water disappears and then reappears as rain. Read those interesting verses from your Bible.

The Earth Possession Question

The earth is the Lord's, and everything in it, the world, and all who live in it. (Ps. 24:1)

Try to solve these mind-teaser questions:

- How much dirt is there in a hole 100 feet square and 100 inches deep? (None—a hole is empty.)
- An eight-year-old boy is on an airplane that is flying 275 mph at 25,000 feet. If the boy jumps 2 feet straight up in the air, where will his feet land? (Right where they were when he jumped.)
- Does the earth belong to man or does man belong to the earth?

Read what the Bible says about that last question in 1 Corinthians 10:26.

Man was not made to own the earth, nor can the earth own people. The earth was made for man to enjoy as his home, to take care of, and to be

in charge of. (Read Genesis 1:26, 28.) God made us to be his gardeners, conservation officers, trash control officials, clean water controllers, and recyclers. The earth belongs to God, and we are its caretakers.

You'll Never Guess What Happened

Many, O Lord my God, are the wonders you have done. (Ps. 40:5)

Here are clues about exciting events that happened in the New Testament. Guess who the clues describe and what happened to him.

- I felt myself being lowered down through a roof (Luke 5:17-20).
- I saw a big sheet full of different kinds of animals (Acts 10:9-12).
- I had the strange experience of some people thinking I was a god and trying to worship me (Acts 14:11).
- I got bitten on my hand by a poisonous snake, and God saved my life (Acts 28:3).
- I saw a vision of all the beauty and wonder of heaven while I was stranded on an island in the sea (Rev. 1:9).

What Went On Here?

Before the mountains were born or you brought forth the earth and the world, from everlasting to everlasting you are God. (Ps. 90:2)

Go outside with your family or a friend. Try to imagine back a hundred years in time and guess what your yard and street may have been like then. Name the things you see that were not there a hundred years ago and guess how the land looked, what kinds of animals and people may have lived then, how they looked, and what they did. Treat everyone's opinions as equally important, since you do not actually *know* what went on there a century ago.

Have a What-happened-before-I-was-born? discussion with your family. If your grandma and grandpa live nearby, be sure to include them in this family rap time. Ask your mom or dad and grandparents to share with you some of the interesting events that happened in the world and in their lives before you were born. If you have younger brothers or sisters, *you* can tell them what happened before *they* arrived on the home scene.

How far back does God go? When was his beginning? When will he end? Read Psalm 90:1-2 together and pray as a family to your everlasting heavenly Father.

From Sea to Shining Sea

There is the sea, vast and spacious, teeming with creatures beyond number—living things both large and small. (Ps. 104:25)

Take an investigation walk through your house, listening with your ear close to the walls and the floors to try to find hidden water pipes. You may need to run a little water in the bathrooms or kitchen, or flush the toilet, to be able to follow the sound of the water through the walls. Count how many places you actually *hear* the hidden water, and find out whether your water supply comes from the town's water system or from a well in your own yard.

When God made water, he did an incredible thing! When he placed the water in the lakes, rivers, and oceans, he did something absolutely awesome! If there were no oceans, there would be no rain; if there were no rain, no life.

Here are a few water facts:

• There is enough water in the oceans to completely cover the land. If all the land and the ocean bottom were level, we would live under a mile and a half of water! Water *did* cover the whole earth one time—in Noah's day. In fact, fossils of sea life have been found practically everywhere on earth since that time.

• God keeps the water controlled in the places where he put it. Read what Job says in Job 38:8, 10-11.

• The oceans are absolutely full of plant and animal life. Genesis 1:20 tells us what scientists have discovered over the years—that the oceans *teem,* or have enormous numbers of living creatures in them.

What an awesome God we love, serve, and obey!

The Bible Is a Hidden Treasure

I have hidden your word in my heart that I might not sin against you. (Ps. 119:11)

Here are three simple treasure hunts you may want to try as a reminder that the greatest treasure of all is God's Word:

• Hide a small Bible in the room for another person to find. Chant the word *treasure* over and over quietly as he searches, repeating it faster as he gets close to the hidden Bible and slower as he moves farther away from it.

• Go on a hidden word search through your house, carrying with you a pencil and a tablet of paper. Write down the different objects you see that begin with the letters *B-I-B-L-E* or *G-O-D'-S W-O-R-D*.

• Search for these verses and books in your Bible and write down the numbers of the pages where they can be found: Genesis 5:1, Ruth, Ezekiel, Daniel 1:1, Jonah, John 3:16, Revelation.

Be sure to hide God's treasure in your heart often by memorizing and understanding Bible verses.

Secret Message on a Wall

Suddenly the fingers of a human hand appeared and wrote on the plaster of the wall, near the lampstand in the royal palace. (Dan. 5:5)

Write a secret message for someone in your family to read but write it backwards and from right to left or upside down. Give your message to someone and let him figure out what it says. If you can't think of anything to say, write this message: "God used Daniel in a special way!"

A Mother for Jesus

Mary was pledged to be married to Joseph, but . . . she was found to be with child through the Holy Spirit. (Matt. 1:18)

Pretend that you must write a recommendation (a letter telling good things about a person) for Mary to be chosen to be the mother of Jesus.

The Bible does not tell us very much about Mary except that she was a pure, unmarried girl (Luke 1:27), that she rejoiced in the angel's great news that she would be the mother of God's Son (Luke 1:46-49), that she wrapped Jesus in swaddling clothes (Luke 2), and that later she welcomed the wise men when they came to their house (Matt. 2). We also know from the Bible that Mary worried about Jesus when she thought he was lost in Jerusalem (Luke 2:48) and that she had a part in the wedding feast where Jesus performed his first miracle (John 2:1-5). We know that Mary stood and cried at the cross while Jesus died (John 19:25), and her name is mentioned in a few other verses of the Bible.

Other than that, Mary's personality

and characteristics are a mystery. Use your imagination to write about the kind of young woman she must have been for God to choose her to be the mother of Jesus.

The Human Light Bulb

You are the light of the world. (Matt. 5:14)

Take a flashlight inspection walk through your house, shining the light and searching out things you usually overlook—like tiny designs on curtains or wallpaper, shaggy strands of yarn in the carpet, and the interesting grains of wood on furniture and doors. Use a magnifying glass with your flashlight if you want a really close look.

If several family members have gone on an inspection walk, get together afterward and talk about what you saw. Turn off all the lights in that room and sit on the floor together. Notice the darkness all around you and the big change that takes place when someone turns on a flashlight.

Jesus said that Christians are to be like flashlights in a dark world of sin.

When we shine for Jesus, other people can see to find their way to God's love and forgiveness. So let's shine!

Who Prayed Best?

When you pray, go into your room, close the door and pray to your Father. (Matt. 6:6)

Look for detective clues in the story found in your Bible in Luke 18:10-14 for help solving the mystery question, Who prayed best? Here are some questions to help you find the clues:

- How many people prayed in this story?
- Did both men pray at a good place? At a good time?
- Was looking up to God an OK way to pray?
- Was looking down, with head bowed all right, too?
- Was being grateful to God a good prayer?
- Was being sorry for his sins OK?

Since most of what both men did seems all right, can you solve the mystery of what caused a prayer to go bad?

We should always pray, recognizing what a great God he is and how fortunate we are to have his love and forgiveness.

Don't Worry!

Look at the birds of the air; they do not sow or reap or store away in barns, and yet your heavenly Father feeds them. Are you not much more valuable than they? (Matt. 6:26)

Is your yard a home for birds? Check for clues to solve that mystery by looking around to find a feather or two on the ground; a bird's nest in a tree; broken, empty eggshells; berry stains on tree branches or leaves; and, of course, listening for the lovely sounds that birds make. Write your findings in a small notebook or on a piece of paper.

When your investigation is complete, make your yard a nicer home for the birds by leaving a small container or pile of nest-making materials for them, including bits of yarn, string, cotton, moss, or twigs. Give the birds a personal birdbath by placing several large rocks in a small circle on the ground and a Frisbee or dish containing water upon them. Sprinkle a little birdseed or bread crumbs around the pan to help the birds get over any shyness—and give them a little time to notice your kindness.

Here are some fascinating bird facts:

- Birds are incredible flying machines because of their hollow bones, the shape of their feathers, and their remarkable way of breathing—a large, strong heart and powerful chest muscles to make them high-powered.
- Bird's beaks, nests, and eggs come in a variety of sizes and shapes that are perfectly suited to the kind of food they eat and the environment in which they live.
- Birds can sing and some can even talk!
- Birds can fly thousands of miles to warmer weather and back home again with no map to guide them.

Who designed the birds with their amazing abilities? And who takes care of them—and us? Read Matthew 10:29-31 for the answer.

Sherlock/Watson

Then he touched their eyes and . . . their sight was restored. (Matt. 9:29)

Play this "blind man" game much like you would the water game Marco Polo. Here's how: If you are inside, move the furniture back a little to give yourselves plenty of room and choose someone to be the famous detective Sherlock Holmes. The other players will *all* pretend to be his partner, Watson. Sherlock will be blindfolded, and all players will play the game on their knees if you are in the house. Sherlock will be trying to find his old partner, while all the Watsons are crawling in all directions, trying to avoid being caught.

When Sherlock begins to call, "Watson," all the rest of the players will scatter out away from him as they answer back, "Here I am, Sherlock!" When Sherlock tags another player, that person will put on the blindfold and become the *new* Sherlock, and the game can continue.

On several occasions Jesus helped and healed people who really *were* blind. Read about one of those dramatic times in Matthew 9:27-30.

Hmmmmmm

Who do people say the Son of Man is? (Matt. 16:13)

Ask one member of your family to leave the room while everyone else sits down in a line, side by side, on the floor. When everyone is in place, ask the one person to come back into the room with his eyes closed. As he does, the other players must begin quietly saying, "Hmmmm" to help him locate where they are.

The one player will then sit down, and everyone else must become quiet until he points at one of them. The player he points toward must again say, "Hmmmm," as the one with his eyes closed tries to guess who made the sound. Repeat the same actions several times, until all the "Hmmmmers" have been identified.

Jesus asked his followers a "Who am I?" kind of question one day as he sat with his disciples. Read what his question was in Matthew 16:13-16 and see who gave a great answer.

Tangle/Untangle

Then the Pharisees went out and laid plans to trap him in his words. (Matt. 22:15)

Sometimes the evidence in a mystery can be hard to "untangle" to find the truth. Secret agents must spend many hours trying to discover the facts and understand what they mean regarding a certain event or person. But in the Bible we are told of people who tried very hard to tangle the truth—to trap Jesus in a tangle of words and get him to say something wrong. Look in Matthew 22:15-22 for the events surrounding one of those evil plots and see who was involved. Then read an important verse in Hebrews 12:1 to see what can entangle us if we are not careful.

Here's a "entangling" game to play with your family. Stand at different places in the room, a few feet apart, and toss a ball of string or yarn back and forth to each other. The person with the yarn must hold on to the end of the string and pass the yarn ball around his back before he throws it to someone else, so that the yarn will be unraveling as you play. When you are tangled enough, try *untangling* yourselves by throwing the ball back from where it last came and rolling up the yarn each time it is caught.

Love to the Max

Love the Lord your God with all your heart and with all your soul and with all your mind. (Matt. 22:37)

Be a Bible agent and try to discover which of these Bible characters only *knew about* Jesus and which ones really *loved* him to the absolute maximum. Try to learn how they showed their love to the max. If you are not sure of your answers, look them up in the Bible.

* The wise men (Matt. 2:1)
* King Herod (Matt. 2:13)
* Mary Magdalene (Matt. 27:1, 8-9)
* The rich young ruler (Luke 18:18-24)
* Zacchaeus (Luke 19:8)
* Pilate (Luke 22:23-25)
* John the Baptist (John 1:2)

There are different ways to show Jesus our maximum love—some people have actually died because they loved Jesus, but many millions have lived for him.

All the ways of showing our love to Jesus must come from first giving him our total selves. The Bible says in 2 Chronicles 16:9 that God's eyes are always searching over the whole world to find people whose hearts are completely his (his *to the max!*) so that he can bless them.

Stick 'em Up!

Then the men stepped forward, seized Jesus and arrested him. (Matt. 26:50)

You have probably seen old movies in which the policeman or detective says to the bad guy, "Stick 'em up!" What does the policeman mean by that—and why does he give such a strange command?

Read in the Bible about three people who were arrested in Matthew 26:47-50, Acts 12:1-4, and Acts 16:22-24. Were any of the the men really guilty of doing anything wrong? Did they have a bad attitude about being falsely accused? Who gives strength to his followers to do what is right even when it is hard or unpopular?

Play this "stick 'em up" game and remember that serving Jesus is what matters most in life, no matter what it may cost.

Ask all the members of your family to sit down at the dinner table, with one person sitting across from all the others. He will be the detective who has the authority to say, "Stick 'em up!" Give a coin to the other players, who must begin to pass it back and forth to each other under the table. The detective will "eye" them carefully, since he suspects that they are up to something.

When the detective shouts the command "Stick 'em up!" all the other players must throw up their hands over their heads, with their fists closed. The player with the coin in his hand will try to keep it hidden. If the detective cannot guess who has the coin on his first try, he may then say, "Hands down!" At that command, the players must slap their hands with palms flat on the table, trying not to let the coin be seen nor to make a clinking sound (not too easy to do!). The detective will again try to guess who has the coin, but if he still cannot, the game can be repeated until he does. If you enjoy the game, change detectives and play it again.

The Dozen Disciples

[Jesus] appointed twelve . . . that they might be with him and that he might send them out to preach. (Mark 3:14)

Ask a member of your family to leave the room while you hide twelve short pieces of string or yarn or twelve toothpicks in different places. Bring the hidden player back in and give him his secret agent orders: to find the same number of missing pieces of string or toothpicks as there were disciples of Jesus.

When the player has gathered the missing items, count them and ask him to check to see if his answer is correct by reading Mark 3:14-19. Then try to name some of the things the disciples of Jesus had to do to be true followers of the Lord. Look in Matthew 4:18-22 and Matthew 9:9 for some clues. (Did you name any of these?)

- They believed in Jesus and decided to follow him no matter what it cost them. Some disciples left fishing jobs and equipment behind and one gave up a tax-collector job that could have made him rich.

- The disciples listened to Jesus' teachings and obeyed what he told them to do.
- The disciples told other people about Jesus. Some wrote down their words for us to read in the Bible, others talked about Jesus to one person at a time, and still other disciples preached about him to huge crowds. But they all shared the Good News.

The twelve disciples are all enjoying heaven with Jesus today, but he needs young, bold new disciples on earth right now. Jesus wants you!

Wild Man Legion

This man lived in the tombs, and no one could bind him any more, not even with a chain. (Mark 5:3)

Pretend that it is a bright, sunny day by the seaside. You and your secret agents are enjoying a quiet day relaxing and picnicking away from the busyness of city life when the silence is broken by the sound of a man yelling and making a terrible commotion. Who is this man and what's wrong with him? Here are the clues you notice:

- The man sounds very angry.
- The sound of his voice is coming from inside a cave.
- You can hear the rattling of chains and the sound of rocks being thrown.

• Other people run away when the man yells and throws things.

Use the clues and the story from Luke 8:27-38 to discover who the wild man is, what is wrong with him, and what finally happens to make things a whole lot better in his life.

Men Who Hated Jesus

These people honor me with their lips, but their hearts are far from me. (Mark 7:6)

In a sack, place several of these items:

• an ear of corn (or a few kernels of popcorn) (Luke 6:1-5)
• a coin (Luke 20:20-26)
• a bar of soap (Matt. 15:1-3)
• an outlined drawing of your hand (Luke 6:7-11)
• a heart-shaped paper cutout (Luke 10:25-27)
• a can of some kind of spice (Matt. 23:23)

If you prefer, write the names of the objects or draw their pictures on small cards and place them upside down in a stack on the floor.

Choose one object or card at a time and try to solve the mystery of how it relates to the Pharisees—the religious leaders in Jesus' day who hated him, were constantly trying to trick him, and finally put him to death.

If you need help with the answers, look up the Bible verses beside each object for clues.

When you find yourself in an unpleasant situation because you are a believer in Jesus Christ and some other people are not, remember that even Jesus Christ himself had enemies because of his faith in God.

The Lowly Shepherds

And there were shepherds living out in the fields nearby, keeping watch over their flocks at night. (Luke 2:8)

Investigate why, of all people in the world, God chose *shepherds* to be the first to hear the awesome news that his Son, Jesus, was born.

Were shepherds famous or rich or important in their communities? Could they bring expensive gifts to the newborn King or persuade thousands of other people to come and worship him? Ask each member of your family to tell why he thinks God sent his angel choir to appear to shepherds on the night of Jesus' birth.

Listen to these facts about shepherds and sheep:

• Shepherds in Jesus' day led their sheep where they wanted

them to go—they did not drive them or force them.

- Each sheep—whether a ram, ewe, or lamb—had a name, and when the shepherd called, the sheep came to his side.
- The shepherd's job was to lead the sheep to food and water and to protect them from danger.
- As the shepherd took care of his sheep, he faced hardship and danger himself. The shepherd had to endure the heat and cold, he had little food to eat or money to buy what he needed, and he was always in danger of being attacked by wild animals.
- The shepherd counted the sheep every night to make sure they all came home to the safety of the sheepfold. When all the sheep were home, the shepherd lay down to sleep in front of the opening of the pen, becoming its door.
- Sheep are mentioned about five hundred times in the Bible.
- Jesus said, "I am the good shepherd; I know my sheep and my sheep know me . . . and I lay down my life for the sheep" (John 10:14-15).

Do you understand why the Bible says that Jesus was the Good Shepherd and we are his sheep? Doesn't that help you feel loved and protected?

Forfeit

What good is it for a man to gain the whole world, and yet lose or forfeit his very self? (Luke 9:25)

Ask everyone in the family to put an object belonging to him in a pile in the middle of the room. It can be a shoe or sock, a piece of jewelry, or some other personal item. In order to get his belonging back, each player must solve a mysterious clue to a Bible character's identity. These are the clues:

- It's a good thing that I had four friends who were willing to carry me, or I never would have gotten to see Jesus. (the paralyzed man)
- Wow! Did I ever have some narrow escapes! I had to kill a bear and a lion in order to protect my father's sheep and my own life. (David)
- We went on a long trip, clear across the desert, to see Jesus. We couldn't have made it without that magnificent star. (the wise men)
- You've never slept until you've spent the night with a bunch of lions! (Daniel)
- Some people thought I was foolish to pour out that expensive perfume on Jesus, but I love him so much. (Mary)

Sometimes people very foolishly forfeit, or give up, what is really valuable—knowing Jesus and serving him—for other things that have little or no worth. Can you name some things that people choose instead of following Jesus?

Read in Luke 9:23-25 what Jesus himself said people sometimes *forfeit* when they do not choose to accept the wonderful life he offers.

Good/Better

> Mary has chosen what is better, and it will not be taken away from her. (Luke 10:42)

Pretend that two members of your family are famous secret agents named "Sergeant Good" and "Captain Better." (They may dress up in detective coats if they want to.) It is their job to investigate a group of criminals who are selling people poor-quality watches that they claim are the *best* ever made!

When the watches are bought, within days they fall apart. The glass faces on the watches fall off, and even the tiny springs inside break and fall out! However, when the unhappy customers try to get their money back, the salesman cannot be found anywhere. His claim to have the best watches ever made just wasn't true.

Ask another family member to pretend to be someone who bought a watch from the criminals. Sergeant Good and Captain Better will knock on his door, show him their badges, and ask him questions about the watch and the description of the bad salesman who sold it.

When Jesus went to visit his friends Mary and Martha, Martha was doing a *good* thing, but Mary did something *better*. Find out what they were doing and what Jesus told them in Luke 10:38-42.

The Mysteriously Missing Coin

> Rejoice with me; I have found my lost coin. (Luke 15:9)

See if you can solve this mystery:

A man claimed that he owned a valuable old coin that had on it the date 2000 B.C. How would you know that the coin was a fake? (Look at the end of this devotional for the tricky answer.)

If you have some extra time, try making your family a new system of currency. Make dollar bills and coins out of different colors of paper, cut in whatever shapes you want. Use your great imagination to decide what each kind of currency (money) will be worth. For example, a round, red piece of money might be worth ten triangular pieces of yellow money. Make up names for your currency if you wish; or use the usual dollar and coin names. Play store or bank with your new money.

What would you do if all your family's savings were kept in a jar in the kitchen (not a good idea, since in our day banks are available for safekeeping!) and you accidentally dropped it on the floor, scattering money everywhere? See if you would do what the lady did in Luke 15:8-10. What is Jesus teaching us through this story?

(Answer: B.C. did not appear on coins before Jesus was born, since coin makers did not know when he would be born.)

Heavyweight Necklace

It would be better for him to be thrown into the sea with a millstone tied around his neck than for him to cause one of these little ones to sin. (Luke 17:2)

Pretend to be detectives, putting together "What happened here?" information from the clues listed below. What do you think happened in each case? Was it a crime, an accident, or nothing important?

- a tricycle on its side
- a bag of money hidden in the bushes
- a bug crawling across the sidewalk
- a broken soda bottle
- a container of illegal drugs
- a very small child near the street with no one to watch him

What if someone really were neglecting or abusing a child? How do you think God would feel about that? How does God want children treated? Why? Read Matthew 14:1-6. Does Jesus think it is serious business when someone leads one of his precious children away from

him? Check your answer by rereading his harsh words in Matthew 18:6.

If you are a child, you are extra special and very valuable to God!

Search for the Smallest

[Zacchaeus] wanted to see who Jesus was, but being a short man he could not, because of the crowd. (Luke 19:3)

Pretend to be secret agents, conducting a house search for the five *very smallest* items you can find in each room.

Assign each agent one or more rooms to investigate, and give him a piece of paper, a pencil, and, perhaps, a magnifying "spy glass" to take along in his search. Instruct each agent to record his findings on his paper. (Write down only things you can actually *see*, not tiny atoms or molecules!)

When each agent has finished his investigation, report back to command central (someplace in the house you have chosen for your headquarters) and read your lists to each other.

Zacchaeus was a small man whose size presented a problem for him when Jesus came to his town. Have you ever wanted to see a parade or a show, and there were taller people blocking your view? If so, you can definitely identify with the feelings Zacchaeus must have had on that day.

Open your Bible to Luke 19:1-10 and read or tell the story in your own words. Did you ever stop to think that some day you, as a believer in

Jesus, too, will actually get to see Zacchaeus in heaven and talk with him about that day long ago in Jericho when he met Jesus? Would you be able to tell Zacchaeus about when you "met" Jesus, if he could talk with you today?

Lost and Found

For the Son of Man came to seek and to save what was lost. (Luke 19:10)

If you were a detective who found these missing items, could you figure out what New Testament person they belong to?

- a lunch containing five loves and two small fish
- a fishing net
- two large spike nails and a whip
- a bag containing thirty pieces of silver
- crutches that have been thrown away
- bandages
- two small coins
- a tax collector's money container
- a crown of thorns
- an empty tomb

Now, think about these things that a person today will be "missing" if he gives his heart and life to Jesus from the time he is young:

- a wasted life
- the problems a life of sin causes
- the sadness of not knowing Jesus

- eternal death and being apart from God

Don't you think that being a Christian is the greatest life possible?

I'm Having Trouble Hearing

And one of them struck the servant of the high priest, cutting off his right ear. (Luke 22:50)

Many miracles happened during the time of Jesus' death and resurrection. Here's one that involved an angry swing of a sword and an ear! Do you know the story? Read about it in Luke 22:47-53 and talk with your family about what was happening and why. Then play this "blindfolded mystery hearing" game:

Blindfold members of the family, one at a time, and test their sense of hearing by dropping certain objects that you have already shown to them. Let them guess what the objects are by their sound. You may want to use a ball, a book, a bean, a sponge, a pencil, a coin, a shoe, or a pin.

In the Bible story you just read, Peter reacted quickly without thinking. Do you ever do that? All of us do at times, and our reactions can get us in *trouble!* Or we can take a few seconds, say a silent prayer to God, and think about our actions before we react foolishly.

In each of these situations, what would be the wise and careless way to react?

- Another child calls you a mean name.
- Someone bumps into you in the hall at school.
- Someone you know scribbles on your homework paper.
- Your soccer ball rolls into the street.
- Someone says bad things behind your back, and you hear about it.
- Someone makes fun of you.

We Didn't Know Who That Was!

Now that same day two of them were going to a village called Emmaus, about seven miles from Jerusalem. (Luke 24:13)

Provide a piece of paper for Mom or Dad and one for each child in your family. Play this "drawing and guessing" game like drawing charades, with one person at a time drawing an object and the others being secret agents, trying to guess the mystery object.

The rule to the game is that the person drawing must only draw *one part* of his picture at a time and then wait for the other players to try to guess what the whole object might be. The parts of the drawing do not have to be connected to each other. The one who guesses the object correctly may then make a picture of his own.

On the same day that Jesus' friends discovered his empty tomb and began to realize that Jesus was really alive,

two of his followers walked along a road together, going toward a village called Emmaus. As they walked and talked about all that had been taking place in Jerusalem, especially Jesus' trial and crucifixion, a stranger suddenly joined them.

He asked what they were talking about, and they gave their answer in Luke 24:19-24. Read their words and see how discouraged and confused they sound.

The two people invited the stranger home with them because they were fascinated by all that he was telling them. But just as you may not have recognized some of your family's drawings in the game you just played, the men did not recognize the stranger at first. Look in Luke 24:30-35 to see when and how they discovered who he was.

Follow the Way

I am the way and the truth and the life. (John 14:6)

Mark a trail outside (signs, marks on the ground, broken branches of trees, or sticks arranged in X's) to show the "way" to go to a certain place that you have chosen. Ask a friend or family member to follow the way you have marked.

Read what Jesus says about the "way" in John 14:6. Where is Jesus the "way" to? Are you following this important way?

The Unseen Mystery

> Blessed are those who have not seen
> and yet have believed. (John 20:29)

Write one of these names of a Bible character on a strip of paper and tape it to the back of each player without his seeing it:

- David
- Jonah
- Noah
- Daniel
- Mary

Each player must then try to guess the mystery person on his back by asking questions about him or her that can be answered by a yes or a no. When he identifies the name correctly, he can remove it.

The Bible tells us about a man who had trouble believing what he could not see. Read John 20:24-28 to learn the identity of this mystery person and the wonderful "solved mystery" he experienced. Can you find yourself in verse 29?

The Incredible Dream

> He saw heaven opened and something
> like a large sheet being let down to
> earth by its four corners. (Acts 10:11)

Play the game "what's in this sheet?" Here's how:

Take turns placing an object or objects inside a sheet or a large towel. Do not let the other players in this game see what you have hidden in the sheet

because it is their job to guess what it is from one or two clues you give them. If they cannot guess the object from your clues, they may then ask questions that you can answer with yes or no, such as, "Do you ever wear this object?"

In Acts 10 the Bible tells us an interesting story about a man called Cornelius, a Roman soldier who loved God but did not know much about him. God knew Cornelius wanted to know him better, and the Lord sent an angel with an amazing message for Cornelius. Cornelius was instructed to send for Peter, who could tell him more about Jesus.

The next day Peter was hungrily waiting for lunch to be prepared (you have felt like that before!) and went up on his rooftop to pray while he waited. Praying on a roof seems strange to us, but Bible land roofs were flat and made a good place to be alone.

As Peter prayed, he began to have an incredible dream. He dreamed that a huge sheet was lowered from heaven by its four corners. Inside the sheet were all kinds of four-footed animals, reptiles, and birds, including some that Peter had been taught by Jewish customs never to eat. And a voice told him to do just that—to kill and eat!

When Peter objected, calling the creatures "unclean," the voice warned him that what God had made clean was not to be called unclean!

Peter's dream had a very important meaning that he later understood. As Peter tried to understand the mystery of the sheet and the animals, he got the invitation to go to the house of Cornelius. Cornelius was a Roman, and Jewish people like Peter thought that Romans were unclean people. They believed only the Jews were clean, and the Jews would never go into the house of an unclean person.

But then Peter realized God was showing him that *all people* are the same to God, and he loves us all *equally*. So Peter went to the home of Cornelius and told him about the Lord Jesus Christ. Read Acts 10:44-46 to see what happened when Peter obeyed God.

Secret Angels on the Road

Therefore I want you to know that God's salvation has been sent to the Gentiles, and they will listen! (Acts 28:28)

Pretend to be an undercover secret agent, following a certain New Testament character on a long and risky trip. Put on your imaginary seat belt as you begin your exciting adventure:

Travel down a road where a bright light suddenly shines and then slip over a high city wall in a basket, lowered by ropes, in a daring night escape.

Continue to follow this Bible person in and out of prisons and towns where people sometimes listen to him tell about God and sometimes try to kill him and his Christian friends. Travel much of the time by walking and sometimes aboard ships, once even surviving a dangerous shipwreck and a poisonous snakebite. End your journey in a dingy, dirty dungeon in Rome. Who have you been following?

Check your answer in Acts 28:17. Just for fun draw a make-believe map of the world on a piece of paper. Make the continents all round, all square, or all different shapes (remember, this is an imaginary map), and write these names of some actual places Paul visited wherever you want to put them on your map:

- Syracuse
- Rhegium
- Puteoli
- Troas
- Cyprus
- Asia
- Thessalonica
- Crete
- Rome

Take a few minutes to pray for people who are serving God as missionaries right now, and ask the Lord to help you be his missionary in your neighborhood and school.

Rumors

Therefore each of you must put off falsehood and speak truthfully to his neighbor, for we are all members of one body. (Eph. 4:25)

Play this game as you would the game "gossip," whispering the message from person to person until the last one says the statement out loud. Whisper the "rumor" only once to your listener, unless he heard *absolutely* nothing you said!

Here are the messages to pass on (let only the first person to whisper the statements see them):

- Martha was the mother of Jesus.
- Jesus was buried for six days.
- Jesus had fourteen disciples.
- Peter was a follower of Jesus.
- David was swallowed by a fish.
- Noah built a huge barn.

When the last player has heard the rumor, he may say it out loud. After you have enjoyed a laugh over the mixed-up rumors, tell what they really were—and then identify which rumors are correct and which should be disregarded as false information.

Detectives must determine which information they hear is false and which can be trusted to be true—and we must often do the same. Because we are followers of Jesus Christ, the Truth, we want always to tell the truth

ourselves—so that we may please him and be considered *trustworthy* by other people. Read Philippians 4:8, 1 John 2:21, and 1 John 3:18 to see what the Bible says about the truth.

Mystery Objects

All Scripture is God-breathed and is useful for teaching, rebuking, correcting and training in righteousness. (2 Tim. 3:16)

Divide the family into two cooperating teams of agents with the assignment to try to find six mystery objects in the house and bring them back to the starting place as soon as possible. These are the assigned objects for your teams:

- an eraser
- a battery
- a balloon
- a rubber band or ring
- a Band-Aid
- a flashlight

When both teams have returned to the starting point with their items, lay them out on the floor in front of you. Try to guess how the mystery objects relate to the Bible, God's wonderful Book. Brainstorm with other family members if you want to, since two heads are sometimes better than one! These questions may help you solve the mystery of the words:

- What is an eraser used for? Does the Bible contain mistakes? Read Proverbs 30:5.

- What do you do to get air into a balloon? Read 2 Timothy 3:16a to see what "breathing" has to do with the Bible. Hebrews 4:12 tells us that the Bible is living and active.
- Does a Band-Aid protect an injury from dirt and bumps? Has the Bible ever been attacked by God's enemies? Who has protected it for so many centuries?
- Why do we put batteries in toys? Is there power in the Bible? How did it get there?
- How are a rubber band and a ring alike? How long will the Word of God last? Read 1 Peter 1:24-25.
- How is the Bible like a flashlight? Psalm 119:105 gives you the answer.

Who Is the Victim?

He himself bore our sins in his body on the tree. (1 Pet. 2:24)

A terrible crime has been committed—not just by one person but by many—to an innocent victim. It is your job to discover the victim's name and who the guilty people were. Here are the crimes against him:

- He was refused a decent place to spend his first night on earth.
- There was a serious attempt to take his life when he was only a baby.

- Many of the people in his own town were against him.
- People often tried to play mean tricks on him to try to get him in trouble.
- His best friends ran away and hid when he needed them most.
- One of his good friends said that he had never even known him.
- People made up lies about him in order to try to get him killed.
- Some cruel people hit him, spit in his face, made fun of him, and finally, killed him.
- Every awful crime was done to this person even though he had never done an unkind thing to anyone—ever.

Who was the victim of these crimes? Read them over again and try to tell who committed each one. Aren't you glad people today are not guilty of committing any of these terrible crimes against Jesus? Or are we?

Read 2 Peter 2:24 to see whose sins really put Jesus to death on the cross. Are we guilty too?

How can we escape the punishment we deserve? Read Romans 5:8, John 3:16, and 1 John 1:9 to learn the wonderful way to become "not guilty."

Question Me

Always be prepared to give an answer to everyone who asks you to give the reason for the hope that you have. (1 Pet. 3:15)

Pretend to be secret agents interrogating (asking someone questions) a Bible character to see who he is and what he has done. Someone will need to choose a Bible person to be. (Keep it a secret until your questioners guess who you are.) The other player or players will ask questions, such as "Are you a man?" "Are you a friend of Jesus?" "Were you sick?" The "agent" that guesses the Bible person's identity will become the next person to be questioned.

Here are some ideas of Bible people to get you started:

- Adam
- Lazarus
- Daniel
- Moses
- David
- Noah
- Eve
- Paul
- John
- Peter
- Jonah
- Samson
- Joshua

The Bible tells us to be ready to be questioned in real life about our faith in Jesus Christ. Be ready to answer any questions that come your way with the reasons that you love God, believe

him, and live for him. Your words and your life may lead another person to trust in Jesus, too! Wouldn't that be great?

Eyewitness Accounts

We did not follow cleverly invented stories when we told you about the power and coming of our Lord Jesus Christ, but we were eyewitnesses of his majesty. (2 Pet. 1:16)

What is an eyewitness? When a crime has been committed, it is very helpful to the crime-solvers to have someone who actually saw what happened. Peter was just such a person, but not to a crime. See what kind of eyewitness he was in 2 Peter 1:16-18 and notice what he saw.

Test your eyewitness memory skills with this activity:

Give someone in your family the assignment of loading a tray with about twenty small items he can find in the house, such as a paper clip, a pencil, a rubber band, or a fork. Place the tray in front of the other family members and ask each one to take a good look at the objects on it. Take fifteen seconds to try to memorize as many items as possible that you see on the tray and then take it away. See how many objects you can remember as you name them together.

BIBLE
GAMES &
ACTIVITIES

H ere we are, Ladies and Gentlemen, at the starting blocks—the race is about to begin. *Bang!* They're off!"

Do you just love the fun of doing something active? Do you feel that you were made to move, to run, to jump, to climb—and only to sit down when you have to?

If not, maybe you like to watch somebody else do all those things. You feel so great watching someone run in for the shot, get that rebound, dribble down the court, make that long drive, and run around third base toward home plate. (Not all in the same game, of course!)

This chapter contains lots of active games and other things to do by yourself or with others. Join in the fun, and learn some very important lessons as you play!

Games for One or More

Dirty Dirt

Now Abel kept flocks, and Cain worked the soil. (Gen. 4:2)

Have you ever examined dirt? Try this:

Fill a quart jar half full of dirt and add water to the top. Place a cap tightly on the jar and shake it twenty times. Let the jar stand until the dirt settles into layers. There will probably be three distinct kinds of dirt in the jar: pebbles; smaller, coarse grains; and a fine layer of silt. The water will remain cloudy.

To examine the layers closely, first try to skim off the tiny parts of sticks, roots, and leaves that are floating on top and lay them on several thicknesses of paper towels. This layer of dirt is called humus; and as it decays, the gooey black mixture it becomes helps to make our dirt rich.

Next, slowly pour the water in the jar into a smaller container and use a spoon to scoop up the grains on the top of the dirt. Spread them out on a paper towel to observe with a magnifying glass. What do you see? Those tiny grains of dirt are called silt.

Finally, scoop out the last layer (or layers) of coarser grains of sand. If there are larger grains among them, they are really tiny pebbles.

There are several great spiritual lessons that we can learn from dirt. We can remember that God is three persons (God, Jesus, and the Holy Spirit) in one great God, just as there are three layers in dirt. Next, we can remember that dirt is dirty! And when it gets on us, we are dirty, too. Once we get dirt on us, it usually doesn't just come off by itself. If you have very dirty hands, do you expect to look down and suddenly find them clean?

We have to wash the dirt off—and we have a similar problem with the sin in our lives. Can we get rid of the sin inside our souls by ourselves? It's

much like dirt—it sticks and won't come off by itself. We need God's help to clean us up. Look in Psalm 51:1-2, 9-10 to see what special kind of soap power we need to become clean in God's sight.

Rainbow Bubbles

I have set my rainbow in the clouds. (Gen. 9:13)

Do you think a bubble can be a reminder that God always keeps his word? Definitely! To prove it you will need a jar of bubble mix solution—the kind that has a plastic bubble blower inside. Add a tablespoon of sugar to the bubble mix to give longer life to the bubbles you blow. To make your bubble holder, bend a thin piece of wire or pipe cleaner to form a ring at one end. Wind the straight end of the wire or pipe cleaner around a pencil and stick the pencil into the center hole of a spool of thread. Then adjust the loop so it is parallel (going the same direction) with the table top you set the bubble holder on. Dip it into the bubble solution, blow gently into the plastic bubble blower, catch a bubble, and gently shake it onto the bubble holder. Now you can get a good look at the bubble. In a few minutes you should be able to see a rainbow of colors on it!

What does a rainbow have to do with God's promises always being kept? Read Hebrews 10:23 and Titus 1:2 to see what God does about his promises. Has there ever been another worldwide flood to destroy the earth since Noah's day? Will there ever be? How do you know?

Jacob's Hard Pillow

Taking one of the stones there, he put it under his head and lay down to sleep. (Gen. 28:11)

Imitate Jacob's camping-out-under-the-stars experience by collecting several different objects to try out as pillows. Some choices might be a large book, a cardboard box, a bowl, a stuffed animal, a tennis shoe, and a ball. See how each object would feel if you had to sleep on it all night! Did you prefer one or two objects over the other choices?

Jacob had the hardest pillow imaginable one night as he slept out under the stars! If you were going to use a stone for a pillow, what kind of stone would you choose?

As Jacob slept, he had a spectacular dream! What did Jacob do when he awoke? What did Jacob promise God? Read about it in Genesis 28:12-22.

The Itsy, Bitsy Spider

What he [the person without God] trusts in is fragile; what he relies on is a spider's web. (Job 8:14)

Have you ever been fascinated by a spider's web?

Our great God designed spiders so that they can manufacture a sticky silk thread, right in their own little body factories! That tiny thread is their life-support system. Without it, they would have no home and no good way to trap their dinner. And if spiders didn't act as excellent bug exterminators, our world would be overrun with unpopular insects!

You can make a play spider's web in your own room by weaving a roll of string or yarn back and forth between pieces of furniture, attaching it to

doorknobs and table legs. Crawl under your web and read Job 8:13-14 and imagine how foolish a person would be to put his trust in something fragile like a spider's web instead of our mighty God!

The Water Eraser

You will surely forget your trouble, recalling it only as waters gone by. Life will be brighter than noonday, and darkness will become like morning. (Job 11:16-17)

Try the water eraser trick to see the effect water has when it washes over sand or dirt. Write a message in the dirt of your yard and spray it with water from a garden hose or pour a glass of water over it. Did the words remain, or did the water wash them away? What happens to a message or a sand castle that we leave on the beach when high tide comes?

Job said we need to remember that the problems we face will soon be gone, as waters wash over the sand at the seashore. Read some other beautiful verses from Job 11:13-19 that God wrote to encourage us.

Love a Tree

He is like a tree planted by streams of water. (Ps. 1:3)

Do you know a tree that you just love? Some of you immediately have an answer to that weird question because you really do have a tree that you would never want anything to happen to. It may be your favorite climbing tree, a tree with a swing or tire hanging from its branches, or a tree in the backyard that keeps your house cool in the summer. It may be a big leafy tree whose shade is perfect as a picnic spot.

Others of you may seriously think that loving a tree sounds a little strange! Would you consider adopting a tree? Yes, really!

Find a tree in your yard, in your neighborhood, or at church to adopt as your own. Of course, you shouldn't try to take it home with you, unless it is a little seedling (baby tree) and does not belong to someone else. You may want to buy a small tree from a plant nursery and be its human mother or father in your own yard.

Get acquainted with your adopted tree: Make crayon rubbings of its bark, measure the distance around its trunk, take notice of its special markings (scraped spots, knotholes, or nicks where birds have pecked), press and preserve a leaf or two in spring and again in the fall, and write down some of your observations beside a photograph or a drawing of your tree. If your tree is small, have someone take your picture beside it each year to see how you both have grown. Don't forget to water your tree and feed it occasionally with some kind of soil enrichment from a gardening shop.

Read the beautiful picture of a tree in Psalm 1:1-4. Who is the writer of the psalm describing? Are you that kind of tree?

Shadow Tricks

He who dwells in the shelter of the Most High will rest in the shadow of the Almighty. (Ps. 91:1)

Shine a flashlight at a wall in a dark room. Try several objects to see what kind of shadow they make; then try making hand shadows of a bird, a swan, a butterfly, or a dog.

Try performing these shadow tricks with a friend: Jump on your shadows, shake hands, and make your shadows as tall or as short as possible.

There are wonderful shadow Scriptures in the Bible, and many of them contain promises for us. Read Psalm 57:1-2, Psalm 63:7; and Psalm 91:1-2. God is so powerful that even in his shadow we are safe! The shadow of a person could never protect us, could it? But God's protective shadow over our lives gives us great security!

Rules to Live By

For I delight in your commands because I love them. I lift up my hands to your commands, which I love. (Ps. 119:47-48)

Can you imagine someone loving *rules?* We may think they are a good idea to have, and certainly we should obey them, but *love* them? Most of us would have to admit that we *don't!*

Here are some commands to obey and the rules to go with them:

- Take ten steps forward. (The rule: You must balance a book on your head as you walk.)
- Put five coins in a glass. (The rule: You must pick them up with a fork.)
- Kneel down on both knees. (The rule: You must keep your arms folded behind your back and get up without losing your balance!)

Those rules were pretty silly, weren't they? But the rules of the Bible are never silly! They are always good, wise, and loving, and they can be completely trusted and fully obeyed to give us a happy, satisfying life on earth and life forevermore in heaven! God's rules rule!

Remember

Remember your Creator in the days of your youth. (Eccles. 12:1)

Let's see how good your memory is! Below is a list of three things to do. Look at them for ten seconds and then do them from memory.

- Stand up and stretch.
- Touch a wall.
- Clap five times.

Good! Now let's try a little more challenge! See if you can remember five instructions that well! You may look at them for fifteen seconds.

- Sit down.
- Crawl forward.
- Get up.
- Turn around.
- Take a bow!

Great job! Or even if it wasn't quite as great as you hoped for, it doesn't matter, since those commands weren't really important to remember, were they?

There are some things that we should definitely remember! Can you find them in these Bible verses?

- Numbers 15:40
- Deuteronomy 8:18
- Psalm 77:11-12
- Ecclesiastes 12:1

Share the Good News

How beautiful on the mountains are the feet of those who bring good news. (Isa. 52:7)

Ask a family member to take apart the pages of a section of the newspaper—or the whole newspaper, if you want a real challenge—and stack them in a pile, out of their proper order. At the "Go!" signal, see how quickly you or your team can put the paper back together correctly and fold it!

Now look through the newspaper and count how many articles are on the front page or section that tell good news and how many report bad news of some kind.

If you have time and interest, make your own family or neighborhood paper, sharing only good news or information about good opportunities that are available to help people in need.

If God wrote a *Good News Gazette*, what would *he* announce in the front page headlines? Read Romans 1:16, and remember that the "gospel" of Jesus Christ is the Good News about his life, death, resurrection, and second coming!

How Could He Know?

But you, Bethlehem . . . out of you will come for me one who will be ruler over Israel, whose origins are from of old, from ancient times. (Mic. 5:2)

Try your luck at predicting what will happen a hundred years from now.

Write or tell your answers to these questions:

- Who will be president a hundred years from now?
- What will be the middle name of your first grandchild?
- What will cars look like and be called in the year 2100?
- What will be the most popular children's movie a hundred years from now?

Could you answer the questions? Of course not! It is impossible to accurately predict what will happen a hundred years from now, but many prophecies about Jesus were spoken *seven hundred* years before he was born.

Look up a few of the prophecies about Jesus in your Bible. Remember, the words were spoken hundreds of years before Jesus came to earth!

The Prophecy	The Fulfillment
Micah 5:2	Matthew 2:1-6
Zechariah 9:9	Matthew 21:1-9
Isaiah 53:6-8	Luke 23:1-25
Psalm 22:7-8, 14, 16-17	Matthew 27:35
Psalm 16:10	Acts 2:22-32

The Terrible, No-good, Really Bad Guy!

For Herod is going to search for the child to kill him. (Matt. 2:13)

One of the worst "bad guys" in the whole New Testament was the evil king Herod. You probably have no friends with the name *Herod*, because parents do not want to attach that name to the children they love! For each letter in the name *Herod*, give a word that could describe that wicked man, such as "Herod was *horrendous!*" If you cannot think of words that begin with the letters of his name, use any other letters to start your words.

Now think of words that describe people who love God and do what is right.

Secret Praying

But when you pray, go into your room, close the door and pray to your Father. (Matt. 6:6)

In Bible days, people often prayed at the altar. An altar was usually made outside from a pile of stones, and the person praying would kneel down nearby and talk to God. Sometimes the altar would be left there so that people could return and pray each time they passed by. The altar helped them to remember that praying to God is a very special event.

You can make your own miniature altar by gluing small rocks or pebbles together on a piece of cardboard. Place small toy people (like G.I. Joes or a dollhouse family) beside the altar, even dressing them in Bible-day clothes made from a tissue or cloth if you would like to make the scene look more authentic.

If you prefer, make a life-size altar by piling up larger rocks, paper bags stuffed with crumpled newspaper and taped shut, several pillows, or even rolled-up "sock rocks."

The important thing to remember when you pray is not *where you are* as much as *who you are talking to*. Everywhere you pray—on your bike as you ride down the street, at your school desk before a big test, or in your bed when you are alone at night—becomes your special prayer altar.

Wring Out the Worry

Do not worry about your life, what you will eat or drink; or about your body, what you will wear. Is not life more important than food, and the body more important than clothes? (Matt. 6:25)

At the kitchen or bathroom sink, hold a washcloth under the running water until it is full of water and can hold no more. Guess how much water you think the washcloth is now holding (one cup, half a cup, etc.). Place a measuring cup under the washcloth and begin to wring and twist the washcloth until you can't get one more drop of water out of it. Measure the amount of water in the cup, and see how nearly right your guess was.

Try to name five things that people sometimes do when they are worrying about something. One strange thing that some people do when they are worried is to wring or twist their hands together. Jesus wisely told us not to worry, because he knew that we would only make things harder on ourselves by our worry. He had a much better plan!

The Bible says, "Do not be anxious about anything, but in everything, by prayer and petition, with thanksgiving, present your requests to God" (Phil. 4:6).

Great Head of Hair!

Even the very hairs of your head are all numbered. (Matt. 10:30)

The next time you shampoo your hair, turn yourself into a work of art in front of the bathroom mirror. Place a towel around your shoulders to catch the drips, and see how many creative ways you can style your sudsy hair. Watch yourself become a living soap sculpture before your very eyes!

God considers you his magnificent work of art—just as you are. He planned for you, he created you, he constantly watches over you, and he knows you even much better than you know yourself. He even knows the exact number of those sudsy hairs on your

head! Isn't it great to have a friend like God?

Oxen-Oxen

For my yoke is easy and my burden is light. (Matt. 11:30)

Try one or both of these tests of strength and balance:

• Walk with one lightweight book on your head, and then try adding more.
• Crawl on your hands and knees across the room with a book or pillow on your back. Let someone add more loads to your back each time you crawl past.

In ancient days oxen were used to carry heavy loads for people, and many countries still use oxen today. Often two strong oxen were placed side by side and held together by a wooden collar or yoke that had holes for the oxen's heads to fit through. The animals could then pull very heavy loads for the people who owned them.

Jesus tells us to come to him when we feel like we're carrying a heavy load of sadness, tiredness, or worry, and he'll give us his rest. When we serve Jesus, he gives us an easy load to carry because he himself helps us to carry it!

Weeds

When the wheat sprouted and formed heads, then the weeds also appeared. (Matt. 13:26)

Imagine that you are going to plant your very first garden. You have a hoe for digging, a garden hose for watering, packages of carrot seeds, cucumber seeds, corn, and beans. You dig, plant, and water your seeds, and soon they come up in neat little rows.

One day, however, you notice other, different looking plants growing up between the rows. You know you did not plant seeds there. What are those little plants, and how did they get there? Will they cause a problem if they stay? If so, what will you do about them?

Jesus often told stories about everyday things that people knew about and understood like plants and weeds. His story is found in Matthew 13:24-30, and the meaning of it can be read in verses 36-43. The lesson of the weeds is an important one because it is our choice whether we become Jesus' own good plants or become weeds.

Is there a flower bed or garden in your own yard—or your neighbor's—that needs a little weeding? Offer to do the job!

The Whole World Is Mine!

What good will it be for a man if he gains the whole world, yet forfeits [loses] his soul? (Matt. 16:26)

In 1803 a famous business deal took place between France and America. France agreed to sell a huge piece of land called the Louisiana Territory to America for 15 million dollars. That may sound like a lot of money, but that land could not possibly be bought today for less than billions or trillions of dollars, if it were even for sale!

Imagine that the whole world is for sale—and you have a chance to buy it! Name the countries you would buy first and the amount of money you would be willing to pay for them. (Pretend that you can afford whatever it costs!) Then name any parts of the world you would rather not buy and tell why.

Jesus said that even if someone could own the whole world, it would be worthless if the person lost his soul. Jesus was trying to help us understand what is really valuable in life and what is not. Read his words of warning in Matthew 16:26-27.

Humility? What's Humility?

Whoever humbles himself like this child is the greatest in the kingdom of heaven. (Matt. 18:4)

Humility is a big word—and an important one, too.

To help you understand what it means, look around the room for the smallest opening you can find that you think you could fit through. What would you have to do to get in? (Kneel or bend down?)

Now spend the next five or ten minutes doing everything from the kneeling position. If the phone rings, walk or run on your knees to answer it; if

Dad calls you, hurry to him on your knees (unless he is outside!).

The Bible tells us that one day every person on earth will fall to his knees. When? Find out by reading Philippians 2:9-11. What did Jesus give up to show us what humility means? Philippians 2:5-8 explains to us what the mighty Creator of the whole universe was willing to do.

I Forgive You, I Forgive You, I Forgive You . . .

Lord, how many times shall I forgive my brother when he sins against me? Up to seven times? (Matt. 18:21)

Choose a number from 1 to 10. Add 6 to it. Now take 4 away from the number you now have. Add 5 more to it and then take away the number you started with. Your answer is 7. Right? If it isn't, try the game again, writing down your numbers if you need to. No matter what number you start with, you should always end up with 7!

Seven is an important number in the Bible because it usually stands for God or for something that is perfect. Jesus once used the number 7—in fact, he used the number 70 x 7!

Jesus was helping his disciples to understand that even when people have done us wrong and treated us badly, we are still to forgive them over and over again—not just 7 times, but 70 x 7 times! He didn't mean for us to actually count up our forgiveness and stop at 490—but to forgive as often as we need to! Jesus knew how to do just that. Do you remember his prayer for his enemies from the cross? You can read it in Luke 23:34.

Have you had a chance to try out your forgiving skills today? Good for you! Some of the very hardest words we will ever have to say to someone and really mean are these: "I'm sorry. Will you please forgive me?" But even harder are the words, "Yes, I forgive you," especially if we are still hurt and angry, if the person has already done the same wrong thing many times before, and especially if he is not even sorry!

If you have been able to use any of those hard words recently, consider yourself congratulated! You have done right.

Who's in Charge Here?

Well done, good and faithful servant! You have been faithful with a few things; I will put you in charge of many things. (Matt. 25:23)

Ask your mom or dad to give you a penny at the beginning of the day tomorrow. Tell her or him that you will keep it with you and be in charge of the coin, that you will keep it with you at all times, and that you will give it back in great shape tomorrow evening. Ask your parents if they will then exchange the penny for a dollar (or a quarter or fifty cents if they think that a dollar is a little too much to ask) that you can keep—but only if you have done a good job of being in charge of the penny all day. Explain to them that the real purpose in doing this activity is to help you remember the Bible truth in Matthew 25:23.

Remember that God promises to reward you someday for doing a good job in little things like finishing your homework on time, doing your chores well, dusting the school chalkboard erasers, or taking care of your younger brothers or sisters now and then. Part of God's reward comes in the form of giving you bigger and even better responsibilities and privileges because you can be trusted!

Food and Clothes for Jesus

I tell you the truth, whatever you did for one of the least of these brothers of mine, you did for me. (Matt. 25:40)

Place a suitcase filled with clothes on the opposite side of the room from your starting line. Include some of these kinds of items in your suitcase: hats or caps, mittens or gloves, socks, a jacket, a shirt, and perhaps pajama bottoms or sweatpants that are easy to put on. Ask someone to time you to see how long it takes you to run to the suitcase, put all the clothes on over your clothes, take them off, and run back. Then try it again (after you catch your breath) to see if you can beat your time!

If two or more people are playing the game, enjoy the race as you both run and put on your own suitcase full of clothes at the same time. Don't get carried away with who wins the race. The fun of this game is in watching and trying the crazy, hectic clothes changing!

Playing this game reminds us that we have plenty of clothes to wear—though we don't normally wear them *all at once,* do we? There are many people, though, who have very few clothes to wear and not enough nourishing food to eat. Some of these needy people may go to your church or school.

Jesus loves the people in need just as much as he loves you, and he wants us to help make sure they have what they need. The Bible teaches that God does his work through his people, especially when someone needs food, clothes, and loving care. In fact, Matthew 25:25-40 shows us that when we do good deeds for other people, we actually are doing them for Jesus himself!

Blow Up a Storm!

A furious squall [storm] came up, and the waves broke over the boat, so that it was nearly swamped. (Mark 4:37)

Blow up a small storm of your own to give you a picture of the day when Jesus calmed the storm in Mark 4:35-41. Read those verses from your Bible.

Fill an eleven-by-thirteen-inch pan with water and place it on a cabinet near a sink or on a table. Stand at one end of the pan and begin to huff and puff and blow into the pan until waves start to form and move across the water. You have created a small storm!

Sudden storms often came up on the Sea of Galilee like the one that happened in the story Mark told. But who calmed and quieted the storm that day?

Sometimes small or big storms seem to come into our lives, too. We don't usually get wet, but we often get worried! Sometimes our storm is a bad grade on a report card, our dad's loss of his job, our mom's struggle with the flu, or problems with a friend. But just as Jesus calmed the big storm during the disciples' trip across the lake, Jesus will calm our hearts when storms of life come our way. And he will give us his quiet peace.

Elizabeth's Family Tree

Your prayer has been heard. Your wife Elizabeth will bear you a son, and you are to give him the name John. (Luke 1:13)

Make a family tree for your family, beginning with a drawing of a tree trunk and branches. If your family is small, make only a few branches; if it is large, include many branches growing from the trunk. Write your own name on the tree trunk and the name of every relative (aunt, uncle, cousin, or grandparent) that you can think of on a branch.

If you can remember five or more relatives, congratulate yourself on having a big family that has helped make you the very important person you are. If you are a member of a small family, thank God for making you one of an extra-special small group!

Elizabeth was also a part of an extraordinary family tree—the family of Jesus! She was the relative of Mary, the mother of Jesus, and her son, John the Baptist, was born only a few months before Jesus was born in Bethlehem. God had a wonderful plan for John the Baptist to tell everyone ahead of time that Jesus, God's Son, would come and be the Savior of the world!

Before bed tonight, say a prayer for every member of your family tree by name, even if you have to read them from your paper as you pray. Especially pray for those who do not know Jesus Christ as their Savior and Lord, for those family members who are sick, and for those who are having any special problems. God will hear your prayers!

Speechless!

He kept making signs to them but remained unable to speak. (Luke 1:22)

Play the "silence game" for fifteen minutes (or for longer if you can stand it!). During that time, don't say anything out loud. You may move your lips, or you may use hand gestures or write notes to get your messages across, but don't make a sound!

Silence was not a game for Zechariah when he lost his ability to speak. Who was he and what happened in Luke 1:5-13, 18-20? Look in Luke 1:57-64 to see the joyful ending of Zechariah's story.

Farmer Luke

Still other seed fell on good soil. It came up and yielded a crop, a hundred times more than was sown. (Luke 8:8)

In Luke 8, Jesus told a story about a farmer who was tossing seeds from a bag he had hung over his shoulder. He was hoping that all the seeds would grow well wherever they landed on the ground; but his hopes, unfortunately, did not come true.

Some of the ground was rocky, other spots were full of thorns, and the hungry birds who hovered nearby had plans of their own for eating some of the seed. To get the feel of tossing seeds, try this "cotton-tossing game."

Make a line on the floor with a piece of masking tape, a yardstick, a belt, a piece of string, or an extension cord. Stand several feet behind the line and try to toss a cotton ball as far as you can over the line. Stick a piece of tape on the floor where your cotton ball landed. Try another toss and keep trying to improve your distance each time.

Read the interesting story in Luke 8:5-8, 11-15. See if it has a happy ending and talk together about what it means. Did you know that we all are some kind of dirt in Jesus' story?

Knock, Knock. Who's There?

Knock and the door will be opened to you. (Luke 11:9)

Try this game with a balloon near a door or wall. (Warn the members of your family that they may hear some knocking for the next few minutes—so they won't wonder what is going on!)

Give the balloon a little tap straight up in the air above you and knock on the door or wall before the balloon comes back down. Then tap the balloon and knock two times. Repeat the action over and over, adding an extra knock each time before the balloon comes down. You may wish you had a higher ceiling!

Jesus compared prayer to knocking on a door. Read the important lesson he taught in Luke 11:5-10. Read this story about the midnight caller, and talk with your family about what Jesus is teaching. Determine to be a believer who keeps on knocking on the door of prayer. The Bible says that the door will open!

The Bent-Over Lady

She was bent over and could not straighten up at all. (Luke 13:11)

For five minutes, pretend to have a bad back that keeps you from being able to straighten up. While you are bent over, like the poor lady in Luke 13:11, try to do these five things:

- Reach a book or something else that's on a high shelf.
- Remove a cup or dish from a high kitchen cabinet.
- Look up at the ceiling or sky for five seconds.
- Talk to someone taller than you as you look straight into his face.
- Hang up a shirt or coat in the closet.

Now straighten up again and be very thankful for the many things your body can do! Remember to show special kindness and compassion—a friendly smile like Jesus would do—to those you meet who have physical handicaps of any kind. If you are handicapped, let Jesus shine through your wonderful life! Read Luke 13:10-13.

Identify the Guy!

If you hold to my teaching, you are really my disciples. (John 8:31)

Write a name of one of these twelve New Testament Bible characters in each section of an egg carton:

- John the Baptist
- Peter
- Zacchaeus
- Paul
- Stephen
- Mary
- Lazarus
- Philip
- Bartimaeus
- Judas
- Herod
- Dorcas

Place a penny inside the egg carton, close the lid, and shake the carton several times. Open the lid and see where the penny landed. Tell all you can about that New Testament person.

Bible people were just like you are in many ways. They had feelings, opinions, happy days, sad days, and often made mistakes. Some were Jesus' followers and obeyed him willingly; others chose to disobey him and to go their own way, bringing sadness to their lives and dishonor to God. The Bible shows us both kinds of people so that we can see that serving Jesus is the most wonderful, rewarding life of all! And that is what he wants for you!

The Great Going-Up Miracles

He was taken up before their very eyes, and a cloud hid him from their sight. (Acts 1:9)

Try to make something go up and touch the ceiling of your house without throwing it, lifting it, hitting it, or pushing it with your hands. The object you use may be lightweight—a tissue, a balloon, a feather, or a bubble—and you may blow it, direct a fan toward it, fan it with a piece of paper, or bop it with a folded sheet of paper or a flyswatter.

Did you find it hard to make something go up and keep going up? Would it have been easier if you had been able to sit on the ceiling and make the objects go down?

Jesus went up in the process of two incredible miracles: his resurrection from the dead and his ascension to be with the Father in heaven. Read about those amazing events in Matthew 28:2-7 and Acts 1:9-11.

Beggar by the Gate

Silver or gold I do not have, but what I have I give you. In the name of Jesus Christ of Nazareth, walk. (Acts 3:6)

Sometimes we take for granted those things we have with us every day— like our feet! If you have ever had trouble walking for any reason, you know how important feet can be.

Try these actions, using only your feet—no hands allowed!

- Pick up marbles and drop them in a jar.
- Take both your socks off without using any part of your body except your feet.
- Pick up a pencil and hold it with your toes as you walk across the room.
- Place a large piece of paper on the floor and draw a picture on it, holding the crayon or marker between your toes.

Acts 3:1-10 shows us the wonderful story of a man who had never been able to walk. Note where he was sitting, who saw him there, and how they helped him. Was the man excited about what happened to him?

A Face like an Angel

Stephen, full of the Holy Spirit, looked up into heaven. . . . "Look," he said, "I see heaven open and the Son of Man standing at the right hand of God." At this they covered their ears and . . . rushed at him, dragged him out of the city and began to stone him. (Acts 7:55-58)

Have a "rock fight" in the house, with your parents' permission.

This "rock" fight is really quite harmless, since the stones are crumpled-up newspapers or paper towels. Besides that, they do not need to be thrown at someone—you may set up a bucket or laundry basket and play "rock basketball" or "rock soccer" instead. If you choose to toss your "rocks" in the basket, perhaps Dad or Mom will let you use rolled up "sock balls" instead.

This kind of rock-throwing is fun, but can you imagine purposely throwing a rock into a group of people, knowing that somebody is sure to get seriously hurt? Even that thought makes you feel terrible. Only Satan gives somebody the idea to hurt another person with a rock, and that is exactly who was behind the actions of the crowd who hurled heavy stones at Stephen in the shocking story found in Acts 6:8-15; 7:54-59.

Read the story to discover whether Stephen had done anything to deserve that treatment, how Stephen looked, and what Stephen said as he was put on trial and then stoned to death.

How's Your Aim?

Aim for perfection. (2 Cor. 13:11)

Choose an acceptable target in your house—a doorknob, a spot in the woodgrain on a door, or a smudge on the wall. Aim and shoot a rubber band, a paper airplane, a piece of wadded-up paper, rolled-up masking tape, or a "sock ball" at your target. See how many hits you can get. "Real close" scores 1 point, and "hits" score 10! If you wish, take turns with another player and try to reach the score of 100 points together!

When you shot the rubber band or threw the paper ball at the target, was your goal to hit about five feet away from it, or to hit a bull's-eye? When an archer shoots an arrow, does he try to land it in a nearby tree, or in the center of his target?

The apostle Paul encourages us in 2 Corinthians 13:11 to aim straight for the bull's-eye in life: perfection! He doesn't tell us to do *fairly well*, to be *kind of good*—but to be the *best!* To go for the gold! Even when we miss the bull's-eye, or fail to even hit the target, let's keep aiming to be perfect, like Jesus.

Sweet Savor

Live a life of love, just as Christ loved us and gave himself up for us as a fragrant offering and sacrifice to God. (Eph. 5:2)

In Bible days, when a sacrifice was burned on the altar in an act of worship to God, God was pleased when he smelled the sweet fragrance of their obedience. We know that God was pleased with Jesus' great sacrifice of himself in our place as an act of love. Jesus' offering of himself unselfishly was a sweet fragrance to God the Father!

Here are some ways to make a "sweet smell" in your house:

- Put a small pan of water on the stove, turn it on low heat, and add some cloves and cinnamon.
- Make potpourri from crushed dried flowers and leaves by sprinkling them with perfume or potpourri oil.
- Melt potpourri wax in a flat pan in the oven (with the help of an adult). Carefully roll pinecones in the liquid wax to cover them. Place the potpourri-covered

pinecones on a piece of waxed paper or newspaper to dry, and place them in the rooms of your house as a "sweet fragrance."

How Much Do You Know?

I want to know Christ and the power of his resurrection. (Phil. 3:10)

Play this ring-toss guessing game in one (or both) of these ways:

Write each of the numbers from 1 to 5 on separate pieces of paper and lay them on the floor. Toss a beanbag or rolled-up sock at the papers, trying to make it land on one of them. Read and answer the question on this page beside that number.

Or, cut five six-inch strips from lightweight cardboard or poster board and write a number from 1 to 5 on one end of each of them. Tape the strips to the sides of a table so that the number end of each strip stands up above the tabletop. Toss a ring cut from a paper plate or an unbreakable round bracelet at the cardboard strips, trying to make your paper ring or bracelet land around one of them. Answer the question that follows that number on this page.

- 1. What did the little boy have in his lunch the day he shared it with Jesus and five thousand people?
- 2. Who was a great missionary in the Bible who went to many cities preaching about Jesus?

- 3. What kinds of sicknesses did Jesus heal?
- 4. What miracle did Jesus perform at a wedding?
- 5. Did Jesus have any enemies? What was the worst thing they did to him?

Answers: (1) five loaves, two fish (2) Paul (3) all kinds (4) He turned water into wine. (5) Yes. They nailed him to the cross.

"Stick" in There

. . . being strengthened with all power according to his glorious might so that you may have great endurance and patience. (Col. 1:11)

Here are two silly ways to get across a very important lesson from the Bible:

- Tape a piece of paper to the bottom of each of your feet. Pretend to be a bug that has stepped on sticky sheets of flypaper. Walk around like that for a while, and then pretend that you are tired of the pesky flypaper. Try to shake it off any way you can!
- Pretend that you and someone in your family have been stuck together back-to-back or side-to-side with glue or Velcro. Go everywhere and do everything together until you get tired of this game.

What do these silly games have to do with a great Bible truth? What was the "flypaper" doing? What were your backs doing? (Read 2 Timothy 3:14.)

The Bible uses a couple of big words to mean "stick" in there! That means now that you have given your life to Jesus, keep on and on and on living for him, day after day, when days are great and days are rough, when your faith is gigantic and when it's tiny. Keep on going!

When to Pray

Pray continually. (1 Thess. 5:17)

The Bible tells us to pray continually. That sounds hard to do! If we are always praying, when do we get to eat, go to school, play, or sleep? Does God want us to be a perpetual "praying machine," doing nothing else?

The Bible contains verses about eating, sleeping, working, walking, running, and studying (yes, that, too!) and gives us guidelines about how we are to do all those activities and please God at the same time. So where does praying fit in?

The Bible teaches us that it is good to have a particular time to pray—perhaps in the morning as we start our day, at mealtime, or at bedtime. But it also tells us to always be ready to pray at any minute during the day, whenever we especially need God's help or want to tell him thank you.

You probably already do that! Haven't you sometimes prayed at school during a big test, when someone got hurt, or maybe when you were afraid you might get in trouble? God

wants us to be ready to talk to him anytime.

Here's a game to try to help you think about what it means to do something *continually:*

Write your name and address on a piece of paper. Sound easy? As you write, balance on one foot and keep the other turning in a circle *continually*—don't let it stop! Then write your name and address again as you lightly tap a balloon *continually* to keep it up in the air as you write.

Games for Two or More

Which Is It?

Play this get-acquainted game with the Old and New Testaments of your Bible. Since a get-acquainted game is meant to be the start of a great friendship, plan right now that you and your Bible are going to become the very best of friends!

Ask some member of your family or a friend to read this list of events that happened in the Old or New Testaments of the Bible. If you know which part of the Bible the event is from, great! If you don't, it's fine to guess the answer. This game is not for shy folks, and it works best when you are in a silly mood. If the event happened in the Old Testament, cup your hand around your ear and say, "What's that, Sonny?" pretending to be an old person. If you think that the New Testament is the correct answer, look sad and say, *"Waaah!"* like a new baby.

- The story of the creation of the world (Old Testament)
- The story of Jesus' birth in Bethlehem (New Testament)
- The life of Moses (Old Testament)
- The stories about King David (Old Testament)
- The story of Jesus calming the storm on the sea (New Testament)
- The story of Daniel and the lions' den (Old Testament)
- The beautiful picture of heaven (New Testament)

Turnabout

In Bible days, the Jewish people often used games to teach God's Word. The Jewish teachers, the rabbis, would repeat the Scripture as they walked along together. One would recite verses for a while, and then the other rabbi would immediately continue saying the verses when the first one stopped for a rest. Back and forth, down the street, the teachers would continue the Scripture exchange.

Play this turnabout game as you walk around in a circle in your room like the Jewish rabbis. Ask someone to read the list of Bible books from this page, one at a time, slowly. If the Bible book is from the New Testament, keep walking forward. If it is found in the Old Testament, turn around and im-

mediately continue your walking in the opposite direction. Here are the books from the Bible:

- Genesis
- Revelation
- Exodus
- Psalms
- Proverbs
- Daniel
- Matthew
- Luke
- Deuteronomy
- Job
- Acts
- Romans

If you are still enjoying the game, add more books to your list.

Old or New?

Here are some games to play to help you remember which Bible books are from the Old or New Testaments:

- "Beanbag toss." Label two boxes, one *Old Testament* and the other *New Testament,* and place them in the middle of the floor. Ask Dad or Mom to read the names of Bible books from the Old and New Testaments, but not in order. Players should then take turns tossing a beanbag into the correct box after the name of each book is read.
- "Old and new tic-tac-toe." Play a game of tic-tac-toe with two or three players. The third player may read the list of Bible books to the others, or if only two people are playing, one can read the Bible books and also play the

game. One player may move his *O* only if the book can be found in the Old Testament, the other player may move his *X* (the letter *X* sometimes represents Jesus) if the book belongs in the New Testament. Players need to decide before the game begins which part of the Bible they will represent. Here is the list of Bible books to use:

- 1 Peter
- Acts
- Malachi
- Ezekiel
- Matthew
- Jeremiah
- Hebrews
- 1 Corinthians
- Joshua
- Joel
- Numbers
- Ruth
- Luke
- Psalms
- Ephesians
- 3 John
- Isaiah

Bible Book Scrabble

Make ten straight vertical lines about a half-inch apart on a piece of paper. Then make ten lines across the paper, forming small squares.

Take turns with a member of your family writing the names of books from the Bible in the squares. Each book name that is added must join or cross another letter in a name already on the paper, like in a crossword puz-

zle. For example, if the name *Daniel* is written across the paper, the next player could write *John* going down, placing it so that the two words share the letter *n*. Or, the name *Proverbs* could cross *Daniel* at the *e*. See how many books of the Bible you can include.

Create-a-Man

So God created man in his own image. (Gen. 1:27)

Play this "create-a-man" game like the game hangman. Think of a Bible person and make short lines in a row, representing the number of letters in his or her name.

The other player must name one letter at a time until he can guess who the Bible person is. Each time he guesses a correct letter, write it on the short line representing where the letter fits in the name. When a wrong letter is chosen, begin to "create" a man by drawing the parts of him, one part for each wrong letter.

The Bible tells us about the experiences of many different kinds of people: some old, some young, many poor, and a few of them rich. Some of the people in the Bible are kings and soldiers, others are beggars and carpenters. Children are some of the very special people in the Bible, and Jesus used them to teach some of his most important lessons. Aren't you thankful that God made and loves people?

Walking by Faith

Leave your country, your people and your father's household and go to the land I will show you. (Gen. 12:1)

God told Abram (later called Abraham) that he was going to take him to a brand-new home in a different land, but he didn't tell Abram where it would be. That would almost be like your dad or mom packing the family in the car with all your furniture and belongings in a trailer behind it and saying, "OK, we're on our way"—not even knowing what direction to go!

Not knowing where home would be didn't bother Abram, though. He trusted God. And he knew that wherever God took him in life would be great!

Here's a walking-by-faith game for you to try with a friend. Play this game outside or in a large room where you won't run into things. One player should close his eyes or wear a blindfold. The other player will give him directions saying where and how to walk. Here are some ideas:

- Walk two steps, hop one step, etc.
- Walk one step and clap, one step and clap, etc.
- Walk facing backwards two steps, facing forward three steps, facing backwards two steps, etc.
- Walk forward two steps, sit down, walk forward two steps, sit down, etc.

Good job of walking by faith!

Red Sea?

Then Moses stretched out his hand over the sea, and all that night the Lord drove the sea back with a strong east wind and turned it into dry land. (Exod. 14:21)

Play this game called "color plus." One person must give clues to another player (player #2) in order for that player to guess the secret color and the word that goes with it. Here are the clues and the answers for player #2 to guess:

- This is the color of the sky or water plus something that shines at night. (blue moon)
- This is the color of an apple or cherry plus a common name for a dog that starts with R. (red rover)
- This is the color of butter plus the name of a beautiful flower. (yellow rose)
- This is the color of coal plus the

name of the sticky blacktop on roads. (black tar)

• This is a common color for sports cars plus another name for an ocean. (Red Sea)

Was the *color* of the Red Sea the important thing about it? Its water was greenish, bluish, or brownish like most rivers are. What happened at the Red Sea when God's people needed to get across in a big hurry to escape Pharaoh's army? Tell the story in your own words, or read it from Exodus 14:19-29.

We Spy!

Let us send men ahead to spy out the land for us and bring back a report. (Deut. 1:22)

Play the game "I spy" with someone in your family. Describe an object in the room that you have actually seen, but be careful not to look straight at it. If the other player guesses your object correctly, he gets to spy. If you stump him, you get to spy again!

Real-life spying can be dangerous business! Joshua and Caleb were sent out with ten other men from Israel to spy out the land of Canaan that God had promised to give to his people for their new home. Their assignment was risky business because their enemies lived in Canaan. If they had been caught, their fate would have been sure and sudden death! Read the intri-

guing story from Deuteronomy 1:21-25.

What a Name!

When Mephibosheth son of Jonathan, the son of Saul, came to David, he bowed down to pay him honor. (2 Sam. 9:6)

Out of all the Bible's wonderful stories, the one involving Jonathan's son, Mephibosheth, is one of the most beautiful.

One day King David was sitting in his magnificent palace, thinking about those wonderful days gone by when he and his best friend, Jonathan, had played and laughed together as boys. Jonathan had already died, and David asked a question about him. Read it in 2 Samuel 9:1, 3. What was the answer to his question in verse 3? What was Mephibosheth's handicap?

Play this happy game, "hop tag," to remind you of Mephibosheth:

The person who is "it" must try to tag the other players, but everyone must hop instead of running. Also, each time a bell is rung or a whistle is blown (or someone claps) all players must change feet and hop on that one until the next bell rings!

Read the rest of the touching story in 2 Samuel 9:5-13. Mephibosheth didn't believe he deserved David's kindness, did he? Do *we* deserve God's kindness and grace toward *us*? Read Ephesians 2:8-9.

Partners for God

*Elijah and Elisha were on their way
from Gilgal. (2 Kings 2:1)*

Elijah and Elisha were great men of God, mighty prophets in the days of the Old Testament. God used them in very special ways and to perform miracles to prove to the people that their messages really were from the almighty God.

Here is a partnership game to play with someone in your family to remind you of the partnership of Elijah and Elisha. It can be called "racquet balloon" and needs these supplies:

- an inflated balloon
- four pieces of paper (even junk mail papers will do)
- a stapler or tape
- a string or yarn
- a few sheets of newspaper

Tie the string across the room or between the backs of two chairs. Hang the sheets of newspaper, still folded in half, over the string. Now you have your racquet-balloon net.

To make a racquet, staple or tape together three of the edges of two papers, leaving one edge open. Slip your hand inside the opening and you have your racquet! (Do the same with the other two papers to make one for the other player.)

Have a great time hitting the balloon back and forth over the net!

Then sit down and read these verses from the Bible: 1 Kings 17:24 and 2 Kings 2:1-2, 7-15.

Lost/Found Bible

Hilkiah the priest found the Book of the Law of the Lord that had been given through Moses. (2 Chron. 34:14)

One of the most exciting and touching events in the Old Testament happened during the days of King Josiah, who began to reign at the age of eight. The Word of God, which had been lost for many years, was found! Can you imagine how the people felt? Now they would know what God expected them to do to please him, and they would gladly obey! See what happened in 2 Chronicles 34:14, 19, 21, 29-33.

Play this lost/found game with a small Bible or New Testament. Ask one player to hide the Bible in a room when another person is outside the door of the room. The player outside must then come in and try to find the missing Bible.

As he enters the room, he sings (to the tune of "Are You Sleeping, Brother John?"): "Am I close now? Am I close now? Am I close? Am I close?"

The other players answer, "You are very close [or *far*] now, you are very close now. You are close. You are close." They should sing louder as the searching player gets farther away from the lost Bible, and more quietly the closer he gets to it. When the "searcher" touches the Bible all music stops!

The Bible Is Truth

For the word of the Lord is right and true; he is faithful in all he does. (Ps. 33:4)

Play this truth or dare game as you determine which of the list of statements are truth from the Bible and which are not. You will need at least one player to guess and someone else to read the statements. If they are the truth, the player must nod his head. If they are not true, he must perform the next daring feat from the list of dares! (There is no penalty for wrong answers.)

Here are the statements:

- John the Baptist was a relative of Jesus. (true)
- Moses was the baby boy whose mother put him in a basket on the river. (true)
- Elijah was the shepherd boy who played his harp. (false)
- Adam and Eve were the parents of Peter. (false)
- Daniel was thrown into a den of cobras. (false)
- Jonah was swallowed by a huge fish. (true)
- Samson was known for his great voice. (false)
- Jesus will come back to earth one day. (true)
- Shadrach, Meshach, and Abed-

nego were thrown into an ice-covered pond. (false)
- Jesus performed many miracles during his ministry. (true)

Here are the dares:

- Try to fold a paper napkin or a piece of paper in half more than seven times.
- Put a bottle in front of a lighted candle. Blow the candle out with the bottle in the way.
- Place several pennies on the inside of your elbow as your arm is held straight out at shoulder height, with the palm of your hand facing down. Try to drop the coins off the elbow and catch them with the same hand.
- Blow a feather or a tissue across the room.
- Put a pen on the floor in front of you. Stand with your toes almost touching it, and hold on to your toes as you try to jump over the pen.

These were some of the silly ways to help you remember that you are taking *no dare* when you put your trust in the absolute truth of God's Word.

Throw Them Away

Cast your cares on the Lord and he will sustain you; he will never let the righteous fall. (Ps. 55:22)

Try one of these throwing games for fun!

• "Juggle toss." Stand across from another family member (or in a circle with several people) and throw two balls back and forth at the same time. If you prefer, use rolled-up socks, balls of masking tape, or beanbags (old socks filled with dried beans and closed with a rubber band) instead of balls.

• "Foot-to-foot toss." Fill a trash bag with inflated balloons and toss it back and forth with your feet as you and other family members or friends lie on your backs on the floor.

What does Jesus want us to cast, or throw, upon him? Read 1 Peter 5:7 to find out.

On Your Knees

Let us kneel before the Lord our Maker.
(Ps. 95:6)

Have a kneeling race with someone just for fun. Before you start, tie old long socks around your knees for cushioning, and mark the start and finish lines. Declare the winner of your race camel of the day! (Why? Have you ever seen a camel's knees?)

If you are still having fun on your knees, stay on them and try your luck at indoor soccer. (Find a room that you won't demolish!) When your knees wear out, flip over onto your backs to the "crab walk" position (front side up, hands on the floor) and continue the game.

There is a word used often in the Bible for kneeling and bowing before the Lord our God. See if you can find it in Matthew 23:11-12 and James 4:10. After reading those verses, what do you think it means to "humble yourself"? Can you think of a word or an idea that would be the opposite of humbling yourself? Do you think a person can really come to God to be forgiven of his sins without humbling himself before God? What if he has the attitude, "Sure, I've sinned—so what's the big deal?" Read James 4:6.

Joined Together

[Those] who bind [join] themselves to the Lord, to serve him, to love the name of the Lord, and to worship him . . . I will bring to my holy mountain.
(Isa. 56:6)

Try these two joined-to-a-friend activities:

• Sit on the floor beside your parent or friend, lock your arm with his, and get up together to a standing position. Then sit back-to-back on the floor with your arms joined at the elbows and try to get up together!

• Tie a bandanna around your leg and your partner's, joining together for a three-legged race. The two requirements in the game are these: (1) You must move a pillow across the room and back while joined together, and (2) you cannot stand up! Move the pillow first by crawling together, then by squatting like frogs (but you don't have to hop), and then in the "crab walk" position (front side up, hands on the floor).

Who does the Bible say that we should join our lives with? (Check your answer by reading Isaiah 56:6.) What is our reason for doing that? Look in Ephesians 4:16 to see who else is joined together with us and the Lord Jesus Christ.

J-E-S-U-S

You are to give him the name Jesus, because he will save his people from their sins. (Matt. 1:21)

Give each person a piece of paper. Ask everyone to write the letters *J-E-S-U-S*, one under the other, down the left side of his paper, leaving about an inch between each letter.

When each player has his paper ready, count to three and say, "Go!" Players must then write down as many Bible names as they can think of that begin with the letters in Jesus' name. After two minutes have passed, tell everyone to stop. If someone has already started writing a name, he may finish it and then stop.

Let everyone add up his own points. Each correct Bible name scores

one point, every name a person has written that no one else has on his paper earns five more points, and anyone who was able to write a Bible name for the letter *U* wins ten extra points! (Look in 2 Samuel 11:17 and Isaiah 1:1 to find *U* names.)

Congratulate each other for the good job you did, and remember that Jesus is the most important person in all the Bible. Just as people in Bible times chose either to follow Jesus or to turn away from him, all people today must do the same!

Make Things Right

Leave your gift there in front of the altar. First go and be reconciled to your brother; then come and offer your gift. (Matt. 5:24)

Find a small box to represent a gift. Then choose a spot in the center of the room where you will place your gift when this game begins. Ask another family member to turn his back to you, say, "On your mark, get set, go!" and then begin to count slowly to ten.

When he says, "Go!" you are to quickly lay down your gift, do the following actions, and then be standing, holding your gift—before he says ten! Here are the actions you must do:

• Turn around three times.
• Rub your stomach and pat your head.
• Pat your head and rub your stomach.

* Do three jumping jacks.
* Run in place.
* Touch your toes.
* Pick up your gift and stand up, holding it!

The actions do not have to be done in that order, but they all must be done in time. Read over the list several times before starting the game to get them in your mind.

After the game, read Matthew 5:22-24 and see what the verses have to say about laying down a gift. More important than the gift itself is what Jesus is saying about the problem of staying mad at someone else. What does he want us to do about that?

Yes, Yes, No, No!

Simply let your "Yes" be "Yes," and your "No," "No." (Matt. 5:37)

Did you ever hear someone say, "Cross my heart, hope to die, stick a needle in my eye?" What that little rhyme really means is, "If I'm not telling the truth, I'll do all those awful things to myself—so you can believe me!"

Jesus said that our "yes" should mean yes and our "no" should mean no! We shouldn't have to make all kinds of unreasonable promises to persuade someone that we really are telling the truth. It is important for people to be able to trust us and believe our words.

Ask a member of your family to ask these yes-or-no questions, and you try to answer them. Try to get them all read and answered in only *ten seconds!*

* Are you at home?
* Are you feeling well?
* Did you go to school (or work) today?
* Do you ever go to church?
* Do you like to play sports?
* Do you ever get your feelings hurt?
* Do you have any loose teeth?
* Have you ever gotten hurt playing outside?
* Do you have any pets?
* Do you know anything about the Bible?

Forgiveness Swap

For if you forgive men when they sin against you, your heavenly Father will also forgive you. (Matt. 6:14)

Play this "trade-off relay" with someone in your family or neighborhood. Find a handkerchief or bandanna of one color for yourself and one of a different color for the other player in this relay. Stand facing each other from across the room (if Mom approves) or on opposite sides of your yard or driveway. Mark two finish lines with masking tape, an object, a piece of string, or a chalk line if you are out in the driveway. At the word *Go*, begin to run toward each other, quickly trading handkerchiefs in the center of the room or yard, and then trying to be the first one to reach the opposite finish line. You are disqualified if either handkerchief falls, and you must then start all over again.

Maybe you have seen a relay race or have been in one yourself. In a relay race a stick, or baton, is quickly passed from the hand of one runner to the next, who then carries it to the runner ahead of him or to the finish line. In God's forgiveness race, however, all runners have in their hands the baton of forgiveness. They can give their forgiveness away and be winners in God's important race, or they can refuse to give forgiveness to others and watch it become an ugly, twisted stick of unforgiveness in their lives. God's children can never be the big winners he wants them to be and get to enjoy the thrill of victory unless they offer their hand of forgiveness to other people.

Look What I Found!

The kingdom of heaven is like treasure hidden in a field. (Matt. 13:44)

Crumple up pieces of newspaper and pack them into a shoe box until it is full. Then, hide a coin in the box among the newspapers. Ask someone in your family to close his eyes and see if he can find the hidden coin in ten seconds or less without looking. If he can, ask him to hide the coin and let you try to find it.

How is the kingdom of heaven like a great treasure to be found? Jesus

compared his wonderful kingdom to hidden treasure and beautiful pearls in Matthew 13:44-46. How does being a part of God's great kingdom compare to having great riches?

Hey! That's Not Fair!

Shouldn't you have had mercy on your fellow servant just as I had on you? (Matt. 18:33)

Try this game with a friend, and see how you like its rules!

Use a box or laundry basket for a goal and toss a ball, a rolled-up pair of socks, or a wadded-up newspaper into it as many times as possible. The first player will get to try five times. Each time he lands the ball in the basket, he will get one point. The second player will get to move closer to the basket than the first player. He gets to try ten times to throw the ball into the basket, and every basket he makes will score ten points. (If there is a third player, he may stand right beside the basket and get fifty points for every time the ball goes in!) The player with the highest score wins.

How does the game sound to you? Were the rules fair enough to please you?

Are you good at detecting unfairness? Most of us can spot it a mile away!

Jesus made sure to include in his Word a valuable lesson on fairness and forgiveness in Matthew 18:23-35. Read the story—or better yet, act it out as someone reads the words like a narrator.

The man in Matthew 18:28 was totally unfair and completely unforgiving, wasn't he? What warning does Jesus give in verses 34 and 35 about being unfair and unforgiving?

The Scattered Sheep

I will strike the shepherd, and the sheep of the flock will be scattered. (Matt. 26:31)

The game "wolf and sheep" is fun with only two players, but more fun with three or more, especially if they are a dad, mom, and kids!

Choose a place to be the sheepfold, and one player to be the wolf. The others will be sheep. The wolf stands with his back to the sheep, who begin to sneak toward the wolf from the safety of the sheepfold. When the sheep say *Baa!* the wolf can turn around and try to catch them! The sheep's goal is to get as close as possible to the wolf to say *Baa!* and then scatter and run back to the sheepfold without getting caught.

Jesus predicted that on the night when he would be crucified, his disciples would all scatter, running and hiding because they would be afraid. Read what Jesus said in Matthew 26:31-32. Look in Matthew 26:56 to see if what Jesus predicted came true. There is a happy ending to this sad story, however. Read John 20:19-20 to see how the disciples felt.

All Bandaged Up!

A man with leprosy came to him and begged him on his knees, "If you are willing, you can make me clean." (Mark 1:40)

To get the feel of being a leper, ask someone to completely wrap your hands in elastic bandages or cloth strips until you cannot move your fingers. Then try to do these actions:

- Tie your shoes.
- Brush your teeth.
- Look through the pages of a telephone book.
- Button a shirt completely up and then unbutton it.
- Find John 3:16 in your Bible.

Lepers in Bible days often wore bandages to cover their scarred and deformed hands. They not only had to suffer the horrible sickness; they had to leave their homes and families and be completely disgraced by their whole town. People who had been loved and respected were now outcasts!

Read about Jesus and his great compassion toward a poor sick man in Mark 1:40-42. What did Jesus do in verse 41 that nobody else would do?

Two by Two

Calling the Twelve to him, he sent them out two by two and gave them authority over evil spirits. (Mark 6:7)

Play the game "partner-partner" by

choosing a partner in your family or one of your friends to do these twelve things with you.

- Put your shoulders together.
- Put your heels together.
- Place the tops of your heads together.
- Place your elbows together.
- Put the soles of your feet together.
- Place a pillow or a ball between your backs and walk across the room with it there.
- Carry a pillow across the room between your heads.
- Play miniature "soccer" by rolling a ball back and forth across the room to a goal, using only your heads or shoulders.
- Sing "Jingle Bells" together.
- Pretend that one partner is a wheelbarrow and the other is pushing it.
- Sing "Jesus Loves Me," each partner taking turns singing one line at a time.
- Before you go to bed tonight, pray with your partner.

When Jesus sent his disciples into their world to do his work, he sent them in pairs—two by two. It is still a great idea to find a good Christian friend to help you be strong as you live for Jesus in your own world of school, the neighborhood, and your hometown!

Two Christian friends (or more) can help each other be stronger and more determined to live for Jesus when the devil tries his wicked best to make them weak. Besides that, they can each pray for the other and pray with each other, and a "team" of Christian kids can be a powerful force for God!

Think of a good Christian friend and determine right now that you two together are going to be serious disciples for Jesus Christ in your own important world.

Sight for Blind Eyes

The blind man said, "Rabbi, I want to see." (Mark 10:51)

Play a blind-man game in a line (or in two competing lines if you have four or more players). You will need one or two blindfolds, two glasses of water, paper, and a pencil for each team. Blindfold the first player(s) and watch him (them) try to perform these activities:

- Pour water into one glass from the other.
- Write his name on a piece of paper.
- Cross out the name you wrote.
- Walk back to the next player, who must then put on the blindfold and repeat the four actions.

After everyone has been the "blind man," talk about how you felt about not being able to see what you were doing. Open your Bible to the story of blind Bartimaeus in Mark 10:46-52 and read this interesting story out loud. Discuss what the blind man must have felt to make him shout so loud and long for Jesus. Tell why you think some people told Bartimaeus to be quiet and why Jesus asked the blind man what he wanted.

Catch

From now on you will catch men. (Luke 5:10)

Play catch with someone you like. To make the game more interesting and challenging, turn your back to the thrower and try to catch that way—or throw and catch from between your legs in a bent-over "hike the ball to the quarterback" position.

Here's how to make a catching mitt:

Cover a round piece of cardboard with flannel, and use a stapler or heavy tape to attach a strap for your hand on the back of it. Glue Velcro circles to several sides of Ping-Pong balls or to small round balls of crumpled-up masking tape. Take turns being the thrower and the catcher with someone in your family.

What did Jesus mean when he said that his disciples should "catch men"? That would take a big catcher's mitt, wouldn't it? No, just a big heart of love for our Savior and for the people he loves. Think of some specific ways that you and your family can "catch" someone for the Savior—and begin right now to do it!

The Tender-Foot Treatment

As she stood behind him at his feet weeping, she began to wet his feet with her tears. (Luke 7:38)

Mom and Dad, this job's for you! To show your love and care for each of your great kids, give this "tender-touch" foot treatment. Ask your child to sit on a chair with a towel on the floor under his feet. Place a bowl of comfortably warm water on the towel, and let him soak his feet for a few minutes as you talk about his day and all its happenings.

Next, lovingly dry his feet with a soft towel and begin the foot massage, putting a small amount of lotion or cream on your hands and rubbing his feet. If your child really wants to experience a little of what Jesus felt when Mary wiped his feet in Luke 7:36-38, finish your foot treatment by applying a small amount of perfume or aftershave lotion.

Read the Bible story of Mary's loving foot treatment of Jesus and discuss why you think Mary felt like doing such an unusual thing in front of some people who definitely did not approve of her actions! What are some times Christian kids or parents might have to show their love for Jesus when other people around them do not love him as they do?

Bragging/Denying Peter

Lord, I am ready to go with you to prison and to death. (Luke 22:33)

Choose a trick you would like to try

from the list on this page. Tell the other people in the room what you will do and say it like this:. "I will [name the activity] and I will do it very well!"

- Write the name of my state backwards on a piece of paper.
- Drink a glass of water with a raisin or a marshmallow balanced on my nose.
- Walk around the room on my hands and feet.
- Push a penny across a table with my nose.
- Say the alphabet backwards.

Do you enjoy hearing someone brag? What happens to the person who says he will do something great, and then he doesn't do well at all?

Peter learned what it is like to brag and then to really mess up. In fact, he *totally* failed to do what he said he would. Read Peter's boastful words in Luke 22:33 with the expression in your voice that a bragging person would use.

Then read what Peter actually did as he warmed his hands by the fire on the night Jesus died (Luke 22:55-62).

Pray that God will help you be a strong and bold Christian when other people are watching to see if you are a follower of Jesus.

The Drink That Lasted Forever

Whoever drinks the water I give him will never thirst. (John 4:14)

How good are you at thinking fast and concentrating hard? Try this test to see if your skills are quick—or if you think better with more time and less noise!

All you have to do is answer these questions by giving your opinion. Does that sound simple enough? The difficulty may lie in the fact that you must stand facing your questioner, look straight into his eyes, answer the question in ten seconds or less, and, to make matters worse, he must ask you the question, "Well?" over and over again as you are answering!

Here are the questions. Please give them to your "questioner" and take your positions.

- Who is your favorite Bible character and why?
- Who are two of your best friends and why?
- What is the most exciting story in the Bible, in your opinion?
- What is your favorite color? Name some things you own that are that color.

Tired of hearing (or saying) the word *well?* Read about a conversation in the life of a Samaritan woman and Jesus that took place at a "well" in John 4:4-15, 25-26, 28-29.

Do you think that the Samaritan woman kept the good news about Jesus Christ to herself? John 4:39, 42 tells us the answer: "Many of the Samaritans from that town believed in him because of the woman's testimony. . . . They said to the woman, 'We no longer believe just because of what you said; now we have heard for ourselves, and we know that this man really is the Savior of the world.'"

Do you have a friend or neighbor who needs to know the Good News about Jesus?

Light of the World

When Jesus spoke again to the people, he said, "I am the light of the world." (John 8:12)

Play the game "darkroom art." Here's how:

Give each player a tablet or several sheets of paper, a book to use as a "table," and a pencil. Make a list of objects to draw and write the name of each object on a small card. Here are some possibilities: car, baby bottle, zipper, watch, porcupine, pretzel, spider, tennis shoe, flower, camel. Place the cards containing the words upside down in a pile, and take turns picking one to draw in the dark.

Give each player a turn at drawing the object on a card in thirty seconds or less with the lights off. The other player's job is to guess what picture he drew. If you do not have a dark room, blindfold the person drawing each time.

Read Psalm 27:1, Psalm 56:13, and 1 John 1:7 to see what life is like when we know the Light of the World!

I Will Obey

Jesus replied, "If anyone loves me, he will obey my teaching. . . . He who does not love me will not obey my teaching." (John 14:23-24)

Play "I will obey" like the game "Mother, may I?" with a few changes. Pretend that one of you is a robot and the other is its master. As the robot is programmed by the master's voice to perform the following commands, he

must immediately obey each order as soon as it is given, repeating the words, "Yes, Master. I will obey, Master." (If you want to really challenge your robot, cut armholes and a neckhole in a large box for him to wear—and a smaller box to fit over his head—and see how well your machine can obey its master now!) Here are the commands:

- Make circles with your right hand on a table in one direction while you try to make a circle with your foot on the floor in the opposite direction.
- Balance for thirty seconds on one foot with your eyes closed.

• See how long you can keep your balance on one knee. If that's too easy, try tying a bow in a piece of string as you balance.

It is important to God for his children to obey him—and to obey their parents. Read Ephesians 6:1-2 and see the incredible promises there for obedient children.

Thomas, the Doubter/Believer

Unless I see the nail marks in his hands and put my finger where the nails were, and put my hand into his side, I will not believe it. (John 20:25)

Play this "I doubt it" game. Someone will need to be the reader and another person the doubter. The reader will read the following statements and the doubter will say to each one, "I believe it" or, "I doubt it."

• Jesus died on the cross between ten thieves. (I doubt it.)
• John the Baptist wore a hat and tuxedo as he preached. (I doubt it.)
• There was more than one Mary mentioned in the Bible. (I believe it.)
• Peter tried to walk to Jesus on the water. (I believe it.)
• Jesus will come back to earth someday. (I believe it.)

Thomas was one of Jesus' disciples who had some trouble believing that Jesus was really alive again after he had died. But Thomas's doubt led him to know the truth, because God's great truth is greater than any doubt anyone can ever experience.

When you find a doubt coming into your mind, go right to God and his Word for help and strength.

Nonstop Talking

Day after day, in the temple courts and from house to house, they never stopped teaching and proclaiming the good news that Jesus is the Christ. (Acts 5:42)

Think of a subject you know a lot about. It can be baseball cards, dinosaurs, soccer, skateboarding, books, or any other subject you like to talk about. Ask someone to time you as you start to talk as fast as you can about your subject. Try to tell them at least five things before ten seconds have gone by. Now let another person in your family tell you some interesting things.

Do you ever just feel like talking and talking to someone you like? Does talking ever get you in trouble at school or somewhere else where it would be better to be quiet?

The Bible tells us that the apostles did some nonstop talking, too, but their talking was definitely the right thing to do! Read Acts 5:42 to see when and where they did all their talking.

Let's do what the early followers of Jesus did—keep on and on and on telling other people the Good News of Jesus Christ!

Imitation Charades

Be imitators of God. (Eph. 5:1)

Pretend to be the shadow or the mirror for someone in your family, imitating everything he does.

Then, perform four different actions and let someone else see if he can imitate what you did. Next, play an "imitation charades" game together with one player acting out good qualities or deeds he has seen in other people and the other player guessing what they are!

We are supposed to be imitators in our real lives. Read Ephesians 5:1-2 to see whom we should imitate.

Put It On

Put on the full armor of God so that you can take your stand against the devil's schemes. (Eph. 6:11)

Blindfold a member of your family and lead him to his closet and drawers to pick out an outfit to put on by "feel" only. When he has chosen a shirt, pants (or a skirt), socks and shoes, go out of the room and let him get dressed. Tell him that he must not remove his blindfold until he is completely dressed. How does he look?

God has chosen an "outfit" for us to wear as Christians, and he describes it to us in Ephesians 6:10-17. Pretty impressive, isn't it? It should be! Our

outfit is God's armor, complete with the

- belt of truth
- breastplate of righteousness
- boots of the gospel of peace
- helmet of salvation
- shield of faith
- sword—the Word of God

He has prepared us for battle and for victory over the devil!

Bubble Bursting

Therefore encourage each other. . . . Encourage the timid, help the weak, be patient with everyone. (1 Thess. 4:18; 5:14)

Have you ever heard the statements "Don't burst his bubble" or "Don't hit him when he's down"? Do you have any idea what they mean? Both statements mean "Don't discourage someone; *encourage* him!"

Our ideas are among of the most valuable gifts we have to share, and we must be very careful to encourage others and not pour cold water on them when they have been nice enough to let us listen in on what they could have kept secret in their minds. If you are an encourager, you may soon find others frequently encouraging you too!

Try these games to help you remember not to burst others' bubbles and not to hit them when they're down.

- "Bubble bursting." Use a small

bottle of bubble solution (or make your own by mixing one part liquid dishwashing detergent to two parts water). If you have no bubble blowers, use empty thread spools.

Let one player be the "bubble blower" and the other the "bubble burster." At the word *go,* begin to blow bubbles for the burster to pop, and count how many hits you score together. Then trade positions and try to beat your last number of bursts.

• "Knock 'em down." Make a bowling set from empty paper rolls, paper cups, or empty tin cans and a ball or a large wad of paper, taped to keep it round.

Hold On

Hold on to the good. (1 Thess. 5:21)

Ask someone to hold on to the two handles of a jump rope while you hold the "loop" section. Begin to both pull on the rope in opposite directions like a tug-of-war. Be determined to hold on and not turn loose! (If one player is an adult, he may want to hold on using only one hand to make the competition more fair.) Count how long you can each hold on.

Now ask a parent to hold on gently but firmly to your ankles or wrists (not tight enough to hurt) while you try to get free from their grip. Or you do the holding on to your parent's wrists or ankles. Were you able to get free? Wouldn't it have been a lot easier if he had just turned you loose?

The Bible says that we are to hold on tightly and never let go of "the good." What are some things that are definitely good?

The problem is that some people think it's all right to catch hold of a little bit of evil for just a short while, thinking they can let go of it any time they want. But what they often do not realize is that when they are holding on to the evil, it is tightening its iron grip around them, and when they are ready to turn loose the evil, it is still tightly holding on to them.

So grab hold of everything good and hold on with all God's might! He will give you the strength. Read 2 Thessalonians 2:16-17.

Avoid the Wire

Avoid every kind of evil. (1 Thess. 5:22)

Try this "avoid-the-wire" challenge:

String a piece of rope, yarn, or twine about three feet off the floor, between the backs of two chairs. Pretend that the string is an electrical wire. The players must crawl or slide under it without touching it. Let each player try again and again, lowering the string each time that every player has crawled under it at that height.

When a player touches the "wire," let him sit down to "recover" for a minute and then try again the next time it is his turn, so that no one will feel left out.

The Bible warns us about the danger of sin and tells us to stay away from anything that even *looks* evil. Unfortunately, some people try to see just how *close* they can get to sin, and before they know what's happened, they are *trapped*—just like getting stuck on flypaper or Velcro. So stay far away from evil!

Grandma, Mom, and Timothy

I have been reminded of your sincere faith, which first lived in your grandmother Lois and in your mother Eunice and . . . now lives in you also. (2 Tim. 1:5)

Play this game called "Grandma." If your real grandma is there with you, let her play in the starring role. If she is not present, appoint someone to be "Grandma." Timothy, Paul's special missionary helper and young friend, had a wonderful mother and grandmother who loved him and told him about God.

The player that is Grandma stands with her face to the wall. The other player stands across the room from her at the starting line. (If more than two are playing, the players stand side by side at the starting line.) The object of the game is for the grandchild to sneak up and touch Grandma without getting caught moving. Grandma may look over her right shoulder, then her left, and back and forth, alternating shoulders. Grandma may not move her feet or her body. The grandchild may stay put each time Grandma turns her head, as long as she does not catch him moving (and grandmas must always tell the truth!). Otherwise, he must go back to the starting line!

Do you have a grandma or mom who tells you about Jesus, takes you to church, and prays with you, like Timothy did? If so, you have the very best kind of mom or grandma in the world!

If your mom or grandmother does not know Jesus for herself, you can be the one who loves her, prays for her, and looks for chances to take her to church (maybe to Christmas or Easter programs). If you go to church alone, or if you have no grandma nearby, find a lady to be your own Christian adopted grandma. No one can have too many grandmothers who love him!

I'm Not Leaving!

Never will I leave you; never will I forsake you. (Heb. 13:5)

For the next few minutes (or as long as you can stand to do this!), pretend that you and someone else in your family are super-glued with your backs or shoulders together or your feet side by side. Go everywhere together until you are ready for a little less togetherness!

The people we love most cannot always be with us. We go to school, to scouts, or to church choir; our mom and dad go to work or to meetings, or stay home while we are gone somewhere else. Even the greatest times of fun with our friends come to an end, and we have to go to our separate homes. Sometimes our whole family must be apart for hours or even days at a time.

But, as Christians, we have a very best friend who never, ever has to leave us—not even for the time it takes to blink an eye or take a breath. The Bible calls him our friend who sticks closer than a brother, our Lord Jesus Christ.

The Tortoise and the Hare

Everyone should be quick to listen, slow to speak and slow to become angry. (James 1:19)

Perform a repeat of the famous tortoise and hare race—right in your own home. You will need two contestants and a place under a table or behind a chair for each to call "home." Mark a starting line and a finish line and let

the race go through every room in your house, representing the hills, valleys, rocks, and trees encountered by the hare and tortoise in the story. The tortoise must crawl all the way, and the hare must hop. You may even design costumes if you like!

In this version of the race, both contestants win—because there is a time to be fast (when we are to run away from everything that looks evil), and there is also a time to be slow! Read about it in James 1:19.

Games for the Whole Family

Bible Land Trip

Pretend to be planning a Bible Land trip with your family as you sit in a circle on the floor. Place a Bible on the floor that players can use any time to find answers. Take turns naming who you will be going with (a character from the Old Testament, either man or woman). Give everyone ten seconds to think of someone from the Old Testament to have as a traveling companion. (You don't want him to have to go alone!) After everyone has had several tries at Old Testament people, change to New Testament men and women. If you wish, take turns naming what you want to do while you are in Israel.

Pretend to be in Israel during Bible days and make your answers actual activities or events from the Bible, such as "I'm going to visit Mary, Martha and Lazarus at their home" or "I'm going with Mary to see the empty tomb!" How about, "I'm going to see the skin of the lion that David killed to protect his sheep"?

Dividing Up the Old Testament

The thirty-nine Old Testament books can be divided into five groups, sort of like the card catalogue or computer system at your library. The Old Testament groups are:

- The Books of the Law: Genesis, Exodus, Leviticus, Numbers, and Deuteronomy
- The Books of History: Joshua, Judges, Ruth, 1 and 2 Samuel, 1 and 2 Kings, 1 and 2 Chronicles, Ezra, Nehemiah, and Esther
- The Books of Poetry: Job, Psalms, Proverbs, Ecclesiastes, and Song of Songs
- The Major Prophets: Isaiah, Jeremiah, Lamentations, Ezekiel, and Daniel
- The Minor Prophets: Hosea, Joel, Amos, Obadiah, Jonah, Micah, Nahum, Habakkuk, Zephaniah, Haggai, Zechariah, and Malachi

Here is a game to help you learn and remember the Old Testament divisions: Write the words *Law, History, Poetry, Major Prophets,* and *Minor Prophets* on cards or pieces of paper. Mix them up and hang them with clothespins in the correct order on a string tied between the backs of two chairs. Take a good look at the words and the order they are in.

Now take the words down from the clothesline and mix them up, face-down on the floor. Let each family member see how quickly he can turn the cards over and hang them up in the right order. Then do one of these five things (to remind you of the five Old Testament divisions) together as a reward for the great job!

- Have a dish of ice cream together.
- Make a cup of hot chocolate or lemonade for everyone.
- Play a table game together or listen to music.
- Read the newspaper Sunday comics or a chapter in a book together.
- Play leapfrog or hide-and-seek as a family.

Animal-Naming Game

Whatever the man called each living creature, that was its name. (Gen. 2:19)

Choose one family member to be Adam. He will stand across the room from the animals (all the other players). It will be Adam's job to name the kinds of animals you are. All players will secretly choose the particular animal they want to be, but they will tell no one else. The animals will walk forward and line up a few feet in front of Adam, and he will begin to name off all the animals he can think of. When he says the animal's name that one or more players have chosen to be, they must run back to their base, with Adam trying to tag them. When he does, the tagged animal must then become a part of Adam's family. The last one to be tagged gets to be Adam for the next round.

Crime in the City

The Lord said, "The outcry against Sodom and Gomorrah is so great and their sin so grievous." (Gen. 18:20)

Unfortunately, cities have crime because cities have people, and people have sin in their lives without God's help and forgiveness. Sodom and Gomorrah were two such cities, full of wicked people who refused to serve God. These two cities were so evil, in fact, that they had to be destroyed. God knew the hearts of the people and that they would never honor him. So he told Abraham the sad plan.

What did Abraham ask God? Read Genesis 18:23-26. God said OK to Abraham's request, but he could not find fifty good people in the whole big city! Look in Genesis 18:28, 30-32 to see Abraham pleading with God to save the two cities. Was God very fair? He would have saved a city of probably thousands of people if only ten good people had lived there, but they didn't. Read 2 Peter 3:9 to see why God is so patient, even with wicked people. Then read what happened to the cities in Genesis 19:24 and what happened to Lot's wife when she disobeyed God (Gen. 19:26).

Do one or both these activities to help you remember the story of Sodom and Gomorrah:

• Lay your local newspaper on the floor. Use a crayon to circle the articles that have something to do with money or drugs. Then use a different color of crayon to circle the good news about your town.

• Play "salt statue." Let Dad, Mom, or somebody strong in your family swing the others carefully around in a circle by their arms and then let go. The person being swung around must then stop in a silly statue position and not move until the leader says, "Melt!"

Funny-Sounding Names

He named it Rehoboth, saying, "Now the Lord has given us room and we will flourish in the land." (Gen. 26:22)

The Bible has many funny-sounding names of places and people! Have a family "naming bee" like a spelling bee. Write the funny names listed below on sheets of paper. Line up the contestants and ask someone to hold up the papers for the others to pronounce. Let any reasonable pronunciation of the names be accepted. The only way to be put out of the naming bee is not to say anything at all! Here are the words to say:

• Abimelech
• Rebekah
• Isaac
• Philistines
• Sitnah
• Esek
• Rehoboth

- Beersheba
- Gerar
- Beeri Ahuzzath
- Shibah
- Basemath

All those unusual words came from Genesis 26. Read the story of Isaac and his experiences in the Valley of Gerar from Genesis 26:17-22.

Take Off Your Shoes

Take off your sandals, for the place where you are standing is holy ground. (Exod. 3:5)

God told Moses to take off his shoes when he was standing in God's presence as a way to honor God's holiness. Ask several family members to take off their shoes and join you in a game of "find your shoes." Each player must place his shoes in a mixed-up pile in the middle of the room. Add extra shoes if you want a greater challenge.

Blindfold each player and start at equal distances away from the shoe pile. At the signal *go,* hurry to the pile of shoes, find your own shoes by feel only, and put them on. When your shoes are properly tied and fastened, stand up.

Please Pass the Ice

The breath of God produces ice, and the broad waters become frozen. (Job 37:10)

Try one of these frosty activities:

- Play "please pass the ice" like you would play hot potato. Sit in a circle on the floor with your family and pass an ice cube around from person to person. If someone drops the ice cube, his penalty will be to hold it for ten seconds! The object is to see how many times the cube can go around the circle before it melts. (Provide paper towels for wet hands.)
- Freeze a bubble! Take your bubble blower and bubble solution outside on a very cold day and gently blow a large bubble. Hold the bubble still on the blower and protect it from blowing away in the wind. If the air is cold enough, you will be able to see tiny crystals forming all over the bubble. Soon it will turn into a frozen ball!

Read Job 38:22, 25-30, where Job is describing the amazing frozen creations of God.

Give Thanks

Give thanks to him and praise his name. For the Lord is good. (Ps. 100:4-5)

Place your dining-room chairs in a circle facing out. Tape a small square of construction paper under two of the chairs. Play this game like musical chairs, starting and stopping the music whenever you wish. When the music stops, the players must sit down in the next chair they come to. (Make sure that there are enough chairs for each player to have one, and do not remove any chairs during the game.)

Each person who is on a chair with a paper square under it must name something he is thankful for, beginning with the next letter in the alphabet. For example, the first player on one of the special chairs must name something he is thankful for that begins with the letter *A*. When the music stops, the next player will name something beginning with *B*, and so on until the end of the alphabet is reached and the game is over.

Read Ephesians 5:19-20 together as a family. What should we be thankful for?

The Circle of the Earth

He sits enthroned above the circle of the earth. (Isa. 40:22)

Play a game with your bare feet and a beach ball or a big balloon. Form a line of people in your family, lying on the floor on their backs. Pretend that the ball is the earth and you are passing it from one end of the line to the other using only your feet. When the last person in line receives the ball, he must grab it and run to lie down at the front of the line, starting the game over again. Keep going until you run out of floor space.

Do you know in what year Christopher Columbus discovered America? (1492) When do you think God inspired Isaiah to write the incredible verse found in Isaiah 40:22? Approximately seven hundred years before Jesus was born! Columbus's discov-

ery that the world was round came over two thousand years later. That means that God knew about the world being round long, long before Christopher Columbus—not surprising, considering he made the whole gigantic universe, including our little round earth.

He Kept On Praying

Three times a day he got down on his knees and prayed, giving thanks to his God, just as he had done before. (Dan. 6:10)

Play a rowdy game of "lion hunt." It's simple. Just assign someone in the family the job of being the lion and send him off to hide in the bushes (somewhere in the house or yard). The other family members must then go searching for the vicious cat. When he is spotted, he may pounce out from his hiding place and tag them! If the lion is successful in tagging his prey, the tagged person must come back to the hiding place with him. Whoever was not tagged can be the next lion!

You may prefer to play "sleeping lion." Here's how to play:

Choose a lion to lie on the floor, pretending to be asleep in his den with his back to the other players. (This would be a good job for Dad or Mom.) The players must try to sneak up to the lion and pet him without being caught moving. The lion can turn his head often to try to catch someone on the move, but he cannot roll over toward him. If the lion sees someone moving, the person must go back to the starting line and begin again. The first one to pet the lion joins him in his den, and the other players start the game again—but this time they are being watched by *two* sleepy lions!

One of the great lessons from Daniel's lions'-den rescue (in Daniel 6:6-23) is that our God is mighty and rescues his people! But another very important lesson for us has to do with Daniel's practice of praying. Can you discover what it is in Daniel 6:10-11?

Daniel kept on praying under all circumstances. He prayed when times were good to thank God, and he prayed when times were bad to ask for his help. Daniel would not stop praying for anything or anyone because he knew that prayer is so important!

Do we sometimes let tiny things like embarrassment that someone might hear us or see us praying keep us from praying at a restaurant or when a friend comes home with us? Do we pray only around people whom we know also pray? Someone who doesn't know how to pray really needs to see someone like you praying, or he may go through his whole life without a prayer of a chance!

Spin the Person

Joseph her husband was a righteous man. (Matt. 1:19)

Pretend that one person in your fam-

ily is a "spinner" with his legs tucked up close to his body, one arm wrapped tightly around them, and the other arm pointing straight ahead. On the floor around him, place pieces of paper, each containing one of these New Testament names:

- Lazarus
- John the Baptist
- Judas
- Luke
- Paul
- Peter
- Barabbas
- Lydia
- Joseph

Hold on to the spinner's shoulders and spin him around until he stops. Find which New Testament name he is pointing toward and tell something interesting about that person. Did you remember that there is a Joseph in the Old Testament and a Joseph—Mary's husband—in the New Testament? Do you know what famous Bible king was in both Mary and Joseph's family history? Read Luke 1:27 to find out.

It was absolutely necessary that Mary would come from the family of King David. Do you know why? Find out by reading Isaiah 9:6-7.

The Christmas Chronicle

Jesus was born in Bethlehem in Judea, during the time of King Herod. (Matt. 2:1)

A "chronicle" is an ongoing story,

written one sentence at a time, usually telling something important that happened in history. If a chronicle were on television, it would be called a serial or a miniseries. Each new program begins where the last one ended and then goes on to show what happens next in the story. Sometimes newspapers are named the *Chronicle*.

Write a family chronicle telling the story of Jesus' birth. On a sheet of paper write the title "The Chronicle of the Birth of Jesus." Place the paper where it can remain for several days, and ask your family members to each add one sentence to the story every day until it is complete. Begin with the angel's appearing to Mary and Joseph, and end with the wise men's visit, but let every family member decide what he wants to add to the story when it is his turn to write. The story of Jesus' birth can be found in the Bible in Luke 1 and 2 and in Matthew 1 and 2.

Remember that the "Christmas Chronicle" is a wonderful story to hear all year around!

Sh! Don't Tell My Right Hand!

When you give to the needy, do not let your left hand know what your right hand is doing, so that your giving may be in secret. (Matt. 6:3)

Here's a silly game for three or more players:

Ask everyone to get in a circle holding the right hand of someone else, but not someone beside you. Next, grab hold of someone else's hand with your left hand. There! Are you all tied up together? Now try to untangle yourselves without letting go of anyone's hand. (This is a time when long arms would come in handy!) You may climb over and under each other's hands until you are all in a circle again.

Isn't it strange for Jesus to say, "Don't let your left hand know what your right hand is doing"? How could anyone possibly keep a secret like that? What could Jesus have meant? Jesus meant that when we do good things, we are not to spread the news around about how great we are, because that kind of bragging does not please God. Instead, we should do good things even when nobody but God ever finds out about them!

God sees all the good we do, even when our actions are kept secret from everyone else, and he is the one who matters most anyway!

Treasure Hunt

Store up for yourselves treasures in heaven, where moth and rust do not destroy, and where thieves do not break in and steal. (Matt. 6:20)

The Bible tells us that we all have something we treasure in our lives—a favorite toy, a pretty rock or shell, money in the bank, or even a friend or family member who is very important to us. Jesus knew that our treasure—whatever it is—would be very dear to our hearts—and *he* wants to be our *most valuable* treasure. Jesus wants your heart to belong to him and for you to treasure his wonderful Word, the Bible. Read Matthew 6:21 to see where your heart will be.

Find an empty shoe box, old jewelry box, or something else that can be used as a treasure chest. Ask Mom or Dad to put some special treats in the box that you can eat or keep. Then ask each member of the family to give you something of his own (pictures he has drawn or pennies from his own savings, perhaps) that can be added to the treasure. Hide the treasure chest somewhere in the room or house without the treasure hunters seeing you. Ask everyone to find the hidden treasure and to share what is inside the box. Remember as you share the treasure together that the very best treasure of all is Jesus!

Fruit Inspecting

By their fruit you will recognize them. (Matt. 7:20)

Pretend that your mom or dad is the fruit inspector and everyone else is the fruit. Decide which kind of tasty orchard-grown or straight-from-the-tropics variety of fruit you are and tell what qualities your fruit needs in order to pass inspection. For example, a banana should be yellow with no black spots, easy to peel, and soft enough to taste good, but not mushy! Each kind of fruit must give his name and good qualities before the inspector begins his inspection. He may then check the fruit by poking or twisting it, lightly thumping it, sniffing it, pinching it gently, or whatever will not damage the delicate fruit!

Read Matthew 7:16-20 together to see what kind of fruit inspecting Jesus was discussing. If you are not sure, look for some help in verse 21.

Jesus had a hidden meaning to his important statement. He was really talking about people as well as trees. People whose hearts are made good by God produce good fruit in their lives—fruit like kindness, love, joy, unselfishness, and peace. Those unfortunate people who do not allow God's goodness to live in them find themselves bearing rotten fruit like hate, unkindness, selfishness, mean words, and angry actions.

Sometimes the bad kind of fruit shows up even on good trees, but when it does, it doesn't belong there. We can ask God, our Master Gardener, to pick it off, throw it away, and help us grow good fruit instead. He will!

Jesus' Very Own Brother

Isn't this the carpenter's son? Isn't his mother's name Mary, and aren't his brothers James, Joseph, Simon and Judas? (Matt. 13:55)

Play the game "I know my brother." If you have no brother, you may substitute your sister, mother, father, or any other member of your family for a brother in this game. Give your brother (or another person) a piece of paper and a pencil and ask him to number from one to ten down the left side of the paper. Then instruct him to answer these questions about himself. (If there is more than one brother in your family, play this game with only one person at a time answering the questions about himself.) As your brother is writing the answers to these questions on his paper, the other family members should answer them on their papers in the way they think their brother will.

- 1. How old are you?
- 2. What is your birthday?
- 3. How tall are you? (Make a guess if you are not sure of the answer.)
- 4. What is your favorite color?
- 5. Who are two of your very best friends?
- 6. Which shirt that you wear is your favorite?
- 7. What is your favorite "free time" activity?
- 8. What do you like to do after school each day?
- 9. What is your favorite "fast-food" restaurant?
- 10. What do you think you want to be when you grow up?

As your brother reads his answers, everyone gets one point for every correct answer he has written. The person with the highest score knows his brother best!

If you have several brothers or other family members who would like to answer questions about himself (or herself), continue to play the game. You may all get better acquainted as you play.

Jesus had several brothers in his own human family (read Matthew 12:46). Imagine what it would have been like to grow up with God's perfect Son as your brother, eating at the table with you and sleeping in the same room at night! How do you think you would have felt?

James was one of Jesus' brothers, who later wrote the New Testament book of James that we read and try to obey today. Read the very first verse of the book of James and see how James introduces himself to us. Does he say, "I am the brother of Jesus Christ"? He realized that we all must choose to be Jesus' followers and servants, including Jesus' very own brother!

James made the best choice in the world when he became a "servant of

Jesus Christ." Have you made your choice?

To Follow or Not to Follow?

If anyone would come after me, he must deny himself and take up his cross and follow me. (Matt. 16:24)

Do not follow the crowd in doing wrong. (Exod. 23:2)

Play a different kind of follow-the-leader with your family or friends. Line up one behind the other, leaving about three or four feet of space between each of you. The leader of the line will do some action, like scratching his head. The person behind him must copy that action and then do a new one of his own. Each person down the line must repeat what the person in front of him has done and then do something new. When the last person in line has copied the one in front of him, he must go to the front of the line as leader and start the process all over again.

The Bible tells us that we should *follow* and *not follow*, depending on who is leading. Right now is the very best time to decide who your leader in life is going to be. There will be a time when the crowd will try to get you to do wrong and dishonor God—so do not follow them! Instead, read 1 Peter 2:21 and do what the Bible says.

Where Is It?

You will find a donkey tied there, with her colt by her. Untie them and bring them to me. (Matt. 21:2)

Play the game "where is it?" by thinking of an object in your house or yard and describing to someone else where it is, what it is near, what other objects are around it, and what it lies or sits on. The other players must guess the object and then take turns giving the whereabouts of an object of their own.

Jesus, who knows everything, knew exactly where to find the donkey that would carry him into Jerusalem to fulfill a prophecy made hundreds of years before. Read the story from Matthew 21:1-11 and listen to the shouts of praise. These shouts, unfortunately, will change to angry jeers in only a few days when Jesus will have to die.

Big Supper

And the wedding hall was filled with guests. (Matt. 22:10)

Plan a special meal or a friendly visit in your home for people who have no family nearby (foreign exchange students, college students from other states, elderly people, new people in town).

There is no need to prepare a fancy or expensive meal. The important thing is that you are giving yourself and your time to them and sharing your food and your home. If you prefer, take a meal to someone else who needs it—just to be nice. Some people who might enjoy your kindness in their own homes are sick people, shut-in people, or families with very small children. Sometimes it is easier for them to eat and visit in their own homes. By your kindness to other people, you will be pleasing Jesus very much! See what Jesus says in Matthew 22:1-10 about his big meal and the people he invited. He is telling us about his invitation to come to the banquet feast that will take place in heaven one day and about the people who will choose to accept or reject his kind invitation. Those are the only two choices there are.

Let's Brag!

For whoever exalts himself will be humbled, and whoever humbles himself will be exalted. (Matt. 23:12)

Play a silly "boy, am I great!" speaking game. Someone in the room must stand up as though he is about to make an important speech. He should use lots of action and enthusiasm as he tells everyone what he has done, what he is good at doing, why he is wonderful, and why everyone should be very impressed by him. After he finishes his speech, another person will get his chance to speak. (Don't hold anyone's bragging against him. Remember, this is only a game!) Now, answer these questions:

• When you were the bragging person, how did you feel as you talked? Were you a little embar-

rassed? Did you really *enjoy* bragging?
• When you were listening to someone brag, how did you feel? Do people usually enjoy hearing someone else brag?

When Jesus gives us a command, it is always because he knows and wants what is best for us. So, why not brag? See if you agree with these statements about bragging:

• It doesn't please God. He said to humble ourselves, which is the opposite of bragging.
• It makes other people uncomfortable, angry, or jealous.
• It causes people to not listen to us—and they may not want to listen if we try to tell them about Jesus.
• It does not lead to the reward that humbling ourselves does. What is the reward that God promises us?

They Should Have Planned Ahead

Five of them were foolish and five were wise. (Matt. 25:2)

Play the game "I'm planning to go on a space-shuttle trip." Take turns finishing the sentence with an action that begins with a letter of the alphabet, in the correct order. For example, one family member would say something like, "I'm planning to go on a space-shuttle trip, and I don't want to forget to *ask my mom*." The next player could then say, "I'm planning to go on a space-shuttle trip, and I don't want to forget to *bring a suitcase.*"

Can you think of a time in real life when you went on a trip and forgot to take along something you needed or wanted?

Jesus told a story about ten unmarried women. Five of them were wise and remembered what they needed to do, but five others were foolish. Why? Look for the answer in Matthew 25:1-13.

This story is a picture of something that will happen someday. Who will the Bridegroom be? Who will the wise and foolish people be?

Sheep, Sheep, Goat

He will put the sheep on his right and the goats on his left. (Matt. 25:33)

Do you remember the game Duck, Duck, Goose? Most little children love that game! Even if you are a big kid now, play the game with your family for old time's sake. Instead of ducks and geese, however, this game involves sheep and goats.

Sit in a circle on the floor (far apart, to make a bigger circle) with one person walking around the circle gently tapping each head as he says, "Sheep, Sheep, Sheep . . ." When he chooses to say "Goat!" that person must quickly get up and chase the first person around the circle, trying to tag him before he gets back to the goat's place in the circle and sits down.

When you're tired of playing, read Jesus' words about sheep and goats in Matthew 25:31-46. What is he really talking about? Do you want Jesus to call you a sheep or a goat?

Give Him a Hand!

And his hand was completely restored. (Mark 3:5)

Here is an idea to try that involves using your hands. Place several objects in a sack. Pass the sack around to everyone in the family and let each one try to tell what is in the sack by feeling it. Ask everyone to write down what he felt in the sack and then compare lists.

Have you ever been in a situation where you could not use one or both of your hands? Perhaps you have that kind of problem right now. If you do, you have probably had to learn how to use other parts of your body to help you out. Joni Eareckson Tada is a wonderful Christian who learned to use her teeth and tongue to hold a pen and a paintbrush when she lost the use of her hands. Perhaps you know someone like that.

Our hands are an incredible gift from God! Think of all the things they do for us in just one day! Can you name a few?

Jesus healed a man's crippled hand and brought great joy to his life. Read the inspiring story in Mark 3:1-6. Almost immediately, people began to criticize Jesus for doing good. Do you sometimes get teased or talked about when you have done right? Jesus knows how you feel!

A Lunch That Grew

> Taking the five loaves and the two fish and looking up to heaven, he gave thanks and broke the loaves. . . . And the disciples picked up twelve basketfuls of broken pieces of bread and fish. (Mark 6:41, 43)

Give members of your family a piece of paper and a pencil and ask them to write down (or draw) what they would like to have in a lunch to share with Jesus, if he needed more food. Share your answers with each other.

Then begin to tell the story of the feeding of the five thousand in a chain story, with one person beginning the story and another picking up where the first person stops and continuing around the family circle in that manner. Don't tell too much of the story at a time or some people may not have any story left to tell when their turn comes around! Refer to Mark 6:35-44 or John 6:5-15 if you want to be sure you have the details correct.

Words That Don't Wear Out

> Heaven and earth will pass away, but my words will never pass away. (Luke 21:33)

Give everyone in the family a pencil and a small piece of paper. Ask each person to think for a minute and then write down a brand-new, never-before-heard-of word that he has made up. If a child in your family is too young to write, let him or her say the word to you. The new word can be made from words or parts of words that he has heard (like *sandcorkjokefrogger*) and it must be between fifteen and twenty-five letters long.

What do everlasting words (they really are not *that* long, are they?) have to do with the Bible? Read what Jesus said about his long-lasting words in Luke 21:33.

You Do It

> I . . . have found no basis for your charges against him. Neither has Herod, for he sent him back to us. (Luke 23:14-15)

Play this "you do it" game with other members of your family. Take turns reading the "orders" from this list of things to do. After each person reads his order, he must then decide whether he will do what he has read or will say, "You do it" to another player. (That player must then cooperate and perform the action.) Here is the list of things to do:

- Eat a bite of something sweet or salty.
- Whistle or sing a verse of "Yankee Doodle."
- Do the splits (or stand with your legs as far apart as they can stretch).

- Do five jumping jacks.
- Balance a penny on your nose and walk across the room.
- Do the "crab walk" (knees bent, face up, back toward the floor, "walking" on hands and feet).

If you told your game partners, "You do it" about any of the six commands, why did you? Tell which of the six activities you would not like to do.

Pontius Pilate and Herod were two rulers in Jesus' day who played a tragic game of "you do it" when Jesus' life was at stake. The Sanhedrin—the Jewish court—had decided that Jesus should be killed for the "crimes" he had supposedly committed.

In spite of the fact that they could find no real reason to put Jesus to death, the Sanhedrin sent him to Pilate to do their dirty work for them. Read Luke 23:1-4, describing Jesus before Pilate, and Luke 23:6-7, describing when Pilate tried to make Herod be the one to put Jesus to death.

Look in Luke 23:11 to see what Herod did. Did either ruler find any reason to have Jesus killed?

New Life Butterflies

No one can see the kingdom of God unless he is born again. (John 3:3)

What do you know about butterflies? How do they start out in life? That's right—as a tiny egg! Does the egg

hatch into a beautiful butterfly? No? How does it happen?

Show the life cycle of a butterfly by playing a silly game on the floor. (Yes, parents, too!) Provide sheets or blankets for every member of your family and roll up in them like cocoons.

Roll around on the floor (remove all hazardous obstacles), bump into each other, and have a great, silly time trying to escape your cocoons. When you do, act as butterflies do when they are finally free and beautiful. They are beginning a brand-new life!

John 3:1-18 tells about a conversation between Nicodemus and Jesus about the new birth and everlasting life. Read or tell the story with your family and share together about what the new birth and everlasting life through Jesus means to each of you.

The Great Escape

So Peter was kept in prison, but the church was earnestly praying to God for him. (Acts 12:5)

Play "great escape" much as you would hide-and-seek with a few changes. Choose somewhere in your house to be the jail. It can be under the kitchen table, inside a circle of chairs, or inside a ring of pillows. Choose a jail keeper, who will be permitted to carry a flashlight. (Make sure it works!)

The prisoners must begin inside the jail, where the jail keeper gets comfortable, puts his feet up, and pretends to go to sleep while he is silently counting from one to fifty. He must close his eyes and count the first five numbers aloud so that the inmates (prisoners) will know he is counting.

The prisoners will quietly sneak from the jail and find new hiding places of their own. When the jail keeper finishes counting, he will suddenly realize the prisoners have escaped and begin to search for them. When he finds them, he must shine his light on them. They must return to the jail when found and stay there until all the prisoners have returned.

Then read the true story of Peter's miraculous jail escape from Acts 12:5-19.

Get Together

May the God who gives endurance and encouragement give you a spirit of unity among yourselves as you follow Christ Jesus, so that with one heart and mouth you may glorify the God and Father of our Lord Jesus Christ. (Rom. 15:5-6)

To help you remember that God wants us to "get together" and work to-gether, play this version of hide-and-seek. It is more fun with several players, so try to involve the whole family, from the youngest to the oldest. One player hides in a large enough space to hold several people, while one of the others counts to fifty with his eyes closed. He searches for the hidden player and hides with him when he is found. The third player then hides his eyes, counts to fifty, searches, and hides with the growing group! Each player in turn, does the same until all are together in the hiding place. The hardest part of the game is not giving away the location of the hiding place from the sound of all the shuffling and snickering!

When the game is over, read together in unison (all together out loud) Psalm 133:1.

Watch Out

Be on your guard; stand firm in the faith; be men of courage; be strong. Do everything in love. (1 Cor. 16:13-14)

The Bible warns us to be on our guard. Why? Two important reasons can be found in Mark 13:32-37 and 1 Peter 5:8-9. Read these passages and discuss what they mean with your family.

Try one of these "watch out" activities:

• Play "laser tag" in a dimly lit house or yard, using one flashlight for beams to "tag" players. When someone is tagged above the waist, he must sit down where he is (or in a safe place) until everyone else is tagged. Then the first person who was tagged gets to be "it" with the "laser beam."

• Play "dodge pillow" like the game dodgeball with a few changes. One player must run back and forth along a wall that is free of furniture and breakables while someone else tries to hit him below the waist with a small, soft pillow. When the runner is tagged, he must trade places with the one throwing the pillow and continue the game.

Amnesia

I thank my God every time I remember you. (Phil. 1:3)

Amnesia is a condition people sometimes get from a serious accident or sickness that causes them to have trouble remembering things—sometimes forgetting even their own name!

Pretend that you are suffering from amnesia and cannot remember who you are. In this game, one player must leave the room while the others decide what New Testament person he should be. When the player comes back into the room, he must say, "Who am I?"

Each person to whom he asks that question must answer by giving him a clue to his identity (the person he is), such as, "You are a disciple of Jesus" or, "You are a tax collector."

When the person with amnesia guesses who he is, the last person who gave him a clue becomes the one to leave the room and the one who is now not able to remember who he is.

Look in Ecclesiastes 12:1 and Psalm 25:6 to see two things we should always remember!

Influence

Don't let anyone look down on you because you are young, but set an example for the believers. (1 Tim. 4:12)

Here is a game called "influence." It requires three or more players, since influence is shared with people.

One player leaves the room while the others decide who will be the influencer (leader). The leader will then begin to clap, which is the signal for the player outside to come back in the room. The influencer will keep changing the group's actions from clapping, to knee slapping, to finger snapping, or whatever he chooses. The player who was outside must guess which person is the one leading the changes. The other players in the circle will follow the influencer's actions by looking at him with their "side vision" and trying to fool the outside observer into thinking that they are really the influencer.

Do only adults have influence on other people? Actually, young people generally have much more influence on each other than adults do on their friends! That kind of influence in youth is often called peer pressure, and it is often a bad influence. But you can be a tremendous influence for

God and for good, and other people will respect you, even if they don't tell you so. Read Titus 2:7 and especially 1 Peter 2:21. (Maybe there is a person older than you whom you can influence for Jesus!)

The Bible Is Sharper than a Sword

For the word of God is living and active. Sharper than any double-edged sword, it penetrates even to dividing soul and spirit . . . it judges the thoughts and attitudes of the heart. (Heb. 4:12)

Have you ever been in a sword drill? No, not the swashbuckling, Three-Musketeers kind of sword drill that involves danger and the clash of steel. This sword drill is really a *Bible* drill— a friendly contest to sharpen your skills at locating verses in the Bible. Hebrews 4:12 tells us why God's book is called a sword. Talk with your family about the meaning of the verse and how God's Word can judge the thoughts and attitudes that are deep inside us. Then have your sword drill!

Stand side by side in a line beside family members, each holding a Bible in his left hand, down by his left side. Facing you will be your commanding officer who will give the orders for you to obey. Each time before he gives you a verse to find, the commander will say, "Attention!" and you must stand straight and tall, with your Bible on your left side. Next, he will say, "Draw swords!" and you will hold your Bible flat on your right hand in front of you with your left hand on top of it.

Your commander will then tell you what Bible book or verse to find, but you must not open your Bible until he has repeated the Scripture and says, "Charge!"

Here are some Scriptures to find:

- Genesis 1:1
- Revelation 3:20
- Psalm 1:1
- Psalm 100
- John 1:1
- Acts 1:1
- Matthew 5:1
- Romans 3:23
- John 3:16

Run the Race

Let us run with perseverance the race marked out for us. Let us fix our eyes on Jesus. (Heb. 12:1-2)

To run this race, you will need a dish or pan, an empty egg carton, and a kitchen spatula. Your family will be an Olympic cotton-ball-balancing team, trying to win a gold medal by each in turn picking up one cotton ball on the spatula and running with it to the opposite end of the room—or around and through several rooms—and placing it in a section of the egg carton. If you lose the cotton ball, you must begin again! Your team wins when it has succeeded in putting twelve cotton balls into the egg carton.

The Bible says that the Christian life is a race. That's great, because a race is full of excitement, challenge, and victory! And sure enough, we will get to experience all those things as we run the race for Jesus Christ! And we already know that we will win!

By the way, did you know that there is a prize for the ones who run the race for God? Find out what it is in 1 Corinthians 9:24-25.

Love Each Other

This is the message you heard from the beginning: We should love one another. (1 John 3:11)

Here are two different versions of the "love each other" game—one rather mild and controlled and the other, well . . . wild and goofy! Take your pick—or do both, since we all need all the love we can get!

• "Spoken love." As your family members are going about their daily activities in different parts of the house, one person should suddenly shout, "I love everybody in this house!" At that "love" signal, every-

one else will repeat the same statement as fast as he can, trying not to be the last one to say it. Make this lively, happy expression of your love and appreciation for your family a frequent tradition.

• "Wild and goofy hugs." Don't play this game unless you want laughs and don't mind a temporary mess! This game is guaranteed to involve the most reluctant hugger! Request that each player put on an old and, preferably, dark-colored shirt. Place a pan containing cornmeal or flour (flour is harder to wash out) on a newspaper in the middle of the floor. At the *"Go!"* signal, everyone must rush to the cornmeal, place the palms of his hands in it, and hug someone, making sure to leave his handprints on the other person's back. Each player may repeat the cornmeal-and-hug process five times, hugging players more than once if fewer than five of you are playing. Compare your backs in the mirror. Then help Mom put the shirts in the wash!

Read what the Bible tells us about love in 1 Peter 1:22 and 1 John 4:19-21.

Do you think that being a Christian and reading the Bible are fun? They should be—that's what the Bible says about the Christian life! Jesus said, "I have come that they may have life, and have it to the full" (John 10:10). That doesn't sound as if he ever intended for us to drag through each gloomy day, grumping along without a smile. Here are some other Bible verses about the happiness of knowing God:

He will fill your mouth with laughter and your lips with shouts of joy. (Job 8:21)

The cheerful heart has a continual feast. (Prov. 15:15)

There is . . . a time to weep and a time to laugh. (Eccles. 3:4)

Be happy, young man, while you are young, and let your heart give you joy. (Eccles. 11:9)

There are times when we should *not* laugh—when someone else is being teased or mistreated, when a joke is told that would not honor God, or when someone with us is sad or hurt. But now is a good time to laugh and be happy, so let's get on with it!

Riddles

Here are some riddles to have fun

with. Remember, God's Word says, "Have fun!"

What is it that you break by even speaking of it?

When we speak, we break silence.

Did you ever notice how quiet everything seems when the electricity in the house suddenly goes off? The quiet hum of the refrigerator, the soft purr of the heater or the air conditioner, the whine of a hair dryer, the buzz of an electric shaver, the *clankity-clank* of the dishes in the dishwasher, the chatter of the television set all are silent. It usually is not long before someone yells, "Hey, Mom, what happened?" and we want the noise back again because we are used to it.

Our brand of silence, however, is not real silence at all. Even in our most quiet moments, the golden silence is always broken by the barking of our neighbors' dog, someone coughing, the phone ringing, or the sweet sound of the birds singing outside.

There was one time of real silence, however. As far as we know, before the time that God created the vast universe and the morning stars began to sing together (Job 38:7), there was absolute quiet. The very first words that broke the silence were the words God spoke in Genesis 1:3. Read the first part of the beautiful and amazing creation story from Genesis 1:1-10. If you do not mind marking verses in your Bible, circle the words *And God said*

every time you see them. Did God wave his mighty arms and do some hocus-pocus to create his world? No! How did he do it, then? The words you circled will give you a good clue to the answer.

In the beginning God created the heavens and the earth. (Gen. 1:1)

Why is it impossible to ever have a whole day?

Because each day breaks early in the morning

Just how long did it take God to make his awesome universe and our world with its beautiful trees and fields of wildflowers? How about the time he spent making us—his most incredible creation of all?

Genesis 1:11-26 continues the story of his powerful display of the creation of all living things. Read these verses from your Bible. They will tell you how long it took God to make each new kind of creation. Look in Genesis 1:27-28 to see his most awesome creation of all.

And there was evening, and there was morning—the first day. (Gen. 1:5)

What did the water say to the land?

Nothing—it just waved!

Water really was a great invention of God's, wasn't it? Read about it in Genesis 1:1-2, 6-9. Make a list of all the problems you would have if God had not created water. Now make another list of problems the whole world would face if there were no water at all! Not a very pretty sight, is it?

God wants his smartest, most important creation to take good care of the other things that he made, and water is certainly one of them. Since we need water so badly, how can we help to conserve it and use it wisely? Think of some good ideas for making sure we put our water supply to good use, and then start to do them.

> And God said, "Let the water under the sky be gathered to one place, and let dry ground appear." And it was so. (Gen. 1:9)

What time of day was Adam created by God?

A little before Eve

Genesis 2 retells the story of Creation in different words and gives the specific explanation of just how God went about making the very first man and woman, Adam and Eve. Read Genesis 2:7 and Genesis 2:21-24 and answer these questions:

- Who did God make first?
- Did he make Adam and Eve in the same way?
- Did Adam seem pleased with Eve?
- In verse 24, what does God tell us about marriage?
- Whose idea was it, anyway?

Whether you are a male or female, be sure to thank God for the extra-spe-cial person he made you to be. Both kinds of people were God's great idea!

> Then the Lord God made a woman from the rib he had taken out of the man. (Gen. 2:22)

What do you call two spiders that were just married?

Newly-webs

Have you ever been to a wedding? What did you think of it? Your answers may range from "beautiful and worshipful" to "long and boring"! Think of a wedding you attended and tell what you liked and did not like about it. Did anything funny happen? Sometimes it does!

Some brides have stepped on their long skirts and gotten all tangled up in them as they climbed up the steps of the church platform; grooms have often forgotten to bring the wedding ring or have gotten it stuck on the wrong finger of the bride's hand. People have forgotten words to songs, people have cried, and lots of people have been nervous at weddings. Weddings are usually happy, sad, beautiful, nerve-racking, wonderful times!

But God knew what he was doing when he made Adam and Eve and united them in marriage: a man and a woman who love God and each other, who marry and live together following God's plan for them and then have wonderful children—what a great plan God created!

By the way, what kind of suits did

ducks wear to Adam and Eve's wedding? Ducksedos!

> For this reason a man will leave his father and mother and be united to his wife. (Gen. 2:24)

Why is a snake so smart?

Because you can't pull its leg!

Does the Bible tell us about a smart snake? Yes! Read Genesis 3:1. That verse says that the serpent was more crafty than any of the wild animals the Lord God had made. When you read the word *crafty*, do you think of the kind of smart that means intelligent, bright, or educated? Don't! The words *sneaky*, *scheming*, and *sly* more accurately describe this evil snake.

Read Genesis 3:1-4 to see the snake's evil plan unfold. Who is about to fall for his lies? Who is the horrible mastermind of this plan to hurt Adam and Eve and all people that would come after them? What happens in Genesis 3:6-7? Don't you wish you could change the ending to this sad-but-true story?

Look what the snake, the devil himself, caused Adam and Eve to do:

- He made them question God's word and God's goodness. (Read Genesis 3:1 again.) He was really saying to Eve, "Did God really say that? Now is that fair?"
- He twisted God's word (vv. 1 and 3). Satan asked, "You aren't

supposed to eat from any tree in this whole garden?" Eve said, "We're not even supposed to *touch* this tree." See what God *really* had said in Genesis 2:16.

- The devil made doing the wrong thing seem more attractive than doing the right thing (Gen. 3:5). And he lied!

The devil has never stopped using his same old tricks because they work so well. Always be on your guard and pray for God's help so you will not fall for crafty Satan's awful plans!

> Now the serpent was more crafty than any of the wild animals the Lord God had made. (Gen. 3:1)

Who was the first woman mentioned in the Bible?

Genesis

Now, is the answer to this riddle really true? Of course not! The first woman did not even have a sis! The first time any woman is mentioned in the Bible is in Genesis 1:27. Read that verse and see what she is called there. In Genesis 2:22, as more specific details are given about how God actually made the first people, he calls her another name. What is it, and why did he choose that name? Now look in Genesis 3:20 to see what the woman's name was and who named her.

Another important word that describes God's woman in Genesis 2:18

is *helper.* Think of some ways that your mom helps your dad and you.

Adam named his wife Eve, because she would become the mother of all the living. (Gen. 3:20)

Why were Adam and Eve never guilty of gambling in the Garden?

Their paradise (pair o' dice) was taken away from them.

No, Adam and Eve were not exactly guilty of gambling, but they were guilty of the sin of disobedience, and all sin displeases God. In fact, it was their sin that separated them from God and made them have to leave the beautiful garden forever. Look in Genesis 3:8-13 to see what happened after Adam and Eve sinned and then had to face God. Did you ever do something wrong and know you were caught? How did you feel right then? Read Genesis 3:12-13 to see what kind of excuses Adam and Eve tried to make when they got caught.

So the Lord God banished him from the Garden of Eden. (Gen. 3:23)

What did Adam and Eve do when they were made to leave the Garden of Eden?

They raised Cain!

Yes, that is exactly what they did. They raised Cain, Abel, Seth, and a number of other children. But let's back up a minute. Let's see exactly what punishment Adam and Eve received for their sin. Read Genesis 3:16-19 to hear the bad news. What did God mean in verse 19, "You [will] return to the ground, since from it you were taken"? Didn't God warn Adam that if he disobeyed him, that would be the result? (See Genesis 2:17.) Would Adam and Eve have had to die if they had obeyed God's plan? Do we have to die? Read 1 Corinthians 15:22 to find the answer and the good news God has for us. If we trust Jesus as our Savior from our sins, we will have life with him forever!

Eve . . . gave birth to Cain. . . . Later she gave birth to his brother Abel . . . and she gave birth to a son and named him Seth. (Gen. 4:1, 2, 25)

What was it that Adam never saw and never possessed, yet gave two of to each of his children?

Parents—Adam was the only man to have no dad or mom.

Draw a picture of your model (perfect) parent and make it as funny as you want. Give him (or her) the size, the face, and even the style of clothes you think he should have. Then make a real list (in case your drawing got a little silly) of characteristics you think a great parent should have. Remember, though, that there aren't any perfect parents and no perfect families in real life—and even no perfect kids! A family is a group of imperfect parents and kids working together to serve an absolutely perfect and awesome God!

> When Adam had lived 130 years, he had a son in his own likeness, in his own image; and he named him Seth. (Gen. 5:3)

Where did Noah hit the first nail in the ark?

On the head

What did Noah hate to hit with his hammer?

His thumbnail

What happens at the end of a dry spell?

It rains.

What goes up when the rain comes down?

Your umbrella

All these riddles have something to do with the man Noah and the huge boat or ark that he built. Most people are familiar with his story from Genesis 6:1–9:19. See if you can answer these questions. Look in chapters 6 through 9 of Genesis if you need help.

- What was the world like in Noah's day?
- How many families were left that served the God of creation?
- What did God tell Noah to do?
- What kind of wood did Noah use and how many stories high was the ark?
- Why did God want it to take a long time to finish the ark?
- What did Noah do as he worked on the ark?
- Did the people listen to Noah's warning?
- Did Noah keep on obeying God even when he was nearly alone and treated badly?

Are there some important lessons Noah could teach us? What are they? Read the best advice Noah could give us in Genesis 6:22!

> Noah did everything just as God commanded him. (Gen. 6:22)

What animals took the least amount of baggage into Noah's ark? Which one took the most?

The fox and the rooster. All they had were a brush and a comb. The elephant brought along his trunk!

Did God intend to destroy all animals in the Flood as well as people? Why or why not? How do you know? (Read Genesis 7:2-3, 14-16.) Did God plan that animals would be useful to man? (Read Genesis 9:2-3.) Besides food, what are some other uses for animals that help people get along better on the earth?

Don't you also think that animals often make nice companions for people? God was kind to make friendly animals to be fun for us. Be kind to an animal friend today. And thank God for his gift of animals!

Did you know that many scholars believe that nearly forty-five thousand animals could have fit into the ark? Quite a zoo!

Pairs of all creatures that have the breath of life in them came to Noah and entered the ark. (Gen. 7:15)

Why couldn't Noah see out the window of the ark?

His windshield vipers weren't working!

Was there a window on the ark?

Perhaps you have heard of a glass-bottom boat, where passengers can actually look down through the transparent floor of the boat to see the plant and sea life and even an occasional scuba diver. There are other ships with windows all around the sides in the form of an open deck or some with tiny round windows called portholes.

Yes, there was a window on the ark—a sort of skylight near the roof of the big boat. Why do you think God wanted the people to look only up instead of down or to the sides where they could see the huge waves?

Do you think Noah and his family had times of being afraid or sad on the ark? Why or why not? Who else was with them on the ark?

Then the Lord shut him in. (Gen. 7:16)

Why did no one play card games on the ark?

Because Noah was always sitting on the deck

But seriously, what do you really think Noah and his family did for nearly a year on board the ark? They definitely took care of animals, but what else might they have done?

Write a list or name some of the activities Noah and his family may have done aboard the ark. If you are good at acting or pretending, make up a skit about the Noah Family's Vacation or The Fantastic Voyage.

Read Genesis 8:1-3, 13-19 to find out what happened when the rain was finally over.

But God remembered Noah and all the wild animals and the livestock that were with him in the ark, and he sent a wind over the earth, and the waters receded. (Gen. 8:1)

Why should you be careful when it's raining cats and dogs?

You might step on a poodle.

What do you call it when a giraffe going one direction bumps into a giraffe moving another way?

A giraffic jam

Which animal could jump higher than the ark?

All of them—an ark can't jump!

What two animals did Noah have with him at all times on the ark?

His calves

Read Genesis 9:8-16 with your family and thank him for his wonderful promise to us!

Never again will all life be cut off by the waters of a flood; never again will there be a flood to destroy the earth. (Gen. 9:11)

Who were the two straightest men in the whole Bible?

Joseph and David—God made *rulers* out of them.

Joseph and David never met on earth, but they have probably enjoyed some great talks during these hundreds of years they have spent together in heaven! When we meet them someday, let's ask Joseph about his experience in Egypt and how God brought so much good out of a bad situation. You can read about how Joseph became Pharaoh's chief officer in Genesis 41:37-43.

It would be great to talk with David, the ordinary shepherd boy whom God made Israel's greatest king and an ancestor of his own Son, the Lord Jesus Christ. You can read the interesting story of Samuel's anointing of David as king in 1 Samuel 16:1,

9-13. David was just a boy when God began to use him. How about letting God start right now with you?

Can we find anyone like this man, one in whom is the spirit of God? (Gen. 41:38)

How did Moses know that the Red Sea was friendly?

Because it waved!

If a purple stone fell into the Red Sea, what would happen to it?

It would get wet!

You probably know that the Red Sea doesn't really have red water. Look at a map in the back of your Bible to see where the sea is. (Hint: It's near Egypt.)

The Bible events surrounding the Red Sea are absolutely incredible! The most familiar story involves the Israelites, Moses, the cruel Egyptian army rapidly approaching with weapons, God's might and power, walls of water, and a strong east wind! Read the amazing story in Exodus 14:15-18, 21-23.

God told Moses: The Lord will fight for you, and you won't need to lift a finger! God will win our battles for us, if we'll let him.

The Lord will fight for you; you need only to be still. (Exod. 14:14)

What's the difference between a thief and a church bell?

One steals from the people and the other peals from the steeple.

Most of us remember that there were two thieves on crosses near Jesus when he died. But did you know that the Bible tells us about other thieves?

One Old Testament thief was a man named Achan. He was a really sneaky thief tiptoeing around at night, digging a hole, and hiding a bar of stolen gold in his tent. Read the gruesome details in Joshua 7:10-11, 22-23.

Two New Testament thieves were a bold, daring man and his wife. They seemed nice enough but were really lying, scheming robbers who thought they could get away with their crime and still look good, but they were wrong—dead wrong! Find out who they were, what they did, and how terribly wrong they were in Acts 5:1-10. It is very important to be honest in every way.

You shall not steal. (Exod. 20:15)

What Bible character besides Adam and Eve had no parents on earth?

Joshua, the son of Nun (none)

What do you know about Joshua, the son of Nun? Look in Joshua 1:1-7 for clues and some great promises from God to Joshua in verses 3 and 5. Verses 6, 7, and 9 all contain the very same words from God to Joshua and to you. What are they?

Joshua could be called "G.I. Joshua" since he was a mighty soldier and commander of the armies of God's people, the Israelites. He led his army in the famous and very success-

ful battle of Jericho, where God caused the walls surrounding the entire city to crumble down!

Read Joshua 1:9 and learn why Joshua did not need to be afraid. Isn't that same great God with you?

Be strong and courageous. Do not be terrified; do not be discouraged, for the Lord your God will be with you wherever you go. (Josh. 1:9)

Who was the most popular actor in the Bible?

Samson—He brought down the house!

Samson was God's strongman—the Arnold Schwarzenegger–type man of the Bible! He could do amazing feats of strength like pulling a heavy iron gate off its hinges or killing a whole army of foxes with only a donkey's jawbone for a weapon! And yes, he actually did bring down the house at the end of his life. Read all about it in Judges 16:25-30.

Then try this strongman (strong-lady) trick on someone in your family. Ask him: "Do you think you're strong enough to lift your finger?" (He will say, "Sure!") Then tell him, "I don't think you can," and prove it to him. Tell him to curl up his middle finger until it touches his palm. Then ask him to put that hand up against the wall, palm down, with the one finger still curled under. Say to him, "Now, lift your littlest finger."

When he has done that, tell him to

lift his pointer finger and then his ring finger. He won't be able to lift *that* finger.

The Bible tells about the sad time in Samson's life when he, too, had very little strength. You can read about it from Judges 16:4, 5, and 21. Read the whole story of Samson and Delilah from Judges 16:6-20 if you have time.

The woman gave birth to a boy and named him Samson. He grew and the Lord blessed him. (Judg. 13:24)

What insect loves music?

A humbug

Do you enjoy music? What kinds? Can you play a musical instrument, or do you like to sing in a choir or at home when no one's listening? If you like music, you would have had something in common with David.

David was a shepherd, a poet, a giant-killer, a killer of bears and lions (read 1 Samuel 17:34-35), a king, an ancestor of Jesus, and a harp player! As David took care of his father's sheep on the hillsides surrounding Bethlehem, he sang praises to God as he played his harp. Read about it in

1 Samuel 16:18. See how God used David's musical ability to help King Saul in 1 Samuel 16:15, 23.

Have you asked God to use your music to bring glory to him?

Whenever the spirit from God came upon Saul, David would take his harp and play. Then relief would come to Saul; he would feel better, and the evil spirit would leave him. (1 Sam. 16:23)

I fly high in the sky, but I'm not a kite or a plane. I hold lots of water, but I'm not a lake. What am I?

A cloud

Do you know the story of Elijah and the very small cloud? His homeland, Israel, was very, very dry. The ground was cracked, the plants were dying, the animals were suffering, and so were the people. They desperately needed rain! So what do you think Elijah did? Look in 1 Kings 18:41-46 to see. Were you right? Did Elijah pray only once? How many times and then what happened? What can we learn from Elijah's experience?

Meanwhile, the sky grew black with clouds, the wind rose, a heavy rain came on, and Ahab rode off to Jezreel. (1 Kings 18:45)

Who was the most popular doctor in the Old Testament?

Job—he had the most patience (patients) of all.

Job got his patience the hard way! If

you ever feel like your day isn't going very well, read about Job's problems! Read the list of his troubles from Job 1:13-22. Things started out bad and got worse and worse for poor Job! But did God leave Job like that? Read the answers in Job 42:7-17.

Color a picture representing Job's tough situation using only color—no pictures or lines. Here's how: Color a section of the paper (a strip on the left side, perhaps) with one bright happy color, very lightly, representing Job's good life at first. Then make more strips of color beside the first, making each section more dark and gloomy than the one beside it until you reach the center of the paper. Color it black. The black stands for Job's darkest, gloomiest days. Make more colored strips, moving toward the right side of the paper with each colored section becoming lighter again as Job's problems began to go away.

Remember the important lesson that God is always with us in times of trouble, and that he will make both good and bad turn out for our good!

In all this, Job did not sin by charging God with wrongdoing. (Job 1:22)

The more you take away from me, the bigger I become. What am I?

A hole

Several Bible people spent time in a hole and almost always for being a believer in God and for living right and speaking about him.

Joseph got thrown into a hole in the ground by his jealous brothers; Daniel's time underground was caused by his practice of praying to God three times daily. Jeremiah was God's special prophet who had to pay dearly for daring to warn about God's coming judgment, and even the great missionary Paul spent his last days in a dirty, damp hole in the ground called the Mamertine Prison! Why were those brave believers willing to go that far for God?

Are we willing to go so far to live for God? Sometimes that can be tough, too. But remember this promise:

God is our refuge and strength, an ever-present help in trouble. (Ps. 46:1)

What color is it when you talk in a loud voice?

Yellow

The Bible tells us about two different servants of God who both spoke in a loud voice for an important reason. One was John the Baptist. What was he yelling about? Find out what important message he loudly spoke in Mark 1:3. At least one of the reasons John spoke loudly was because he was outside, where he had to speak up for his wonderful message to be heard, without a microphone! But the main reason John spoke loudly was because he believed his message with all his heart and knew he had to share it.

Jesus was the other person who

spoke loudly one time. Find out why in John 11:17, 38-44.

Sometimes God's *message* is proclaimed loudly, perhaps by a preacher who believes it with all his heart, but God usually speaks in a still, small voice. Read about God's quiet voice spoken to our hearts in Psalm 46:10.

Be still, and know that I am God. (Ps. 46:10)

The alphabet goes from A to Z, but what animal goes from Z to A?

Zebra

There are many names in the Bible for Jesus. One of the most interesting is the name *Alpha and Omega*. That seems like a strange name to us, but it is strange only because you don't speak Greek! If you were a little preschool child learning to read Greek in school, instead of singing the song, "A, B, C, D, E, F, G, . . ." and so on, you would be singing "Alpha, beta, . . ." all the way to Omega! Does that give you a clue about the words *Alpha and Omega?*

Jesus is the beginning of all things (like the letter *Alpha*) and he will someday end (*Omega*) time and start our everlasting life in heaven with him!

I am the first and I am the last; apart from me there is no God. (Isa. 44:6)

Why do carpenters believe there is no such thing as stone?

Because they never *saw* it.

Can you think of an important Bible person who made things out of wood—a carpenter? Did you think of Joseph, the husband of Jesus' mother, Mary? Joseph took good care of Jesus, but Joseph was not Jesus' real father. You may live with someone who is not your real father, too.

Jesus had a mother, Mary, and he had a real Father, God. Everyone else who has ever lived had a human father, even if he never knew his father or didn't live with him. But Jesus' *real* Father was God, the heavenly Father.

Joseph her [Mary's] husband was a righteous man. (Matt. 1:19)

I have a mouth but I never speak. I have a water bed, but I never sleep. What am I?

A river

Have you ever sailed a toy boat in the rain river that formed on the edge of your street after a sudden hard rain? Have you ever gone down a real river in a canoe or raft? Some people live near such a river and get to ride the river often. Others of us get our taste of river fun from a log ride at an amusement park during summer vacations. Rivers are important as well as fun. What are some uses for rivers? Can you think of a famous American river with a long name that contains several double letters?

The Jordan River in the Bible was especially important because of what happened there one day. Do you remember what it was? You may read about the beautiful and amazing event in Matthew 3:13-17.

Then Jesus came from Galilee to the Jordan to be baptized by John. (Matt. 3:13)

What keys are too big to carry in your pocket?

Donkeys

The Bible tells us an interesting story about a donkey that was at the right place at the right time. Read what happened in Matthew 21:1-7.

What if the Master had had need of a boy or girl who was willing to do whatever he needed and asked. Would you have been the one he could use for his purpose?

Tell him that the Lord needs them, and he will send them right away. (Matt. 21:3)

Why is a diamond ring like eternity?

It has no beginning or end.

It seems like good things always end, doesn't it? Christmas season begins, with all its beauty, excitement, and anticipation. We feel like Christmas day will never come! And it does! Yes! But then it goes for another whole year! Birthdays, parties, holidays all do the same thing. None of the great events we love last long enough!

But the Bible promises us that the greatest experience of all time will last and last and last forever. We won't

have to say good-bye to our friends like we do after summer camp or a great sleepover. We won't have to watch our favorite big sister leave for college or another person we love get married and move away. This experience won't end like recess or lunch break. We won't have to stop our play and go to bed! We'll never have to separate from our friends and go to our own homes after a day of fun together.

Read Revelation 21:2-4 to find where such an experience will take place. Read Revelation 21:23-25 to see what days and nights will be like there.

Every time you see a ring, let it remind you of this Bible verse:

I tell you the truth, he who believes has everlasting life. (John 6:47)

Knock-Knock Jokes

Knock-knock.
  Who's there?
Esau.
  Esau who?

Esau-fully important to do what's right!

Esau would have fit right in with the now generation. What is the now generation? Well, now, the now generation is a group of people who want what they want and they want it *right now!* Have you ever felt like that? Of course you have! Everyone has!

But Esau's life could be a warning to us that it really is risky business to be too much a now person. He gave away his most precious possession, his birthright, because he wanted a bowl of stew *right now!* Read the sad story in Genesis 25:27-34.

Sometimes young people or adults give away their most valuable possessions—their purity, their health, their good name, or their influence for the Lord Jesus—for something that looks fun, exciting, or popular right now, and they are sorry all their lives!

You can do something great right now. You can decide now (when it really counts) that you will live for God, obey his commandments, and keep your whole life clean and pure. You can be a leader in the new now generation of kids who make good choices now and the rest of their lives.

Quick, let me have some of that red stew! I'm famished! (Gen. 25:30)

fluff each piece as you add it, to help it soak up the water better. If you move slowly and carefully, you can probably put all the cotton in the full glass of water without spilling a single drop! Why? Because cotton fibers are hollow cells filled with air. The water moves into the spaces where the air was.

The Bible contains many stories and lessons that have something to do with water. Think of all the possible uses of water by Christians that would please God. Did you include these?

- Drink it.
- Bathe in it.
- Wash dishes or clothes in it.
- Share it.
- Cook with it.
- Water plants and animals with it.
- Use it for baptizing.
- Conserve it.
- Just enjoy it!

He leads me beside quiet waters. (Ps. 23:2)

Knock-knock.
Who's there?
Water.
Water who?

Water you doing for God?

Try this trick using a glass, cotton or cotton balls, and water. Fill the glass almost to the top with water and put two large handfuls of cotton into the already almost full glass of water, bit by bit. Be sure to use real cotton, and

Knock-knock.
Who's there?
Lettuce.
Lettuce who?

Lettuce go to church since it's Sunday.

Do you and your family attend church? Why do you? Give each person thirty seconds to think of five reasons why people of all ages should go to church (and because it's fun is a great reason!). Share your ideas. Now, name some excuses people give for not going to church. What do you think of those?

As good as the reasons are that you gave for being a part of a church, the best reasons of all come from the Bible. Read them together:

- Psalm 122:1
- Ephesians 1:22
- Colossians 1:18
- Hebrews 10:25

In the first century after Jesus died, Christians wanted to go to church so badly that they were willing to meet in secret underground tunnels, called catacombs. Today, many believers in other countries walk miles just to go to church. It really is a privilege to meet with God's family at church, isn't it?

I rejoiced with those who said to me, "Let us go to the house of the Lord." (Ps. 122:1)

Knock-knock.
   Who's there?
Roseanne.
   Roseanne who?

Roseanne the Lily of the Valley are two flower names for Jesus.

You can make your own good-smelling potpourri to use in your room. Collect roses, wildflowers, cloves, or other fragrant flowers or leaves, cut off the stems and leaves, and place only the flowers themselves in a covered box. Put the box in a dark corner of a closet or the garage. Wait ten days and then check to see if the flowers are dry.

When they are, sprinkle them with a few drops of your favorite perfume. Keep your potpourri in a tightly closed plastic bag when you are not using it, and refresh it with perfume as often as you need to.

Read Song of Songs 2:1 to see two flower names for Jesus. Why would he be described like that?

I am a rose of Sharon, a lily of the valleys. (Song of Songs 2:1)

Knock-knock.
   Who's there?
Noah.
   Noah who?

Noah lot of reasons why you love the Lord!

The Bible says we should love the Lord our God with all of the three things that belong to us. What do you think they are? Take a guess, and then check your answer by reading Deuteronomy 6:5. Jesus then names one more part of us that we should add to this loving God experience. What is it? Look in Matthew 22:37 and find out.

You have probably heard the commercial on television that says, "A mind is a terrible thing to waste." It is so sad when children, teenagers, and adults waste the incredible minds that God gave them on drinking, drugs, reading bad books and magazines, and watching shows that dishonor him. Maybe that's why doing drugs and getting drunk is sometimes called "getting wasted"! What do you think?

> Love the Lord your God with all your heart and with all your soul and with all your mind. (Matt. 22:37)

Knock-knock.
  Who's there?
Odyssey.
  Odyssey who?

Odyssey a doctor if your stomach hurts.

Finish these silly Doctor, doctor rhymes:

Doctor, doctor,
  Can you see?
I fell down and
  Skinned my _____!
Doctor, doctor,
  No, oh no!
I walked along
  And stubbed my _____!
Doctor, doctor,
  Sigh, sigh, sigh.
I reached up and
  Poked my _____!
Doctor, doctor,
  I'm a wreck!
I'm afraid
  I broke my _____!
Doctor, doctor,
  What would I do
If I didn't have
  A friend like you?

Think of as many kinds of illnesses or

handicaps as you can that Jesus healed while he was on earth. Try to name at least five kinds.

Anytime a broken bone grows together or a sick person gets well—whether God uses a doctor, a hospital, medicine, or treatments to help—who does the actual healing?

> The people brought to Jesus all who had various kinds of sickness, and laying his hands on each one, he healed them. (Luke 4:40)

Knock-knock.
  Who's there?
Sarah.
  Sarah who?

Sarah reason why you think being a Christian is so awesome?

Sarah is a very pretty and popular name today. How many Sarahs do you know? Perhaps they were named after the Sarah in Genesis 17:15, whose name meant "princess," and who was the mother of the whole Jewish nation that still exists today and an ancestor of Jesus.

Were you named after a person in the Bible, or do you know the meaning of your name? There is another really great name in the Bible, found in Acts 11:26. What is it? It is a great honor to be called that name. Think of as many reasons as you can why being a Christian is so awesome!

> The disciples were called Christians. (Acts 11:26)

Knock-knock.

Who's there?

Orange.

Orange who?

Orange you glad to be a Christian?

There is a simple little song that you have probably sung at Sunday school sometime in the past that goes like this: "If you're happy and you know it, clap your hands."

Let's change the words to say, "If you're glad to be a Christian, tell us *why!"*

Pretend that someone in the room is considering becoming a Christian and you are telling him how he can and why you wish he would. Explain to him the wonderful advantages of being a child of God.

Here are some excellent verses you can use from the Bible: John 1:12, Acts 16:31, and 1 John 1:9.

Believe in the Lord Jesus, and you will be saved. (Acts 16:31)

Knock-knock.

Who's there?

Lion.

Lion who?

Lion can be just as bad as cheatin'.

Knock-knock.

Who's there?

Robin.

Robin who?

Robin can be just as bad as cheatin' and lyin'!

What does it mean to rob someone? Why is that wrong? Read what God says about robbing in Exodus 20:15 and Ephesians 4:28. In the verse in Ephesians, what does the Bible tell us to do instead of stealing and why?

Do you know who one of the biggest/little robbers was in the Bible? Zacchaeus. He even admits it in Luke 19:8! Zacchaeus never actually put on a black mask and sneaked into homes of people who were gone on vacation like the two crooks in the movie *Home Alone.* Instead, he did his robbing by cheating people as he collected their taxes.

We know that bank robbery, pickpocketing, purse snatching, and shoplifting are all kinds of robbery, but here are some other things that are stealing, too. Tell what is being stolen in each situation:

• A group of girls at lunch break are spreading gossip about someone's poor math grade that they weren't even supposed to know about. (The girl's right to privacy)

• Some boys are telling all their friends and their coach that another boy drinks and does drugs, even though they have no evidence that he does, so he won't get to be on the team's starting lineup. (The boy's good name—his reputation)

• You keep the extra change the store clerk accidentally gave you, since he doesn't recognize his mistake. (Money that does not belong to you)

Did you know that breaking another of the Ten Commandments often leads a person to stealing? Find it in Exodus 20:17. Do you think a lot of robbing could be prevented if people would obey this commandment?

Be content with what you have. (Heb. 13:5)

Knock-knock.
  Who's there?
Weevil.
  Weevil who?

Weevil do our best to please God.

Play "Please, may I?" like this:

Someone gives the following commands for a second player to perform as the second player slowly makes his way across the room to the finish line on the other side. The only requirement is that the second player must say, pleadingly, "Please, may I?" each time before he begins to do the command. If he forgets, he must go back to his starting position and begin again. Here are the commands. (Repeat them as many times as necessary until the player reaches the finish line.)

- Take two giant steps forward.
- Balance on one foot as you count from one to ten.
- Crawl forward as you quickly count one-two-three and then step.
- Move forward four steps with one knee on the floor and one foot on the floor at the same time.
- Sneak forward five steps.

Did you remember to always say please? Was this game pleasing to everyone involved in it? Would you like to know what really pleases God so that you can do it? Read together these verses to give you a head start on a life of pleasing God.

- Micah 6:8
- Hebrews 11:6
- Hebrews 13:16

Do not forget to do good and to share with others, for with such sacrifices God is pleased. (Heb. 13:16)

Knock-knock.
  Who's there?
Ron.
  Ron who?

Ron away from every kind of evil!

Ever try a three-legged race? How about a bean-zag race or the farmer and the crow race? Here's how to do each race. In each of them you are trying to get from one end of the room or yard to the other and back.

- Three-legged race. Two players

each tie one leg to the others with a bandanna and run the race together.

• Bean-zag race. Two players toss a beanbag back and forth in a zig-zag pattern as they run the race.

• The farmer and the crow race. The farmer lays five objects such as socks in a row (representing seeds he is planting) as he first runs to the finish line. Then the crow hops along the same race track picking up the seeds and returning them to the farmer, who plants them again!

Running is mentioned several times in the Bible. Sometimes we are told to run *to* something and other times, to run *away*.

Find these verses and see what we should run to or run from:

• Psalm 119:32
• Proverbs 18:10
• 1 Corinthians 9:24-25
• 2 Timothy 2:22 (*Flee* means "run away from")
• Hebrews 12:1

We can even make the devil himself run away from us! How? Look in James 4:7 for the two important things we must do before the devil will run away and leave us alone!

Submit yourselves, then, to God. Resist the devil, and he will flee from you. (James 4:7)

Knock-knock.
Who's there?
Israeli.
Israeli who?

Israeli great to know God loves you!

Who are the Israelis—the Israelites in the Bible? Sometimes they are called the Hebrews, sometimes the chosen people or the Jews. Nearly everything in the Old Testament and much in the New Testament was written about them. They are special people to God. He chose them for a very important purpose on earth. What was it? Read Genesis 22:17-18 to see why God chose to bless Israel. How many other people did God want to help and bless through the Jewish people (v. 18)? Why was God able to use Israel?

Can God use you if you obey him, too? Are you a special and chosen person? Read 1 Peter 2:9 to find out! Who is God talking about here?

But you are a chosen people, a royal priesthood, a holy nation, a people belonging to God. (1 Pet. 2:9)

Ask someone these questions:

• Do you know who I am?
• Will you remember me tomorrow?
• Will you remember me next month?
• Will you remember me next year?

Knock-knock.
Who's there?

See! You've forgotten me already!

What's the difference in knowing *about* somebody and *really knowing* someone? Look at this list of people and decide whether you *know* or *know about* each one:

- George Washington
- Your mom
- Your grandma
- Abraham Lincoln
- Michael Jordan
- Your dad
- Daniel in the Bible
- Jesus

Now, do you better understand the difference in two kinds of knowing? Listen to how the Bible says that God knows you!

- He knows your heart. (Acts 15:8)
- He knows your secrets. (Ps. 44:21)
- He knows where you are going. (Job 23:10)
- He knows your thoughts. (Ps. 94:11)
- He knows everything about you. (1 John 3:20)

Psalm 139 says that God knew you long before you knew him—he saw you and knew all about you before you were even born! (Read Psalm 139:13-17, and then read verses 1-4 and 7-10.)

Since God knows you, don't you want to really know him? Find out how to know if you know him! Read 1 John 2:3, 6 and 1 John 3:23-24.

Whoever claims to live in him must walk as Jesus did. (1 John 2:6)

Knock-knock.
Who's there?

Isadore.
Isadore who?

Isadore handle where I can reach it?

Did you ever try to open a door with no handle? Not easy, is it? There is a famous picture of Jesus standing at a door that has no handle on the outside, and he is wanting to go inside. How can he do it?

Read the beautiful words of Jesus in Revelation 3:20. If Jesus were knocking on the door of your heart and life, would he gruffly say, "I demand that you let me in!" No, Jesus gently says, "I am standing here knocking on your heart's door because I so much want to be with you, sharing your life and lovingly guiding you. Will you please open the door from the inside and let me in?"

The answer is up to you. What will you say to Jesus?

Here I am! I stand at the door and knock. If anyone hears my voice and opens the door, I will come in and eat with him, and he with me. (Rev. 3:20)

Tricky Tricks

A Fishy Coin Trick

Take the first fish you catch; open its mouth and you will find a four-drachma coin. (Matt. 17:27)

Try this coin trick: Place a coin in front of a cup standing on a table. Can you put the coin in the cup without touching the coin? (Yes, by hitting underneath the coin and table with your fist. The coin will pop up!)

Did Jesus ever perform tricks on people? No, he performed mighty miracles! One time his disciples had a special need. Read about their need and Jesus' miracle in Matthew 17:24-27. In this one short event, Jesus taught us at least three important lessons:

- We should pay taxes we owe our government.
- We should try not to offend other people unnecessarily.
- God will provide to meet our needs.

With a Snap of the Fingers

Then Jesus told his disciples a parable to show them that they should always pray and not give up. (Luke 18:1)

Try this trick to fool your friends. You'll need three glasses with water in them and two empty glasses. Line up the glasses in this order: full, empty, full, empty, full. Ask your friend to change the order of the glasses in only one move, with only one hand—to three full glasses on the right, and two empty glasses on the left.

If he cannot do it, snap your fingers over the glasses three times, and simply take the full glass on the right and pour the water into the empty glass that is second from the left.

Sometimes we think of prayer like a kind of magic trick—that all we need to do is pray once, and with a snap of our fingers, God will rush to immediately answer our prayer! We forget that we are God's servants, and that God is not just a Santa Claus in the clouds who should instantly meet our every desire. That attitude would be selfish, wouldn't it?

God loves to hear his children pray, and he sincerely wants to say yes to our prayers. But God always knows what is best for us—to make us good and useful in his service—and he knows that some of our requests are not in our best interest and would actually be harmful to us or to his kingdom. God also knows the very best *time* to say yes to our prayers—and sometimes that is not right now! He wants to teach us patience and trust in him—and he is honored and pleased when we keep on praying to him because we know that at the right time and in the right way, our prayers will be answered.

Blow the Can Down!

The wind blows wherever it pleases. You hear its sound, but you cannot tell where it comes from or where it is going. So it is with everyone born of the Spirit. (John 3:8)

If an empty tin can were sitting on your kitchen table, could you blow it over? Let each family member try to do this trick. Tell them you can blow the can over for sure. Then put a balloon on the table, insert a drinking straw into the end of it, and hold the straw in place with a rubber band. Place the tin can on top of the balloon and blow into the straw, tipping over the can.

Jesus talked about the wind when he explained to Nicodemus about being born again. Jesus said that we cannot see wind, but we know it's there because we can see what it does, and we can hear it. Describe to someone in your family how you know when a day is windy. Read what Jesus said about the wind in John 3:8. What did he mean?

We cannot see wind, and we cannot see the change that takes place (called the new birth) in someone's heart when he gives his life to Jesus, but the new birth experience is very real! Ask someone (or everyone) in your family to tell what happened when he was born again and how receiving God's salvation through Jesus Christ has affected his whole life.

How Strong Are You?

I can do everything through him who gives me strength. (Phil. 4:13)

Ask this question of someone in your family: "Are you strong enough to fold a paper napkin in half?" If he answers yes, ask him if he can fold a paper napkin (or any other piece of paper) in half more than seven times. Let him try.

He will learn that no one can fold any kind of paper more than seven times, because by the time it comes to the eighth fold, the paper will be too thick to budge. That's a trick that can't be done!

Sometimes we have an I-can't-do-that attitude about things that are important for us to do to please and obey God. When he gives us a job to do, or when we need to do something to obey our teacher or parents or to help another person, God has a special promise with "muscles" for us! "I can do everything through him who gives me strength" (Phil. 4:13). That's a great verse to mark in your Bible and remember!

Tongue Twisters

Honesty is honestly honorable.

Honest Ollie often offers aid.

Once-honest Abraham and Isaac did double dishonest deeds.

Honesty is very important to God. Read Titus 1:2 to see how honest our God is. If God cannot and will not ever lie, he's able to help us be honest, too. Trust him to be your strength and truth!

God is not a man, that he should lie. . . . Does he speak and then not act? Does he promise and not fulfill? (Num. 23:19)

A loud, proud crowd is not allowed.

Stealing a meal still jails a male.

Lying leads to denying, sighing, and crying.

Where in the Bible are really wise bits of advice called proverbs found? What is a proverb? Do you know who wrote most of the wise words in the book of Proverbs? Solomon the king, David's son.

How did Solomon get such wisdom to know right from wrong in God's eyes? He asked for it! He knew that he needed God's help and guidance to make the right decisions and be a wise king. Read about Solomon's request and how it made God feel in 1 Kings 3:5-14.

You also need God's gift of wisdom to lead you at school, at home, or on the job. He tells us how we can get his wisdom and know what is right to do in James 1:5.

Listen to some of King Solomon's words from God:

Trust in the Lord with all your heart and lean not on your own understanding; in all your ways acknowledge him, and he will make your paths straight. (Prov. 3:5-6)

[The Lord] blesses the home of the righteous. (Prov. 3:33)

My son, keep your father's commands and do not forsake your mother's teaching. (Prov. 6:20)

The fear of the Lord is the beginning of wisdom. (Prov. 9:10)

The fear of the Lord adds length to life. (Prov. 10:27)

Commit to the Lord whatever you do, and your plans will succeed. (Prov. 16:3)

Whispering walruses wait willingly for watermelon.

The bear's brass band beat the boar's bass bassoon.

Lively leopards look like leaping lions and lazy lizards.

Now that your tongue is all tangled up, let it rest while you make a list of things you should use your speech for—and what you should not speak. Read Psalm 145:5-7 and pray that God will help your speech to please him.

I open my lips to speak what is right. My mouth speaks what is true. (Prov. 8:6-7)

Proud people produce particular problems.

The Bible warns us about being too proud of ourselves. It warns us about what can happen when we become puffed up with pride like the prideful girl who walked with her nose in the air because she thought she was so much better than everyone else. Because she was so occupied with prideful thoughts about herself, she failed to look where she was going, tripped over a rock, and took a nasty fall! Beware of pride!

Pride goes before destruction, a haughty spirit before a fall. (Prov. 16:18)

One begun, two flew, three ski, four roar, five dive, six fix, seven heaven, eight skate, nine shine, ten win!

The important number in this silly number rhyme is seven. There was once a western movie called *The Magnificent Seven*. The heroes were a group of seven tough cowboys who rode into a sleepy little Mexican town and got rid of the gang of bad guys that had been hiding out there and causing trouble.

In the New Testament there was also a "Magnificent Seven" group of men. They were chosen by the early church to help pass out food to the poor widows and to do other important jobs. Even their names were magnificent—or unusual, at least! You can find them in Acts 6:5. Do you recognize any of the names from other Bible stories?

In our churches today there are groups of people we call deacons or elders who do very special jobs of serving and helping people just like the "Magnificent Seven" did in the Bible. When you see any of those serving people at church, thank them for helping your church to run smoothly and for taking good care of the people.

Choose seven men from among you

who are known to be full of the Spirit and wisdom. (Acts 6:3)

Christian children choose charity every chance there's a choice.

What is charity? (Maybe you know a person with that name!) First Corinthians 13 is a whole chapter in the Bible about *charity*. Read verses 4-8 and 13.

Here is an idea for sharing charity—or love—with someone:

Cut out two paper hearts. Decorate them or color them however you wish. Fold them in half and staple them together to form a cone-shaped basket. Attach a paper-strip handle to your basket and fill it with candy or flowers. Include a handmade greeting card or let your gift basket be from a secret friend. Hang your "love basket" on the doorknob of someone's house or room.

Remember who loves you the very most—God!

I live by faith in the Son of God, who loved me and gave himself for me. (Gal. 2:20)

Raps to Try Just for Fun

The Bible Rap

Hey! Yo! Here's the situation:
 God has given us a revelation
Called his Word, so listen to this rap
 About the Word of God from Genesis to maps.
In the beginning God is all ya need to know
 'Cause he created the world, and it was quite a show.
First the light, then the earth, and then the rest of the plan:
 The birds and the animals and finally man.
Now to Exodus, Leviticus, the book of Numbers,
 Where we read about the signs and wonders
God did, when he taught his chosen few
 About the ten laws that still apply to me and you.
Next we read about the history of a nation
 And the people involved in certain occupations
Like prophets, priests, judges and kings,
 Farmers and soldiers and all kinds of things.
Psalms and Proverbs tell us how to live;
 Minor Prophets, of the gift that God was gonna give
Named Jesus—he's the one who sees us,

And he gave up his life so that he could free us.
The B-I-B-L-E, yeah, that's the Book for me,
 And with Matthew, Mark, Luke and John it's easy to see
Who Jesus was and why he died on the cross,
 Dying so that we could live and not be lost.
But wait a minute, brother [or sister], that ain't all!
 Then we read about a fella by the name of Paul
And Timothy and Peter and the early church
 And just a little more if you really search.
Go to the back and make a sharp left turn
 There's a lot you're gonna want to learn
About what's gonna happen at the end of the age
 'Cause Revelation takes you to the last page.
That's the end; now my story is done,
 But if you want to know about the Father, Spirit, and Son,
Don't take my word—read it for yourself,
 And get your Bible down off the shelf!

Jonah and the Whale

Once there was a man named Jonah,
 And if you met him, he would never say, "Glad to know ya!"

'Cause he wasn't—he was just too
selfish!
   So when the Lord spoke, he
   headed straight for Tarshish.
He thought he could run away from
God's command,
   But his luck ran out when he left
   dry land.
A storm came up; it looked like all
was lost,
   Then Jonah spoke up, and over-
   board he was tossed.
He ended up in the belly of a great
big fish,
   But to tell the truth, he made a ter-
   rible dish,
After three long days of being fish
food,

He was spit out on land with a
new attitude.
He went to the city and began to
preach
   A message to the people God
   wanted to reach
About God's love and his judgment
too,
   And everybody listened up—
   wouldn't you?
That's the story of Jonah and the
great big whale,
   But there's a little moral to this
   very famous tale:
When God commands, tell your
friends about him.
   You know Jonah never thought
   he'd go for a swim.

F riends, here's a riddle for you: What is a word that is often spoken of in the Bible but never mentioned by name? Give up? The mysterious word is *character*.

We sometimes hear people called "characters" because they get themselves into mischief and trouble—and the Bible describes a few folks like that—but the word *character* actually means the way we think, behave, and live as we obey God's Word and do his will. A person with good character will be honest, obedient, kind, caring, and humble. He will want to be and to do all that God wants him to. Jesus is our example of someone with perfect character.

Christian boys and girls and men and women should want to be people of character—and God will help to make us that way if we will let him. As you listen to the stories in this chapter or read them to someone else, decide right now to be a person of character that God can greatly bless and use.

Ted

God is love. Whoever lives in love lives in God, and God in him. (1 John 4:16)

Love is usually one of the first words we hear in life, coming to us with smiles and hugs from caring family and friends. What is love, anyway? Spend a few minutes brainstorming about what love means to the members of your family. Is love a feeling? Is it a promise of some kind? When we say we *love* peanut butter, baseball, or kittens, is that the same kind of love we have for our parents, grandparents, brothers, and sisters—or God?

God is the "love expert." He *is* love (see 1 John 4:16)—and he gave his love in the incredible gift of his Son, Jesus, who came to show us how love *behaves* in everyday life. God is the one who puts love in our hearts for himself and for other people—and who shows us how to express this wonderful gift.

The Bible tells us how love *acts* in 1 Corinthians 13:4-7. Read these beautiful verses with your family. Then listen to the story of Ted. As you listen, draw a happy face on a piece of paper every time you hear some expression of love—and a sad face each time something unloving is said or done.

It's not easy to be a mouse; if you could try it—even for one minute— you'd see why. Mice are always being threatened from above. A well-placed swat of a broom, the boot of an unsuspecting passerby, the swooping dive of an owl or hawk, and it's all over. Some human beings set traps for them or lay out poison; some drop them in little glass cages with toys and a wheel to run and run on but never get anywhere. Some (can you imagine?) feed them to snakes. And we haven't even talked about the natural enemy of mice—but wait. Let's not get ahead of ourselves.

It wasn't easy for Ted Tricklefeather to be a mouse. (Yes, it is a strange last name, but it's quite common among mice to have elaborate last names. It's said that's their way of compensating for their small size—and not everyone can be named Mouse.) Ted lived in a time and a place when things were difficult for mice: turn-of-the-century London. It was a time that has gone down in history (for mice) as "Tears and Troubles." You see, Britain was at a grand time in history, and London, its greatest city, reflected that time. London's city officials had pledged to make it "the cleanest city in all the world." For some strange reason they considered mice to be dirty and undesirable. So they "declared war" and did all they could to get rid of all the city's mice. Mice were forced to seek refuge underground, and there was hardly a mouse in London that had not lost a loved one in the conflict. Food supplies ran short, and mice had to make do with less.

Well, as you can imagine, the mice liked this turn of events very little. In fact, they didn't like it one bit. But what could they do about it? Of course the answer was: nothing. So they tightened their belts and prayed a little harder. Most of them tried to get on with life as usual, or as much like usual as they could manage. The

Tricklefeathers were no exception. For Ted, that meant that, troubles or no troubles, he would be starting school. The Tricklefeathers were wealthy mice and were sending Ted to the finest private school for mice in London, which was still open despite the hardships. It was commonly known as RRS, which was short for Rodentia Regent School (Rodentia was the reigning queen, a revered and sweet, dignified old mouse).

The first day of school arrived, a fine fall day, and Ted was dutifully packed off, carrying a bag full of supplies and wearing stiff, uncomfortable clothes. The school uniform consisted of a dark blue wool jacket and shorts, a starched shirt with high collar, a striped tie, black shoes, and a little cap. Ted didn't like the uniform, but it was required at school. He felt very ill at ease, especially since his mother had tied a white ribbon in a bow around the tip of his tail, insisting that it would look, as she had said, "simply adorable." Ted didn't think it was very adorable. He thought it was ridiculous. He felt like other mice were staring and snickering at him as he walked along the shaded lane toward the school. (The mice had streets of their own, well hidden from the view of London's human population.)

As Ted walked, the crowd of mice grew smaller. Soon he was walking by himself, though he took no notice—his mind was on all the strange new things he would surely find on his first day of school. Would he like his teachers? What would his classmates be like? Would he like to study? These questions kept him from noticing *why* the crowd had disappeared. He kept walking, caught up in thought, as a long shadow slipped up behind him. In a moment, one sound, one small sound, made Ted's blood run cold.

It wasn't a growl. It wasn't a hiss. It wasn't even a meow. It was a purr, the very faintest of purrs, coming from behind Ted. He knew instantly what it was: cat, of course. He had seen them before and had even heard one or two in cat fights outside the door of his family's house. He was terrified, and he began frantically searching around with his eyes for a place to hide, a place too small for the cat to reach him. He saw nothing. And so Ted did a very intelligent thing, something his parents had always taught him to do but never expected to be necessary.

Rather than panicking and running, he kept walking, pretending that he hadn't noticed the cat. (Ted's father had had to do this numerous times in his life, having grown up on a farm with five cats; it had always worked for him.) Ted could hear the cat's footsteps coming closer. Soon he could feel the cat's hot breath on his neck. And finally it got to be too much for him.

Ted screamed and began to run in a panic. Behind him he heard a voice shouting, "Wait! Wait!" It had to be the cat, he thought. He ran and ran until he didn't think he could run anymore, looking for hiding places. There were none. Finally he heard a whistle and spotted a sewer drain. Standing at its edge, Ted saw, were three dirty, grungy-looking rats motioning toward him and yelling. He didn't like the looks of them, but he had no choice. He headed straight for the drain as fast as he could go.

Once there he thought he was safe. But two of the rats grabbed him by the arms and began to drag him toward the sewer. The other one stood and laughed mockingly, saying, "That's it, boys. We knows who 'is parents are, we does. He'll bring a pretty ransom!" Ted squirmed and struggled, but the rats were much stronger than he was. They meant to drag him into the sewer with them. They were right at the edge of the black hole when a noise split the air. It was a loud hiss. To Ted's amazement an orange paw shot out and sent the three rats flying into the dark pit of the sewer. Ted closed his eyes and stood there shaking. He was sure it was his turn to go now. He waited. . . .

There was no hiss or growl or sharp claws. Instead, to Ted's great surprise, there was a soft voice. Ted was so shocked he didn't catch what was said. He turned and looked. Sure enough, there was a cat, a small orange tabby. The cat didn't *look* mean, Ted thought, though he was still wary. But the cat had spoken to him, he was sure. He stammered out, "D-d-did you s-say something?"

"Yes," the cat replied, with a big friendly smile. "I said, 'I think you dropped this.'"

Ted looked to see what "this" was. What he saw was his little cap, balanced on one of the cat's soft front paws. He noticed that the cat didn't have his claws out. Maybe he wasn't going to hurt him, Ted thought. No! This had to be a trick. Well, no hat was worth his life. Still . . . Ted finally decided to ask.

"How do I know this isn't a trick? Maybe you're trying to trap me, get me to come over there, then you'll pounce on me!"

The cat seemed really surprised by this. He looked perplexed. "I wouldn't do that, really. I wanted to help you. I really want to be . . . friends."

"Friends? But you're a cat and I'm a mouse."

The cat (who was really just a kitten) said in a shy voice, "Well, yes . . . that's true, but it doesn't really matter, does it? Couldn't we still be friends?"

Ted thought about this for a minute or two. Finally he said, "I guess it doesn't matter so much . . . but we don't have anything in common."

The kitten said brightly, "I like sports!"

"You do? So do I!" said Ted. He took a step or two closer. He was starting to like the kitten more and more. "I also like music."

"Me too!" And so it went.

Ted and Mortimer (that was the cat's name, more's the pity) discovered much that they had in common. This continued for some time until Ted said, "Wait a second. Aren't we supposed to be enemies?"

"I guess so, but you know what? You don't feel like an enemy. Besides, doesn't the Bible say to love one another?"

"*You* read the Bible *too?*" Ted shouted in amazement, bringing on a whole new conversation.

As it turned out, Mortimer and his family faithfully attended church at the famous St. Paul's Cathedral (they waited until the human beings had all gone in and then stood at the back). And *Ted's* family also faithfully attended St. Paul's; they climbed the walls and perched in chinks in the stone. (This way they could see and hear and have less chance of being caught by humans who just wouldn't understand.) Now they *knew* they had something in common. They would have talked for hours more, but Ted remembered something.

"SCHOOL!" he shouted, and snatched up his cap from off the ground where Mortimer had gently placed it. "I've got to go now, but, Mortimer . . . can we meet again sometime?" He looked sheepish, but hopeful.

"I'd like that a lot, Ted," Mortimer replied. "I guess sometimes enemies make good friends."

Ted and Mortimer met often after that and became even better friends. Their families became friends. Soon the mice and the cats of London were all on speaking terms and becoming friendlier all the time. Even the city officials relaxed somewhat, and mice were finally able to, for the most part, come out of hiding. "All this," many wise old mice said, "from one fine fall day and one unusual friendship." Ted heard it said from time to time, and it never failed to make him happy.

Yes, he thought, remembering a Bible verse his mother had taught him as a baby mouse bouncing on her knee, *sometimes God works in mysterious ways.*

Nick

Love your enemies, do good to those who hate you. (Luke 6:27)

Jesus was the most compassionate person who ever lived. What did he do for people who were sick, sad, hungry, or needy in any way? Read about one time Jesus showed great *compassion* in Mark 1:40-41. Jesus is our example of the right way to act in *every* situation—and he wants to help us be compassionate people, like he is.

Do you know someone who has special needs—someone who is elderly, handicapped, lonely, poor—or may not have a lot of friends to care about him? Spend a few minutes talking with your family about people you know who need compassion. Then, with God's help, give them the kind of compassion they need.

As you listen to the story of Nick, try to find three ways that compassion was shown to him when he *badly* needed it. Discuss your answers with the other members of your family at the end of the story.

"Nick! *Nick! NICK!*"

The young man in question was trying his very hardest to do two things: to not be noticed (which of course he already had been), and to pretend not to hear his mother's voice, which was getting louder every time she called his name.

Actually Nick was trying to do something else at the same time. He was trying to tie a burlap sack to a horse's tail. This would have been fairly simple except for one thing: the bag held one fighting mad tomcat. The cat wasn't taking Nick's little joke well; he was scratching and clawing and biting and spitting and hissing—all inside the bag, which made it bulge and shake and made Nick laugh harder. The horse wasn't finding it

that funny either; it was crowding to the far end of the narrow chute it was standing in beside a corral and snorting. As you might have guessed, it's difficult to do something like this without your mother noticing. And Nick's mother had definitely noticed.

She came running out of their farmhouse, moving as fast as only a mother can when her son is either in danger or in trouble, and grabbed Nick by his left ear. Nick's mother had a strong grip; the pain in his ear made him jump down off the chute's fence and at the same time drop the sack. The mouth of the sack fell open, and the tomcat jumped out and ran off, but not before one final hiss at Nick. Nick's mom pulled him toward the house by his ear, scolding him the whole time and swatting at his behind. (Like all mothers, she could do several things at one time.) What she was saying went something like this:

"How many times have I told you not to tease the horses? Think how badly you could have been hurt! And that poor cat! You'll be the death of him."

"But Mama, don't cats have nine lives?" It's very difficult to ask questions when one is being pulled by the ear and swatted and scolded, but Nick managed somehow.

Nick's mother looked like she would have tweaked his nose if she had had three hands. She said, "Don't give me any back talk, young mister! If they do, you've taken at least six away from that cat!" By now they were passing through the door to the kitchen; soon they were in the kitchen itself. Nick's mother had been slowly relaxing her grip, and eventually she let go altogether.

She spoke again, but her voice was softer now. "Nick," she said, "trying to farm in Australia is not so easy. This isn't England. Things are different here, and it's hard for your father and me to get used to it, just like it is for you. The land is wilder and more open here, not like the little fields and villages that we knew back home. It's easier to get hurt. I've got my hands full trying to keep our house in order. It would help if I didn't have to worry about you getting in trouble all the time."

Nick felt ashamed. He wrung his hands and twisted the toe of his shoe on the ground. He could see that his mother was tired. He took one of her hands in his and squeezed it.

"Sorry, Mama. I-I won't cause so much trouble. I promise."

Nick's mother smiled at him and hugged him close. "I know," she said.

Nick's parents, the Whitleys, had moved to Australia from England to farm and to raise cattle. They had fallen on hard times in England, and Nick's father wanted to make a new start in a new land. The people of Australia were more rugged and tough than Nick's family was used to. The land itself was rugged and tough, and it made its people the same way. Most of the farmers and ranchers had also come from England or Ireland or Scotland, but most had also been there longer than the Whitleys. Still, Nick's family was doing the best they could, and it wasn't long before they had also grown stronger and more rugged. Nick learned how to rope and ride as well as the other boys who had started much younger; in fact, he was better than most. Mr. Whitley was proud of Nick and sometimes let Nick go with him on short cattle drives. Nick was discovering many things and learning many things.

The day soon came, however, when it was time for Nick to learn subjects other than farming and roping and fancy riding. Nick had to start school. There was a school at the nearest little town, which was hardly more than an outpost. The community was in a wild part of the Australian outback, and so not many teachers could be convinced to come and live there and teach. The town had to take its chances that someone new would be coming, hopefully soon, after the previous teacher had left. Someone new usually did, though often he or she could not properly be called a model teacher.

Nick was none too excited about starting school. He wanted to stay on the farm or ride out onto the wild and lonely range (though his mother still wouldn't let him go very far, and never by himself). School meant a stiff suit, tight, squeaky shoes, and an itchy collar. School meant sitting quietly and still. School meant girls. Nick would rather have been around horses and cows. Nevertheless he went, having no choice in the matter.

The first day of class was very boring to Nick, and he found it hard to pay attention. In fact, he was dreaming of riding his horse, Dan, all over the outback. Suddenly a word that the teacher had said made him pay attention. It was a strange word, one that Nick had only heard once or twice before and had never understood. There, he said it again.

"How many of you have seen an aborigine?" asked the teacher (whose name was Mr. Thornapple).

Many of the children raised their hands. Nick didn't know what an aborigine was, but he wanted to find out. He waited until his classmates had lowered their hands and then raised his own.

"Yes?" said Mr. Thornapple.

"Mr. Thornapple, what's an aborigine?" Nick asked. Many of his classmates started to giggle and whisper loudly to him, "You don't know?"

Mr. Thornapple scowled at the class. "Quiet!" he said. Then he looked at Nick and said, "The aborigines are a dark-skinned, native Australian tribe. They are dull, dim-witted, and clumsy. They are an inferior class. Civilized people should have nothing to do with them. And that," he added with a firm nod, "is all that you need to know."

Nick never saw aborigines in his school or in the little village. He never saw them near his family's farm or near the houses of his friends. He never saw them at all. He only heard about them from the children at school, and they were always described the same way: stupid, slow, mean, lazy. Nick found himself hoping he would never meet one.

Nick's father still had Nick help him on the farm after school, and some days he let Nick ride with him out onto the range. The days and weeks and months passed, and soon Nick had completed a year of school. It was summertime, and school was out for the term. Nick was glad to help around the house and work with his father, but he longed to take Dan and the cattle out on a drive by himself. He thought about it all the time.

One day when Nick awoke, his father had gone to town for supplies. His mother was sewing in a room at the other end of the house. Suddenly an idea came into his mind. He thought, *I may not be able to go on a cattle drive without Father, but I can take Dan and go exploring!* So he crept out of the house as silently as he could.

Once outside, he went cautiously to the stable and saddled up Dan. He led Dan to the gate and opened it slowly, careful not to make loud noises. He led Dan through and shut it behind them. Then he hopped up onto the horse's back and trotted off, looking behind him all the time to make sure

his mother hadn't seen him. He turned to look straight ahead. What he saw took his breath away.

Nick saw rolling hills and flat plains stretching on for what seemed forever. He saw rocks and sand and patches of grass and scrub bushes. He saw no people, no animals, no houses. He had seen the land before, of course, but he had always seen it from behind a fence or riding beside a few dozen head of cattle with his father right in front of him. Now he was alone, and it was a fantastic feeling. He rode on into the emptiness, and as he rode, he felt like he was the only person in the world. The familiar farmhouse grew smaller and smaller behind him. Finally Nick rode over the crest of a hill, and his house disappeared completely from view.

Nick had intended to ride only a short distance, but the farther he went, the more fantastic sights he saw. There were piles of rocks that looked like they had been stacked by giants. There were strange bushes that Nick had never seen before. There were even . . .

Kangaroos! Nick saw them hopping along, faster than he had thought they could move. They looked so funny that he laughed and laughed. They bounced and bounded, growing smaller, until finally they were gone. Then Nick realized something. It was hot. He looked at the sun. It stood almost directly overhead.

Nick hadn't noticed how hot the day had gotten. He knew by the posi-

tion of the sun that it was almost noontime. He also began to notice that he was hungry. *Enough adventure for one morning,* he thought to himself. *I'd better go home for something to eat. Plus I'm sure Mother knows I'm gone by now.*

Nick turned his horse around and started heading for home. He rode for a while and eventually found himself climbing a hill. "On the other side of this hill," he said out loud, "I should be able to see our farm." So he and Dan rode over the crest of the hill. No farm and no house. Nick didn't think this was so strange. "Maybe I haven't ridden far enough, but it ought to be beyond this next hill." And so he rode to the top of the next hill, but there was no house in sight, only open plains of dust and scraggly bushes as far as he could see.

Nick was hungry and thirsty. He was starting to get tired. The day was continuing to get hotter. He started to worry. *Did I go in the right direction?* he wondered. *Am I lost?* But he felt that he had no other choice, so he continued to go forward. Soon he knew that indeed he was lost.

Nick halted Dan. He tried to think

of what to do. After a moment he notice Dan starting to twitch and quiver. Nick started to lower his head to see what was the matter, but suddenly Dan reared and whinnied, nearly throwing Nick off his back. Nick grabbed onto the pommel of his saddle as hard as he could. He looked down at the ground.

Right in front of Dan's hooves was a long, speckled snake. Nick only got a second's look at it before Dan reared again. This time Nick went flying though the air, landing a short distance away on the ground. Dan, spooked, ran off quickly. Nick saw the tail of the snake disappearing into a hole. He looked at his left leg, which was bent strangely under him. Then he began to feel a terrible pain shooting through him, and everything grew black.

Nick awoke later in darkness. It was so dark that when he opened his eyes, it seemed as though they were still shut. He found himself lying on his back. The air around him was cool. Something soft supported his head. Nick wondered where he was and how he had gotten there. All of a sudden he remembered the snake and Dan, and he tried to get up, but there was a sharp pain in his leg that made him cry out and fall back down.

Immediately he heard voices some distance away, but they weren't speaking any language that he had heard before. He saw a light illuminating rock walls. *So I'm in a cave,* he thought. *But how did I get here? And who's here with me?* He grew frightened. The voices drew closer. Soon figures appeared, silhouetted in torchlight. They approached the place where Nick was lying.

There were two men and one woman. They all had dark skin, curly hair, and broad faces with heavy brows. They were dressed very simply in skins. They looked at Nick and spoke to him, but he couldn't understand them at all.

These must be aborigines! Nick thought. He wondered if they would hurt him. Mr. Thornapple and his classmates had said such terrible things about the aborigines. Nick hoped they weren't true. Nick said out loud, "What am I doing here?" The people just looked at him, not understanding him either. But they smiled at him. One of the men reached out and patted him on the shoulder, and the woman stroked his cheek. Nick saw that they were friendly, and he began to feel better. The other man stooped down beside him and began to draw in the dirt with a stick. He drew a picture of a horse and a snake. Then he drew a picture of a person with a broken leg.

That's me, Nick thought. *It sure feels like my leg is broken.*

The man then drew a picture of other people carrying the boy with the broken leg to a cave. He also drew a picture of other people leading a horse to the cave. *That must mean that they found Dan and brought him here, too!* Nick thought. He looked up at the man and smiled, pointing to the drawing and then to himself. The man smiled and nodded. Nick saw the kindness in his eyes. He realized at that moment that these people were not the mean, lazy, stupid people he had heard about in school. They were smart and kind and gentle.

Someone else came into the chamber of the cave with something for Nick to eat and drink. Nick gladly took it; it had been a long time since he had had food or water. Then the people made signs for Nick to lie down again and sleep. They left him alone, and he soon discovered that he was still very tired. He quickly fell asleep.

When Nick awoke again, it was still dark, but he sensed that outside it was morning. Soon the dark people came back into the room. One man picked Nick up and carried him out, smiling gently at him. Nick realized for the first time that his leg had been placed in splints made of sticks and wrapped with rough cord. The aborigines took him out of the cave. Nick squinted in the bright sunlight. He looked around and saw the same hills and plains that he had seen before. He saw several more aborigines standing around. But he also saw his horse, Dan. He shouted out, "Dan! It's you!" The aborigines laughed and smiled with him.

They had made a pallet with a woven mat for Nick to lie on. The pallet was attached to two long branches that a man was holding. They laid Nick gently onto the pallet. They began walking and pulling Nick carefully along as they went. One of them led Dan by the reins. They made their way in a deliberate manner, as if they knew exactly where they were going. Somehow Nick knew that they did. They traveled for quite some time, periodically speaking to Nick to reassure him. He didn't understand their words, but their soft voices and looks made him feel perfectly safe, although his leg ached. Finally they crested a hill. Nick sat up and looked and found that he was looking at his own house. He saw his father frantically saddling up his horse, and his mother standing and watching his father anxiously. He shouted, "Father! Mama! Over here!"

They both turned and looked, then shouted out, "Nick! Nick!" They flung open the gate and ran to him, falling down to their knees and hugging him tightly. The aborigines stood and watched, smiles on their faces. "Where have you been? What's happened to you?" Mr. and Mrs. Whitley asked over and over. They looked around at the aborigines with wonder.

"Father, Mother, I was so stupid! Can you forgive me?" Nick asked.

"Of course," they said. "All that we care about is that you're safe!"

His father added, "Nick, what's happened? Who are these people?"

So Nick explained all that had gone

on, including the many kindnesses that the aborigines had shown him. Mr. Whitley grasped the hands of the aborigines. "Thank you, friends," he said, though of course he knew they didn't speak English. But it was all right. They knew exactly what he was saying. And they nodded to him and patted Nick's head. Then they began walking back in the direction from which they had come.

After that, Nick and his family never thought of aborigines in the same way again. And any time they heard someone say that the aborigines were lazy or stupid or mean, they knew differently, and they made it clear that none of these things were true. Any time Nick heard the aborigines called an "inferior class" he grew very angry and challenged anyone who thought it was so.

And the aborigines came back to visit Nick and his mother and father often. The Whitleys always received them with great joy.

You see, they had learned the meaning of compassion.

Annette

Pride goes before destruction, a haughty spirit before a fall. (Prov. 16:18)

Jesus once made a puzzling statement: "He who humbles himself will be exalted" (Luke 14:11). What does "humbling" oneself (or having "humility")

mean? Is a humble person someone who walks with his head down, too embarrassed to look anyone in the eye? Is a humble man, woman, boy, or girl someone who feels completely worthless to other people and to God? Definitely not!

Listen to the story about Annette and her problems that all came about because she had not yet learned to be humble. As you listen, sit or lie back on a pillow with your legs, ankles, or arms crossed, *right* over left. When Annette is acting proud and arrogant (opposites of "humble"), leave your legs, ankles, or arms crossed as they are—but when she shows humility in the story, change positions by crossing them *left* over right! Then, when something good actually happens to *you* sometime (and it will!), pray that God will help you to be thankful and humble.

Once little girls were taught all kinds of virtuous behavior (I don't know why they're not anymore). They were taught how to curtsey. They were taught to say please and thank you. They were taught that *yes ma'am* and *no sir* are polite and that *yeah, nah,* and *huh* are impolite. They were taught the right fork to use and the right way to drink tea (with the pinkie pointing out, of course). They knew what a fingerbowl was for. They could recite the names of all the presidents (at that time there were fewer than today). They even knew who Bach and Mozart were. Most of all, they were taught how a young lady should behave: gently, politely, and with humbleness. They had a good guide—the Bible.

Sometimes these young ladies didn't learn their lessons all that well. Sometimes they picked up the wrong fork. Sometimes they kept their pinkies in. Sometimes they drank out of the fingerbowl. Sometimes they left out Millard Fillmore. And sometimes they were most definitely *not* gentle, polite, or humble, to the dismay of their parents, nannies, and governesses. These were the girls that mothers cried over, teachers threw up their hands in exasperation over, and schoolmates whispered about. These were the girls that made the elderly ladies in church shake their heads, cluck their tongues, and whisper to each other, "Pride goeth before a fall, says the Good Book"

Sadly, Annette was that kind of girl. But she didn't think she was all that bad, though other people thought she was. She was mannerly; she didn't giggle too much, or snort, or put her elbows on the table—most of the time. She could be quite polite, on occasion, though only to those whom she liked; to others she could be quite terrible. She only had one glaring fault, one that even she recognized (though naturally she didn't care). She was extremely proud of her long, dark hair. It was naturally curly, and thick, and admittedly it was beautiful. But Annette was very vain, spending long hours combing her hair and gazing at herself in the mirror. Sometimes she would even miss meals or lessons to do this. Naturally, this frustrated others.

Her parents would be sitting down for an elegant meal, only to discover that Annette wasn't there. What usually followed went something like this:

Father: "Annette, dear?"

Annette: "Yes, Father?"

Father: "Aren't you joining us for dinner tonight?"

Annette: "Oh, I'll be there in a few minutes."

Mother: "Why aren't you here now?"

Annette: "Well, Mother, my hair looks so beautiful tonight. I just want to admire it for a few more minutes."

Father:"Why don't you give us a chance to admire it, too—at the *dinner* table?"

Annette: "Oh, Father, you're always so mean!"

And then Father would shout, and Mother would go to get Annette, and Annette would cry. It didn't make for a very pleasant meal.

It was also particularly frustrating for Annette's governess, Miss Peabody, when it came time for lessons. Miss Peabody would be holding forth on the struggle between the proletariat and bourgeoisie (in other words, saying boring things about history), when she would notice a faraway, glazed look in Annette's eyes.

"Young lady, *why* are you not paying attention to this fascinating lecture?"

"Because," Annette would say with a smirk, "I don't know what your prole-whatever and burge-wa-thingy are, and I don't care. They're boring."

Miss Peabody, in a scandalized voice, would say, "Boring? I suppose you have something better to think about?"

"Of course I do!" would come Annette's prompt reply.

"And what would that be?"

"My hair! Don't you think it's just beautiful, Miss Peabody?"

Well, as you might expect, this clearly prevented Annette from learning much about history or English or mathematics, which was just fine with her. To her there was nothing as important as her lovely dark hair. Annette's friends resented her vanity, and often they'd gather in a circle, pointing and whispering things that weren't very nice. Of course Annette put it down to pure jealousy, nothing more. Sometimes the boys would come up with elaborate plots to cut off her dark ringlets or dip the ends in an inkwell, but they were always discovered by Annette or some adult who happened to be near (though those adults that knew Annette were occasionally attempted to let them go ahead with their plans). She always escaped untouched.

One day Annette's parents had business downtown that they had to attend to. Miss Peabody was taking a short vacation (the poor woman needed it, too), and so there was no one to watch Annette. Knowing this, they made arrangements for her to visit one of her friends. Annette didn't want to go, and she sulked and pouted, but it was no use. As you know, when parents make up their minds, there's not much you can do. It was time for them to go, and they took Annette and dropped her off on the sidewalk in front of her friend's house. It was a lovely Victorian brownstone on a peaceful, tree-lined street, only two streets over from Annette's own.

"Annette, dear, you will have a good time, won't you? Father and I won't be gone long," her mother called.

"Of course, Mother, I'll have a wonderful time." And Annette stood on the sidewalk and waved at her parents as they pulled away.

As soon as they were out of sight, however, she did not go up to the door of her friend's house. In fact, she did something quite unexpected. She turned around and began walking back to her own house. You see, Annette didn't like to go over to friends' houses. She didn't really like to play with others. What she liked best was looking at herself in the mirror. And since her parents were gone, and Miss Peabody too, and no one was home at her house, well, it was a perfect opportunity! No one would be around to disturb her, tell her she had to come to dinner or do her mathematics. The closer she got to her own house, the faster she walked, at the last almost running.

She flung open the front door. There was not a sound to be heard. She walked down the hall, past rows of open doors. No one was home. She shouted, "Hey! I'm here by myself! I can do anything I want!" There was no reply except the quiet ticking of a clock in a distant room. She dashed up the staircase to her room and perched herself in a chair in front of her big, ornate mirror. She thought to herself how beautiful her hair looked that morning, how dark and how long. How very long her hair looked!

After Annette stared for a while, a feeling of delight came over her. She cried out, "My hair—it's so long! I do believe it's longer than it was last night!" And it really did seem to be. Normally it fell just over her shoulders; now it appeared to be down nearly to the elbow. *More gorgeous than ever*, she thought with contentment. But she couldn't get over a feeling, slight though it was, that something unusual was going on.

She watched a few minutes longer, and soon she realized that something unusual truly *was* happening. There was no denying it now; her hair was down to her elbows and past the middle of her back. It was growing, and growing fast. Annette's eyes widened. Now her hair was down to her

waist. Now it was nearly to her knees. Now it was just starting to touch the floor. Something was definitely wrong here. Annette ran out of her room, which wasn't easy because her hair was getting heavy. She dashed down the stairs, trailing long dark hair like a rug behind her. She shouted out for her mother and father, but they weren't there. Now that her hair was growing so fast, and she didn't know why, nothing was turning out like she had expected. She had always thought that if her hair were just a little bit longer it would look even prettier.

Now it was a lot longer, and she didn't like it at all. In fact, she was really frightened. She couldn't move very easily at all now because hair was curling around her feet and ankles and tripping her up. So she did the only thing she could do; she sat down at the bottom of the staircase and began to cry. Her hair continued to grow, wrapping around her like a blanket and covering the floor.

In a few more minutes Annette's parents pulled up in front of the house. They had been nearly to their destination, forgotten something, and had to come back. Annette's father wasn't happy about this. Perhaps that's why he didn't notice something strange about the house. But Annette's mother did.

She said, "Darling, what's that?"

"What's what?" Annette's father said gruffly, without looking up.

"What's that sticking out of the chimney . . . and under the front door . . . and out of the upstairs window?"

That got his attention. He quickly looked up at the house. "Why, I don't know . . . it looks like—" and then he leaped out of the car, without even turning off the engine, and ran up to the front door of his house. Annette's mother followed right behind him. Father grabbed the doorknob and threw open the door. Waves of beautiful, thick, curly dark hair came cascading out, nearly knocking him over. He gasped and spluttered in amazement. Mother looked about to faint. And then, from somewhere deep inside the thick mass, a sound could be heard.

It was the sound of Annette sobbing. Her father shouted, "Annette, dear!" and her mother shouted, "My baby!" at the same time.

Annette responded, in a shaky, tearful voice, "Mother? Father? I'm in here."

"In there?" Father yelled. "But how? Annette, is this all your hair?"

"Yes, yes it is, and I don't like it!" she responded. "I always thought my hair was so pretty, and now I don't like it a bit. Oh, if it would just stop grow-

ing, I'd never be vain about my hair anymore!"

All the time that they had been speaking, locks of hair had continued to curl out the front door, spreading out over the steps and growing toward the sidewalk. But as she said the word *anymore* they suddenly stopped. She gave a cry of joy. "Oh, it's no longer growing! It stopped!"

Annette was now shouting with happiness, Father was standing there speechless with his mouth hanging open, and Mother was saying "But . . . I don't . . ." and clinging to the rail. For a moment it was complete pandemonium, and then Father did a sensible thing. He dashed away and disappeared around the back of the house. When he appeared again, he was carrying a large pair of hedge clippers. Mother's mouth opened wide.

"What are you going to do?"

"I'm going in there," he said, a little too dramatically, "to rescue our daughter." And he snipped and hacked away. It wasn't long before Annette was rescued. It was quite a bit longer, as you can imagine, until the house was back in order. And even for years after that strange day, Annette and her parents were always finding locks of beautiful dark hair in some corner or drawer that had escaped their attention.

Annette made a promise that day, one that she kept. In fact, from that day on she hated the sight of mirrors and never talked about her hair except when necessary. And she was much easier to get along with, she loved being with her friends (who had changed their minds about her), she was never late for dinner, and she excelled in her studies, much to the satisfaction of Miss Peabody. She became the kind of girl about which the elderly church ladies said privately, "Such a good girl," and said out loud to her, "Very nice to see you today, little Annette."

Once in a while Annette could be seen taking out a piece of paper and looking at it, then smiling as she put it away and went on. No one paid much attention to this, and no one ever saw what the paper said. But if someone had ever caught a glimpse, he would have simply seen this, written in a little girl's handwriting: Pride goeth before a fall.

Ian

When I am afraid, I will trust in you. (Ps. 56:3)

What is *trust?* If you have a friend you feel you can trust, what does that mean to you? Are you someone who can be *trusted?*

God is the one person we can *really* trust—he is always there when we need him, and he never fails to love and help us! He wants us to trust him enough to put our whole lives in his care. He will always be our faithful friend! Read his message to you in Psalm 56:3.

As you listen now to the story about Ian and *trust,* keep a piece of paper and a pencil in your hands. When something in the story attracts your attention, such as the words *castle* or *suit of armor,* make a simple drawing of it.

If you wish, use your drawings to remind you of the story and retell it (or reread it) to a friend or neighbor. If your friend does not know Jesus for himself, help him to know that Jesus can be trusted completely as his Friend and Savior.

Ian was none too excited about the coming summer. This was unusual because normally he couldn't wait until summer arrived. Ian lived in a large city, so there was much to do: swimming and basketball and amusement parks—you name it. But this summer, he had been told, there was a real "treat" awaiting him. At least his parents considered it a treat. Ian didn't think it sounded like a lot of fun.

The "treat" in question was a trip to Scotland to visit a distant relative of his mother. Ian's parents had wanted to give him a chance to see another part of the world, and this was really a very generous offer, but he didn't see it that way. To Ian the world consisted of the swimming pool and the hoop in his driveway, and not much else. Sure, it was only for a couple of weeks, but that was two weeks away from his friends, who would surely remind him of how much fun he had missed back home while shut up in that old castle.

That's right—a castle. Ian's mother had some kind of great-uncle or someone like that who lived in a full-fledged castle in Scotland, one that had been in the family, apparently, for hundreds of years. For many kids this might seem like a dream come true, but not for Ian. He didn't like things like that (or so he thought). It would just be dark and cold and musty-smelling, he was sure. And there wasn't a chance of a basketball court for miles around. And no swimming either, unless it was in one of the lakes—and weren't those full of monsters, anyway? They were sure he'd change his tune after a few hours in Scotland. That's the reason they were insistent on his going.

School soon drew to an end, and shortly after that the fateful day arrived. Ian's parents (whose names, by the way, were Mr. and Mrs. Boswell) drove him to the airport to see him off. When he was about to board, they hugged him and said their good-byes.

"We'll see you in two weeks, sweetheart," Mrs. Boswell said.

"Yeah, if I don't die of boredom first," Ian replied. His parents winked at each other. Each was thinking the same thing: *He'll change his mind.*

The plane got away safely, and Mr. and Mrs. Boswell went home. Ian pulled out a sports magazine and set-

tled back. It was going to be a long plane ride, to say nothing of the next two weeks. He figured he'd better relax and get used to it. After a short while the soft hum of the plane's engines coupled with Ian's comfortable seat lulled him into a peaceful sleep.

Ian awoke suddenly after a short time. Something had awakened him; what was it? He looked around but didn't see anything that could have disturbed him. All the people on his row were asleep. *Could it have been a dream?* he asked himself. Yes, a dream. That was it! But what had the dream been? Let's see, something about a library, and a book, and suits of armor, too; was that right? But the memory of the dream was fragmented, and Ian couldn't quite put it all together. If you've ever had a dream that you wanted to remember but couldn't, you know how frustrating this can be. Ian slept and woke many more times on that long plane trip, but he didn't have the dream again. They flew for so long that Ian lost track of time. Had it been a day, a week? Had he always been on this plane? (If you've ever been on the same kind of flight, you know how long it is!)

At long last the captain's voice crackled over the plane's speakers. "Good morning," he said in a rich Scottish accent. Ian sat up and noticed. He thought the accent sounded pretty neat. The captain continued, "We're approaching our destination, Scotland's capital city of Edinburgh. The weather today is . . ." But Ian didn't hear because he was curious about something. He had seen the name of the city spelled "Edinburgh," but the captain had pronounced it like "Edinburro." *Why is that?* he wondered. The captain's accent and way of speaking intrigued him. *Is this how everyone talks in Scotland? That's pretty cool,* he thought.

The plane landed and everyone began to disembark. Ian looked at a piece of paper on which his mother had written some instructions. It read:

"Ian, when you get to the airport in Edinburgh, there will be an old gentleman waiting to meet you. His name is Alistair Culligan. He's the cousin of your great-aunt Carolyn. You'll be staying with him. And you'll love his house. Have a great time, sweetheart! We love you and miss you."

Alistair Culligan, Ian thought. *He sounds about three hundred years old.* He folded the piece of paper and stuck it into his pocket, then walked up the ramp and out into the terminal. Once there he looked around for someone waiting to meet him. Sure enough, he spotted an elderly man holding a sign that said "Ian Boswell." The man waved enthusiastically and came quickly over to Ian.

"Is that you, Ian, my boy?" he asked, in that same wonderfully thick accent. Ian was really starting to like the way people talked here.

"Yes, it is . . . Mr. Culligan?" Ian replied sheepishly. They shook hands, and Mr. Culligan threw his arm around Ian, pointing him in the direction of the baggage claim. As they walked, Mr. Culligan told Ian how glad he was that Ian was here. Ian surveyed him while he talked. Mr. Culligan was a short, thin man with steel-gray hair and twinkling blue eyes. His face was weathered and worn, as if he'd spent much time outside, but very kind also. He wore a tweed suit, plaid tie, and a cap on his head, and he carried a gnarled stick for a cane. To Ian he looked like someone straight out of a movie, but Ian couldn't help liking the little old man a lot—he was so friendly.

They collected the baggage and walked out to the parking lot, arriving at a car that Mr. Culligan had waiting. Ian had never seen a car with a chauffeur before. They pulled out of the parking lot and headed away.

During the trip that followed, Mr. Culligan told Ian many things about himself, about his home (which really was a castle), about Scotland, and about God. Mr. Culligan was a faithful Christian and a faithful churchgoer, and he let it be known that while Ian was in his house, he would attend church. Ian went to church back home, but it didn't really mean that much to him.

Ian learned a lot during that trip. He discovered that Mr. Culligan was actually Lord Culligan, a title that had been passed down in his family for centuries. He heard much about the history of Scotland, which was fascinating. But what interested him most were the things Lord Culligan was saying about God. He'd never heard things like that before, or at least not paid attention when they were being said. The trip was over too quickly, as far as Ian was concerned. But soon they pulled onto a circular gravel drive, and Ian got his first look at where he'd be spending the next two weeks. He could hardly believe his eyes.

What he saw was a huge granite structure, with turrets and towers and small windows. It was really a castle! But instead of looking dark and cold, it looked intriguing and exciting. He could hardly wait to see inside. And it didn't disappoint him. There were huge portraits of regal-looking men and women who had lived hundreds of years ago. There were high oak ceilings. There were real suits of armor, stags' heads, and coats of arms, things that he'd only read about before. And now, for the first time, he was really glad that he had come.

Ian spent the next few days exploring, which Lord Culligan happily encouraged. Ian never ran out of new hallways, new rooms, new passages to discover. He also got the opportunity to attend church with Lord Culligan, which, to his surprise, he really enjoyed. It was more formal than his church, but Ian learned a lot because he really listened. The message one time was from Psalm 56, and

one verse really stuck with him. It was verse 3: "What time I am afraid, I will trust in thee." He thought that sounded comforting.

One dark and foggy day, Ian was looking around a wing of the castle that he hadn't seen yet. At its far end he discovered the library, which was full of books that looked old. He went in and started looking at the titles. They weren't at all what he was used to; he read mainly sports magazines. Naturally he didn't recognize any of the books. But all of a sudden something came to him. His dream—yes, it had been about a library. And that suit of armor in the corner had been in his dream, too! How strange! He tried to remember something else, something about a book. He looked around at the shelves. Nothing looked familiar.

But wait! That one—the big one over there. He went up to it and grabbed it to take it down from the shelf. And then something totally unexpected happened. A panel in the wall slid open, exposing a door that had been invisible before. It led to the outside, out onto the vast moors. Ian couldn't believe it! He dashed out through the secret door. Once there he looked around. Behind him lay the back of the great castle; in front was barren moorland, with all of its hills and valleys and rocks. It looked so wild. Ian had seen most of the castle already; this was something he hadn't seen yet. *Well, why not explore it?* he thought. *It's not time for dinner yet, so they won't miss me.*

He set out across the empty wilderness. The castle got smaller and smaller in the background, and after he crested one of the rolling hills, it disappeared from sight. Out here there were no trees, no roads or houses, just vacant places, hills, heather, and rocks. He walked on and on. It was overcast and hazy, making the day darker than it would normally have been. There was no wind at all. Fog was creeping slowly up, making it more difficult to see very far away now. It wreathed around him, cold on his skin. The farther he went, the less he could see. It was getting colder outside, and Ian hadn't dressed very warmly. He soon decided he had had enough of exploring and turned around to go back.

Let's see, which way was back? He couldn't see very well; the fog was getting thicker. And he wasn't sure exactly which way he had come because there weren't any markers of any kind. He walked for some distance in the direction he thought was home, always sure that just over the next hill he'd spot the familiar castle. But he didn't. And soon Ian really began to worry. There was a nagging thought in the back of his head, but he didn't want to think it. He pressed on.

After two or three more hills, he had to admit it. He was lost, and he had no idea how to get back. He was also very cold, and it was starting to get dark outside. Ian was more than

worried now—he was really scared. He started shouting for help, hoping that someone would hear him. No one answered. He panicked and began to run, but he soon wore himself out and collapsed onto the springy ground.

He was scared out of his wits. He just sat there, not knowing what else to do. Very soon something curious happened. He started to pray, something he hadn't really done before. And quick as a flash a voice came into his mind. The voice simply said, "What time I am afraid, I will trust in thee." Ian felt instantly better. He sat back and said, "Okay, God. I'm trusting you. Please help me."

He sat there for a short time. Not long after, he heard distant shouts and the baying of dogs. The voices came closer. He could make out flashlights and lanterns through the fog. Shortly he was looking into the worried eyes of Lord Alistair Culligan.

"Boy, we worried about you! I should have told you how easy it is to get lost out on the moors and warned you about the castle's secret passages. Thank God you're safe. I prayed, and the Lord answered my prayers."

Ian replied with enthusiasm, "I prayed, too, and then I knew you'd find me. I also remembered what I heard in church. I guess God was telling me I'd be okay."

Lord Culligan answered solemnly, "That he was, lad."

The rest of Ian's trip passed without incident. When the day came for him to return home, he didn't want to leave. He had learned much. What he had chiefly discovered, however, was that God is very real and very concerned about him. That was certainly the best lesson of all.

His parents picked him up at the airport after his long flight back, and he was full of things to tell them. As they all walked off with their arms around each other, Ian's excited voice could be heard above the hum of the crowd:

"Hey! Have you ever read Psalm 56?"

Pingo

Children, obey your parents in the Lord, for this is right. (Eph. 6:1)

Obedience is a not-too-popular word with some children—and even with some *adults*—but it is a very *important* attitude that helps to keep us safe and give our lives order and purpose. Obedience helps our homes run smoothly, makes our schools places where children can freely learn, and keeps our whole country from becoming a dangerous land where everyone does only what he wants—even if that means driving the wrong way down the street or taking things that belong to someone else.

Obedience is something we *choose* to do. Other people can encourage us to obey and punish us when we don't,

but the final choice to obey or to disobey is in our own hearts. The Bible gives us some great words about the rewards that come the way of obedient people. Read some of these important words in Ephesians 6:1-3 and Hebrews 13:17—and decide right now to live a life of obedience—first to God, and then to anyone whom the Lord has put in authority over you.

Then sit back, relax, and enjoy the story of Pingo, who learned an important lesson the *hard* way about obeying his parents. As you listen, keep a piece of white paper and a box of crayons nearby. As various colors are mentioned later on in the story, make a design or a drawing using them.

Do you really hate baby-sitting? You don't like it when your mother and father have to go somewhere and you're asked (or told) to stay and watch little brother or little sister? Well, cheer up, because it could be worse. How, you ask?

What if you had to baby-sit, not in the comfort of your own home, but *outside*, with temperatures at about, oh, let's say twenty degrees below zero? Wearing something that looks a lot like a tuxedo? And what if, instead of watching TV or listening to music or whatever you like to do for fun in your house, you had to stand perfectly still and not do much of anything? *And* what if you couldn't put your baby brother on the couch, or in his chair, or his crib, and you couldn't even hold him, but you had to *balance* him on the tops of your feet, so that he wouldn't touch the cold ground? See what I mean?

Pingo found himself having to do all of the above on a regular basis. You see, Pingo lived at the South Pole. Pingo was a penguin. And that's how penguins take care of baby penguins, which are, of course, still in the shell. Pingo's dad, Mingo, and his mom, Jingo (penguins aren't very creative when it comes to names, as you can see), were very busy. They often had to leave for a period of time because of business down on the oceanfront or up on the glacier. And when they left, guess who got to baby-sit little Junior (a name they thought was pretty clever)? That's right—it was Pingo. He griped and moped and pouted, but it didn't work. (If you're smart, you know by now that those things never work.)

His parents would leave with cheerful waves of their stubby little wings, and there would be Pingo, all alone—besides Junior, that is—on a field of ice, going over their last instructions in his head. (By the way, as your parents can tell you, penguins don't mind the cold and the ice; God made them so they could live in cold weather. Pingo just thought he was too big to be told what to do.) His parents generally said the same things each time: "Be good. Be careful. And Pingo, *no horsing around!*"

Well, Pingo had to baby-sit today.

And his parents gave him the same instructions. As usual, Pingo didn't like to hear it. "No horsing around, no horsing around," he said out loud, just like you might say, "Nah, nah, nah, nah, nah, nah." Of course, he waited until his parents were gone to do this. It echoed, so he said it louder. He stood like that for some time, Junior's egg balanced on his feet, talking to himself. Pretty soon, he got bored. And pretty soon after he got bored, he got restless. He was getting a cramp (so he thought) standing like this for so long. He had to do something to entertain himself, anything, before he went crazy.

Pingo did do something. He reached down and picked up the egg between his two stubby wings, examining it. It was very smooth, as most eggs are, and extremely plain. *Hard to believe Junior's in there,* he thought. He looked at it some more. He tossed it up in the air and caught it once or twice. Looked like this thing was pretty tough. He set it down on the frozen snow and spun it on its big end. It spun around for a while and finally toppled over, which made Pingo laugh. "Hey, I'll bet I could have some fun with this thing—I mean, with my little brother," he said aloud to no one but himself. He set it on end and spun it again and laughed hysterically as he watched it. *Boy, bet he's dizzy in there!* he thought. Next he wanted to see how long it would spin without falling over, so he mustered up all his strength and flung it spinning onto the snow.

Unfortunately, Pingo had been standing right on the edge of a high hill, and this last toss had been just a little too strong. He watched in horror as the egg spun, teetered on the edge of the hill, and then did a fast slide down the slope. He watched it go. He was so stunned that he didn't move for quite some time. He just watched the egg gathering speed as it shot down the long, steep slope, up the other side, and over the crest of the next hill, out of sight. A sinking feeling settled in the pit of his stomach. Finally he found his feet and his voice at the same time. "J-J-J-JUNIOR!" he shouted, and started frantically down the slope, following the track the egg had left. About halfway down, he slipped on the ice and fell flat, sliding the rest of the way down on his back. When he got to the bottom, a little valley between the hills, he got back on his feet and waddled up the steep rise in front of him (he waddled because penguins can't run, of course).

Pingo was in a panic by this time.

He remembered what his parents had said: no horsing around. He had disobeyed, and look where it had gotten him. Well, it was too late to mope around. He had to go and get Junior. He was nearing the crest of the second hill. By this time, he had built up some speed and was really moving. He came over the top . . . and scrambled and skidded and threw himself onto the ground to keep from flying over the edge. He found himself flat on his belly, staring wide-eyed over the side of a tall cliff that rose high above the sea. He had nearly gone right off it. He sighed with relief, and then a terrible thought came to him. Junior! Where was Junior? He looked all around. Finally he spotted the egg, but what he saw didn't make him feel much better. The egg was balanced right on the farthest tip of a little spur of ice jutting out over the ocean. Pingo didn't see any way to get to it, but he knew he had to try.

He stepped out very cautiously onto the little spur. It was barely wider than he was. The egg was resting about six feet in front of him. He didn't want to look down. He wished he could make himself lighter; what if he weighed too much? He shuffled out, closer, closer . . . he was nearly there . . . he could almost touch it . . . he r-e-a-c-h-e-d out. . . .

With a loud cracking sound the spur broke off, and Pingo and the egg both started to fall, heading for the sea far below. Miraculously, they didn't fall far, because there was a ledge right in their path. They hit it and stopped, unhurt because of the high piles of snow that broke their fall. Pingo made sure that the egg wasn't broken, then he took a minute to catch his breath. After that, he took stock of his surroundings. The fall had deposited them on a ledge about ten feet wide and long. Beneath them was the ocean, full of chunks of floating ice. And behind them . . .

Behind them was a beautiful sight. It was an ice cave. It went back, back, back into the heart of the cliff, fading from the palest crystal blue at its entrance to a deep, rich sapphire, then midnight blue, and finally black, as black as the darkest night. Pingo was enchanted. He wanted to explore the cave, and besides, he certainly couldn't get back up to the top of the cliff the way he had come. Maybe this would be a way back. So he picked up the egg (still unharmed) and made his way into the ice cave.

Inside, the blue color was even more pronounced, and he saw many other colors as well, in little cracks and crevices and tunnels—red and green and white and purple. The entire interior of the cave looked like it was lined with diamonds. And the sights that Pingo saw amazed him! There were chambers that branched off from the tunnel that were hung with icicles many times taller than Pingo himself. There were weird, fantastic shapes. There was even a frozen waterfall. The

more he saw, the more he wanted to explore. But the tunnel was growing darker, and he hoped he would find a way out soon. He turned a corner and saw yet another chamber. In this chamber there were big white mounds lying on the floor, looking like piles of snow. But this wasn't snow like Pingo had seen before. It was—it was like *hairy* snow! It looked so funny that Pingo let out a loud laugh.

Instantly, the piles of snow jumped to their feet and started to growl. POLAR BEARS! Pingo was terrified. He scrambled off as fast as he could go, down the darkening tunnel. He didn't know where it was leading him, but he had to get away. He could hear the polar bears behind him getting closer all the time. They were gaining on him. Soon they would be right on top of him. He could barely see the icy floor in front of him anymore. It was hard to carry the egg between his wings and travel very fast. The polar bears were so close—but at the last possible minute, Pingo spotted the entrance to a tunnel wide enough for him but too small for the polar bears to follow. He wriggled into it with the bears snapping at his heels.

Once inside and safely away from danger, he surveyed his surroundings. The tunnel was just tall enough for him to stand up straight. Behind him was only darkness. In front of him, from somewhere way in the distance, was a faint light. *That can only mean one thing*," thought Pingo. *A way out!* He shuffled toward the light. He walked like that for some time. The light was growing but still wouldn't allow him to see his own feet. (He barely could anyway, even in the light; penguins are just built that way.) After a while, the tunnel started to slope upward. Pingo began climbing and then felt his feet slip out from under him. He sensed himself sliding down a slippery hole, and he gripped the egg tightly so he wouldn't lose it. Then he seemed to be sliding upward, then downward again, and then upward again. The light was still so dim that he really couldn't see much of anything. If he had known about roller coasters, he would have thought that this was very much like a roller coaster—especially when he took a long, steep plunge into darkness, so steep that for a while he was hurtling downward in midair. The drop seemed to go on forever. Then he was going up, up, up, and the light was getting brighter. Then he burst through the snow and shot into the air, finally coming back to earth with a soft *plop*, the egg (unharmed even after all that) resting beside him. He was back nearly where he had started.

Pingo had had enough adventures for a while. He knew he should never have disobeyed his parents. It had brought him a whole lot of trouble. He stood up straight and put Junior back in his proper place. It didn't seem so bad now just to stand there and wait for his mother and father; in fact, he was very content to do nothing. And soon enough, they showed up, coming over the crest of a nearby hill, waving and smiling.

"Thanks for baby-sitting, Pingo! Did you have any trouble?" his father asked.

"No, Dad, not at all . . . ," he started to say, then caught himself. He didn't want to lie to them, too, after disobeying their instructions. One thing was bad enough. So he told them the entire story. Their faces were stern when he finished. He was expecting some kind of severe punishment, but instead his father simply said,

"Is this the truth?"

"Yes, sir, it is."

Mingo looked at Jingo, then looked at his son and said, "Well, Son, you disobeyed us. But what you've been through is probably punishment enough in this case. And you're safe, and Junior, too. That's all we can ask."

Pingo was so happy, and he promised on the spot never to disobey his parents again. (He didn't keep this promise, but he did a whole lot better after that.) And he never complained again about having to baby-sit. It seemed like a piece of cake from that point on.

And you thought *you* had it rough!

Scripture Index

Page numbers indicate activities related to the verses listed.

Tyndale Books—Helping Parents Nurture Their Children's Spiritual Growth